PLANNING, POLITICS AND COMMUNICATIONS

Planning, Politics and Communications

A Study of the Central Lancashire New Town

GEOFFREY L. WOODCOCK
Associate Director, School of Extension Studies
University of Liverpool

Gower

Published by
Gower Publishing Company Limited,
Gower House, Croft Road, Aldershot, Hants GU11 3HR,
England

Gower Publishing Company,
Old Post Road, Brookfield, Vermont 05036, USA

British Library Cataloguing in Publication Data

Woodcock, Geoffrey L.
Planning, politics and communications: a study of the Central Lancashire New Town.
1. City planning——England——Central Lancashire New Town (Lancashire)——Citizen participation
I. Title
711'.4'094276 HT169.G72C3/

ISBN 0-566-00833-5

Printed in Great Britain by Paradigm Print, Gateshead, Tyne and Wear

Contents

Acknowledgments

The writer would like to thank Malcolm Warner for his encouragement and Bob Houlton for his support throughout the lengthy stages of the fieldwork and the interminable period of writing up the research. Thanks are also due to members and former members of the staff of the Central Lancashire Development Corporation for their patience and to a number of journalists for sharing their working hours and facilities, to Phyllis Kon, Jean Phillips and Jane Burton for undertaking the typing, to Peter Grimshaw and Jenny Lawton for illustrations; but above all, to all the members of the many action groups who generously and openly offered him the access and hospitality to conduct his research in Central Lancashire.
The book is of necessity a distillation of a lengthier document for which the degree of Ph.D. was awarded by Brunel University in 1983.

A CHRONOLOGY OF THE CENTRAL LANCASHIRE NEW TOWN

'Preliminary Plan for Lancashire' published proposing the Leyland and Chorley areas as overspill for up to 47,500 people	1951
'Review of County Development Plan' in which Lancashire renewed its proposal for a new town in the Leyland area.	1962
Preliminary Technical Report of Lancashire County Planning Officer proposed a population intake of 150,000 approximately in Leyland-Preston-Chorley area.	1964
Announcement by Richard Crossman, Minister of Housing and Local Government, of the Government's intention to designate an area for a new town in Central Lancashire based on Leyland and Chorley.	24 February 1966
Consultants' report 'Central Lancashire: Study for a City' published.	May 1967
Consultants' study 'Impact on North East Lancashire' published	February 1968
Draft Designation Order published for an area of 41,000 acres.	December 1968
Public Inquiry into Draft Order held.	May 1968
Minister's decision letter and Inspector's report published. (Designated area reduced to 35,000 acres)	24 March 1970
Central Lancashire New Town Designation Order.	14 April 1970
Secretary of State for the Environment confirmed decision to proceed and establish CLDC.	February 1971
Sir Frank Pearson appointed Chairman of the Board, CLDC.	March 1971
Mr R.W. Phelps took up appointment as General Manager, CLDC.	December 1971
Walton Summit Protest Committee formed.	*25 June 1973*
Planwatch inaugural public meeting	*10 July 1973*
Liaison Committees formed by CLDC.	August 1973
Grimsargh/Haighton C.P.O. Public Inquiry starts.	14 August 1973
Clayton-le-Woods C.P.O. Public Inquiry starts.	17 August 1973
Draft Outline Plan published by CLDC.	November 1973
Moss Side (Leyland) Residents' Association formed.	*December 1973*
Walton Summit No. 2 C.P.O. Public Inquiry starts.	29 January 1974
General Election I.	28 February 1974

Ashton Action Group formed.	*April 1974*
Preston North Action Group formed.	*April 1974*
Resignation of Bernard Davies from new town Social Development Working Party.	*18 April 1974*
Public Participation commences - publication of Outline Plan Summary Pamphlet.	23 April 1974
Road Appraisal Reports made available by CLDC.	23 April 1974
Strategic Plan for the North West published	6 May 1974
Road Appraisal Reports public meetings commence.	16 May 1974
Outline Plan published by CLDC.	31 May 1974
Secretary of State confirms C.P.O.s for Walton Summit, etc.	6 June 1974
Ingol Public Meeting and Exhibition	28 June 1974
Transport Network Public Meeting (Leyland).	1 July 1974
House of Commons Adjournment Debate on lack of consultation on CLNT	*4 July 1974*
Deputation by M.P.s to request postponement of public inquiry.	*24 July 1974*
Fulwood and Broughton Residents' Association formed.	*25 July 1974*
Outline Plan Public Inquiry original date for commencement.	17 September 1974
Public Inquiries into Leyland Moss Side and Whittle-le-Woods District Centre and Community School	17 September 1974
SCRAP launched (Preston).	*September 1974*
General Election II.	10 October 1974
Outline Plan Public Inquiry commences	5 November 1974
Local Groups Joint Working Party formed.	*8 May 1976*
Secretary of State, Mr Peter Shore, makes speech on Inner Cities, Manchester.	17 September 1976
House of Commons Adjournment Debate on CLNT.	*23 December 1976*
Decision letter and Inspector's report published.	5 April 1977
Curtailment of New Town Development Corporations announced.	February 1982

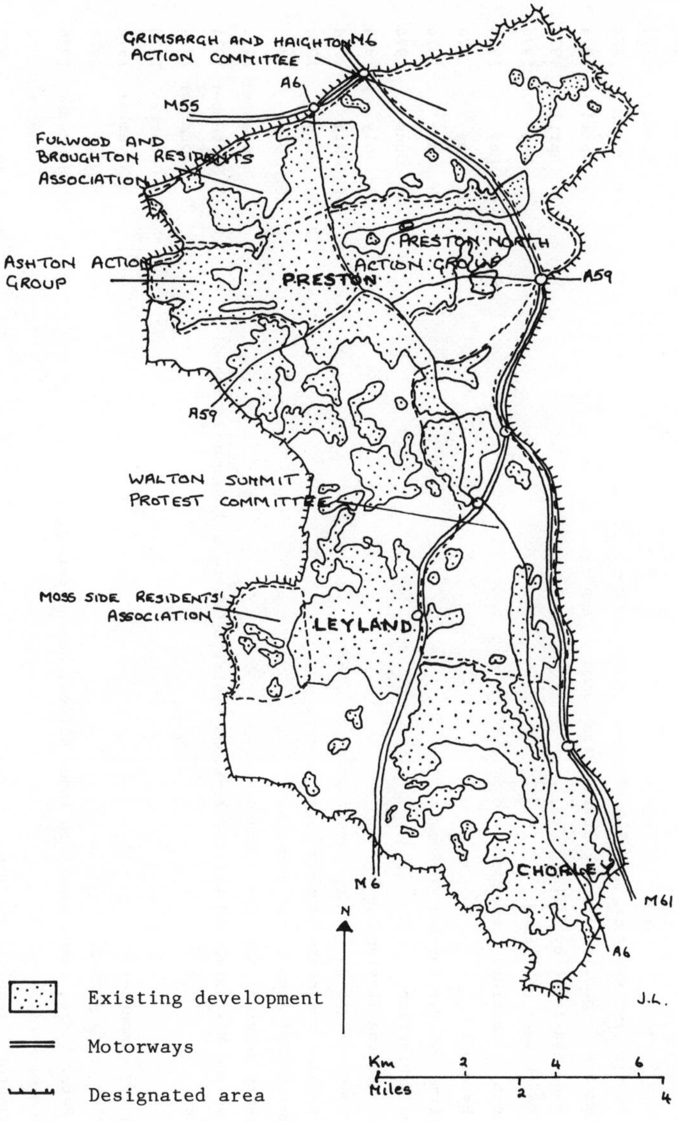

CENTRAL LANCASHIRE NEW TOWN

Areas of Influence of the Local Action Groups

PART I
INTRODUCTION

1 The focus of the study

This study describes and analyses events and activities which took place, primarily in mid-Lancashire, in connection with the Central Lancashire New Town (CLNT) following its designation in 1970. Particular attention is given to the organisational structure of the focal administrative organ of central government for this project, the Central Lancashire Development Corporation (CLDC). The research fieldwork, during the years 1973-1977, concentrates upon CLDCs inter organisational relationships, the procedures associated with seeking ministerial approval of the outline plan and the ensuing process of influencing decision making.

CLNT is especially worthy of attention. (1) This substantial concentration of public and private investment has been regarded as the culmination of an important phase of development in British regional planning and new town policies. Although this was not the last new town to be designated (Llantrisant in Wales and Stonehouse in Scotland were designated in 1972 and 1973), CLNT became the last whose outline plan proposals would be submitted and eventually approved if in a truncated form. (See Figure 5) The Secretary of State's decision on the outline plan in April 1977 coupled with the growing attention to the problems of the inner cities (the Inner Urban Areas Act was passed in 1978 with the subsequent formation of the Urban Development Corporations in London docklands and Merseyside), thus denote a marked policy shift in planning priorities.

A major theme of the study is that of participation in planning. The Skeffington Report 'People and Planning' (HMSO 1969) had aroused the expectations of many members of the general public concerned about planning issues. Differences in perceptions and interpretations of definitions of 'participation' are not uncommon. An understanding of such variations is an aid to deciphering the various stances adopted and a range of theoretical approaches are described and developed in Chapter 4. Attitudes to participation are complex and the concept itself is the subject of various models, typologies, political analyses and justifications. It should be noted that the first new towns were established on 'greenfield' sites and at most negotiations with the owners of farms and small villages would be involved prior to the acquisition of development land. Some later new towns, notably Northampton, Peterborough, Redditch, Runcorn, Telford and Warrington, however were based upon centres with a substantial original population. The admitted autocratic nature of their original tradition (See Crossman, 1975, p.66) does not easily coexist with growing expectations by the public of consultation and participation, particularly since 'Skeffington'. Most important for this study the designation, the

Figure 1 CENTRAL LANCASHIRE NEW TOWN in its Regional Context

subsequent development of CLNT and the relationship between CLDC and its public occurred 'post Skeffington'. The research therefore describes the participation relating to CLNT within the new town designated area in some detail. The expected involvement of some of the interested citizens and main activists are outlined and grievances based upon alleged restrictions of information and the extent of the commitment of the CLDC to participation are detailed.

Closely linked and supportive of the participation theme is the application of communications theory. The extent to which the flow of influence as well as more generalised information links with the concept of social networks and an examination of the activities of interest groups: most specifically in the context of this study, local planning action groups. Such organisations require to be placed within the community power structure literature, based predominantly on the explanations of studies in North America, and also within the tradition of urban social movements which is largely European and British in origin.

A further and predominant theoretical perspective within the study is based upon the sociological analysis of organisations. While it is important to incorporate many of the insights derived from the analysis of organisational behaviour, much more illumination in this research has been derived from the examination of organisational environments and inter-organisational behaviour. From the first, more common, approach of behaviour within organisations explanations for the redefinition of goals of CLNT, from the need to cater for population growth to that of subregional economic regeneration, may be understood. (See Chapter 6). The second, less usual, emphasis focuses upon the external environment or organisations and in particular upon the notion of the 'task environment' (Dill, 1958, pp.442-3). This approach concentrates upon those parts of the environment which are likely to be relevant to the achievement of the organisation's goals. Important here is the organisation's legitimation within its environment. CLDC as an 'imposed' agency of central government is required to succeed in persuading local authorities and other formal organisations of its legitimacy in its immediate environment. More exacting, it is necessary for such an agency to succeed in the competitive environment of its region. An organisation's environment may thus be regarded as both a resource and a threat: the arena for conflicts to exist or coalitions to occur.

Control of the environment is of paramount priority to any organisation attempting to achieve dominance in its organisational relations and within its external environment. This requirement is highlighted by the 'political economy approach to organisations' (Zald, 1970, p.223) which emphasises the interplay of power and the goals of power wielders within an inter organisational network. Concentrating upon the external relations of a large focal organisation, the study examines the interactions between the CLDC, other formal organisations, such as industrial and commercial employers, and voluntary organisations such as interest groups and local planning action groups.

The centrepiece of the organisational environment and inter organisational focus of the study is the outline plan public inquiry. Indeed the public inquiry is itself described in Chapter 4 as 'a symbolic aspect of inter organisational relations'. As with the study of organisations and interest groups themselves this specialised ritual may also be scrutinised and analysed by employed theoretical models. The comprehensive description and analysis of the public inquiry provides material evidence for the inter organisational relations to which reference has just been made. Tensions between local authorities are depicted, not only referring to the uneasy alliances between the constituent districts of a county council, but also between the local authority districts within the new town designated area and the CLDC itself. More explicity observed are the stresses between the voluntary organisations and CLDC together with the differences of emphasis between such groups. These relationships provide insight into the notion of an 'urban relations system' (touched upon in Chapter 11), and an assessment of the balance of influence is evaluated in Chapter 11. Attention is also given to the presiding central figure of the inspector at the public inquiry.

An aspect of inter organisational dialogue which may be observed and monitored is the press coverage of specific events, issues and relationships. The role of the media, and the local press in particular, is described in Chapter 7. Its importance as a source of current views from the leading protagonists is presumed, yet the local press in the context of this study, it is argued, has functioned as 'an observer and filter of events', as 'a promoter of dialogue' and as 'an opinion former'. News in a community, as Warner has pointed out, is 'part of the political process' (Warner, 1969, p.169). The editorials emanating from the pen of the managing editor of the Chorley and Leyland (now South Ribble) Guardians, which circulate in the southern part of the new town designated area, promoted a scepticism of participation, and together with the Lancashire Evening Post (LEP) placed the Strategic Plan for the North West (SPNW) high on the local political agenda. The SPNW was treated by the press as a threat to CLNT. By implication those who supported the proposed concentration of resources within the North West of England upon the Mersey Belt were ipso facto expressing disloyalty to their own sub region and its creature, CLNT.

Two significant events following the outline plan public inquiry form an integral part of the study. First, the formation of a local groups Working Party and the associated lobbying at national level by the Council for the Protection of Rural England (CPRE), and second the 'unearthing' of a critical organisational study of CLDC ('the Morgan Report') by Mr. Ron Atkins, M.P., and his subsequent intervention in the House of Commons. The first of these as a researcher, the writer was most fortunate and privileged to observe and reflect upon. An informal and covert element of the study, the formation of a cohesive federation linking with CPRE from loosely connected and indeed often mutually suspicious local groups, should not be underestimated. This translated a local bargaining relationship, concerned about CLNT, as a major sub regional project, into an issue for national lobbying.

In employing CLNT as a case study, it is argued that generalisations can be made about the processes of influencing decision making in Britain. The project itself, the background and history of which will be described in more detail in Chapter 2, provides an example of the direct involvement of central government in physical planning. The insights provided by an inter organisational approach to CLDC are employed to illustrate the group and organisational dimensions to participation. In particular, the political economy approach to organisational networks will highlight resource and power differences between the voluntary and the statutory and commercial sector.

The overarching within networks of the formal and voluntary in this study will meet with the criticism recently expressed by Lowe and Goyder that, apart from the case of trade unions, organisational sociologists have been preoccupied with large, complex and bureaucratic organisations (Lowe and Goyder, 1983, p.2).

Above all, the unique nature and importance of CLNT mark it out for close scrutiny. As the last and most extensive surviving British new town it was transmuted from its initial overspill population remit to that of a platform for sub regional economic growth with its so called 'spin-off effects' for the region as a whole. From its designation in 1970 the new town was dogged by uncertainty and threatened with reappraisal. Following much argument at Cabinet level, according to Crossman, he and George Brown supported the notion of the 'growth point' against the opposition of Douglas Jay (Crossman, 1975, p.149).

With such unsure initial foundations, subsequent speculations were bound to occur with each change of government during the 1970s. Yet with great skill and no little guile the CLDC managed to engineer its survival against adverse population trends and public expenditure changes. By utilising the powers contained in the New Towns Act, 1965 (which permitted schemes to be submitted in advance of the outline plan to the Secretary of State under section 6(i)) the development corporation devised compulsory purchase orders for land banking and advance housing and employment schemes. Such projects were placed strategically throughout the designated area as shown in Figure 4. Continued support from the contiguous local authorities was also aided by a common opposition to the proposals of the SPNW. Indeed in terms of organisational survival alone, CLDC is worthy of study.

NOTES

1. The location of the new town is shown in Figure 1.

2 An outline history of the Central Lancashire New Town

'The project is Lancashire's brainchild. For at least twenty years it has been a major element in the strategic policies of both Lancashire County and Preston County Borough Councils............' (CLDC, 1974, p.10).

Both Lancashire and Cheshire had undertaken the preparation of advisory plans prior to their legal obligation to produce the Statutory Development Plan under the 1947 Act. Lancashire's county planning officer, G. Sutton Brown, prepared 'A Preliminary Plan for Lancashire' in 1951 and, by being an advisory plan, it managed to escape the limitations of the legal requirement and could consider the problems of the county boroughs which 'punctured' the county in great numbers.

It was at this point that the local authority initiative was made explicit for three possible new towns, Parbold, Garstang, and the first of the triumvirate which now make up the CLNT, Leyland. Garstang was soon abandoned, at least for the immediate future, Parbold was also shelved and later in 1961 the adjacent Skelmersdale was designated, but Leyland was left as a joint county-urban district project.

Both Lancashire and Cheshire development plans proposed a population dispersal in two stages: the first based on short distance overspill to the edge of the conurbation, and the second to take both population and industry beyond the green belt, but within reasonable distance for access. While Manchester encountered protracted political and land use problems in their relationship with Cheshire, notably at Lymm and Mobberley, Merseyside was more fortunate in being offered Skelmersdale. In the event, new town developments were not in favour for a number of reasons during the 1950s (1) and Cheshire's suggestion of Congleton, and Lancashire's of Skelmersdale, were held in abeyance, and only Skelmersdale was revived when national interest in new towns occurred in 1961 - with Skelmersdale being designated that year.

Consistent with this new thinking, the Lancashire county council's 'Review of the County Development Plan' in 1962 renewed its proposal for a new town in the Leyalnd area, and by 1964 a preliminary technical report of the county planning officer, Mr. Aylmer Coates, was proposing the accommodation of an intake of 150,000 people in the Leyland-Preston-Chorley area. (Lancashire County Council, 1962, 1964). This scheme coincided, as Levin points out, with the movement towards the large new cities propounded in the South East Study (Levin, 1972, p.93) and also with the idea of economic growth points: a concept which will be reviewed in Chapter 4.

These developments of overspill estates and a renewed interest in new towns were not viewed within a regional planning framework until 1965, when the North West Economic Planning Council and Board were established. (See Chapter 6). The council produced two reports, and a multi department government team, one study, hardly comprehensive enough to be called plans, and these publications made some general pronouncements on the CLNT. The first, produced by the Department of Economic Affairs, merely stated that the four new towns existing or proposed under the New Towns Act (Skelmersdale, Runcorn, Warrington and Preston-Leyland-Chorley), together with a number of smaller developments, would probably be adequate to meet the needs of Merseyside and Manchester conurbations in the near future. In particular, the CLNT was welcomed in relation to the strategy outlined in the report since 'it would house people from the conurbations, it was well placed for economic growth, and it would aid the regeneration of some of the existing towns'. (DEA, 1965,pp.110-11).

The two council reports, usually referred to as Strategy I and Strategy II, also concluded in favour of the existing new town proposals and developments, though Strategy II did indicate that the overspill problem seemed to be marginally diminishing and suggested that long term schemes for developments in Lancaster-Garstang and mid-Cheshire (Northwich-Winsford-Crewe) should be considered for the 1980s and 1990s rather than the 1970s. (N.W. Planning Council, 1966, 1968).

Although Manchester city council had consistently been of the opinion that Leyland and Chorley would not be sufficiently attractive for their citizens and industry, Richard Crossman, Minister of Housing and Local Government announced on 24 February 1965 that the government had decided to designate an area for a large new town in just that location.

In January 1966, planning consultants Robert Matthew, Johnson-Marshall and Partners were commissioned to advise the Minister and at this time the area to be considered included Preston. Funds were allocated through supplementary new towns legislation later in the year.

The consultants' report, Central Lancashire: Study for a City, was published in May 1967, but probably because of the influence on the surrounding area, particularly north-east Lancashire, the then Minister of Housing and Local Government, Anthony Greenwood, announced that he was commissioning the same consultants and Economic Consultants Ltd. to examine the effects of the new town on the areas to the east. This 'impact study' published in February 1968 formed the basis for concessions for north east Lancashire, such as the provision of a motorway link to the M6, 'the Calder Valley fast route', the M65. The draft designation order was published on 31 December 1968. There were 670 objections to this order and a public inquiry took place into designation in Preston under Sir Andrew Wheatley during May 1969.

The minister's decision letter was published, together with the inspector's report, on 24 March 1970 indicating that the designated area was to be reduced from a projected 41,000 acres to 35,000 acres. Despite this announcement there followed a period of uncertainty associated with the change of government in June of that year and there was a review of the decision to designate. In February 1971, the Secretary of State for the Environment, Mr. Peter Walker confirmed the decision to proceed (2). Sir Frank Pearson, a former member of parliament for Clitheroe, was appointed chairman of the development corporation and by July 1971 the membership of the board of the corporation was completed. The general manager, Mr. Richard Phelps, took up his duties in December and the task of preparing the outline plan commenced.

There was some delay in producing the outline plan. It was stated in the local press that it 'should be ready for Spring' (1973) (LEP, September 1972). In the event a draft outline plan was produced for limited circulation in November 1973, with an accompanying leaflet, and the actual outline plan was published on 31 May 1974. (See Chapter 8).

In the meantime, various local groups were being formed or revitalised (See Chapter 6). Walton Summit Protest Committee was formed on 25 June 1973 and shortly afterwards Planwatch was inaugurated at a public meeting on 10 July. At the turn of the year Moss Side (Leyland) Residents' Association was founded and during April 1974 both Preston groups, Ashton Action Group and Preston North Action Group were formed. Later that summer Fulwood and Broughton Residents' Association was founded (July 1974) and SCRAP (3) launched (September 1974).

The commencement of the 'participation' period may be taken as the date of publication of the free summary pamphlet of the Outline Plan (23 April 1974). Public meetings to discuss the road appraisal reports and the outline plan itself took place during the months of May, June and July 1974 with the original date set for the public inquiry of 17 September 1974. Following representations by the two Preston M.P.s this date was rearranged and the inquiry commenced on 5 November, finishing some three months later on 24 January 1975. (See Chapter 11).

Following a period of quiescence in 1975 local groups became active once more and a local groups Working Party was formed following a conference of delegates on 8 May 1976. Lobbying at national level, under the auspices of CPRE continued that summer, and the campaign culminated in a Commons adjournment debate on 23 December 1976. (See Chapter 12).

The Secretary of State's speech on inner cities in Manchester on 17 September 1976 may be seen as a precursor to the policy shift indicated by the decision letter on CLNT in April 1977, when population targets were substantially reduced and, as Judy Hillman commented, somewhat over dramatically, CLDC was allowed to 'go ahead with the creation of an urban midget in central Lancashire instead of an urban region'. (Guardian, 6 April 1977).

To the date of the decision letter, 5 April 1977, the uncertainty associated with the eventual boundary and proposed population of CLNT had been considerable, as Figures 3 and 6 indicate, yet developments approved or sought under Section 6(i) of the New Towns Act, 1965 at that ime were not insubstantial (See Figures 4 and 5). (4). The development corporation published its 'Implementation Strategy' a year later, which set out the schemes permissible following the Secretary of State's decision. With a limited target population of 285,000 to be reached by the mid 1980s, and the exclusion of development in the Grimsargh/Haighton and Runshaw/Ulnes Walton areas, the modified road and housing schemes increasing stress upon urban renewal are spelled out. (CLDC, 1978). This strategy was interpreted as 'a multi million pound crash programme of homes, roads and factories .... to beat the new town's 1987 deadline'. (LEP, 22 August 1978).

Further uncertainty and speculation of the future of CLNT was linked with the general election in 1979. Trade union leaders in the area expressed their opposition to any further curtailment of the new town and this view was largely endorsed by the Labour Party candidates in the area. The most vociferous opposition to the CLDC was voiced by the Conservative candidate, Mr. Den Dover, who succeeded Mr. George Rodgers as M.P. for Chorley; though Mr. Edward Gardner, M.P. for South Fylde was ambivalent, while conceding that all new towns 'throw up large amounts of discontent', he believed that 'there had been a considerable improvement over the last few years' (LEP, 20 April 1979).

The expectation that an incoming Conservative administration would retain the option to review the new town was confirmed. The lower number of rented houses allowed in 1981 was expected to affect the rate of building, and in view of the transfer of emphasis from the public to the private sector, 'the corporation has been encouraged to roll over some of its existing assets', (Town and Country Planning, 1980, pp.388-9).

By the spring of 1982, new town development corporations had been given dates for their winding up. The CLDCs existence is expected to cease on 31 December 1985 and the Secretary of State has been consulting the Lancashire county council and its constituent borough councils (See Figure 2) about a proposed programme which would provide 'an indication of what would be reasonable for the development Corporation to carry out' (document quoted in LEP, 15 February 1982).

This chapter has provided a brief outline history of CLNT. The following pages contain sketchmaps and diagrams to which reference has been made in the text.

Figure 2 shows the new town designated area superimposed upon the constituent local authorities, Preston, South Ribble and Chorley, together with other local authorities within both Lancashire and Greater Manchester counties which come within the fringe of planning constraints.

Figure 3 provides an outline in sketchmap form of the various boundaries proposed preparatory to the area designated in 1970.

Figure 4 indicates the location and dispersed nature of the various Section 6(i) applications and the extent to which these were approved, awaiting approval or known to be in preparation by CLDC. While Figure 5 indicates the actual development position in 1977 showing the areas excluded from immediate new town development under the outline plan, notably the north east flank of Preston at Haighton and Grimsargh and an area south of Leyland - Ulnes Walton and Runshaw.

Figure 6 emphasises the changing nature of the population targets, with the outline plan decision in 1977 virtually returning to the initial target proposed in 1951 for the Leyland area alone.

A chronology of the events is provided in the appendix of the study.

NOTES

1. Particularly, the political will in the conservative administration in the 1950s and its insistence upon the use of the Town Development Act, 1952 (See Schaffer, 1972, pp.245-7; Hall, et al, 1973, pp.584-595).

2. For a detailed account of the factors involved in the designation see Levin, 1976, pp.130-9.

3. Society for the coordination and reaffirmation of anti new town policies.

4. These sketchmaps and diagram (figures 3,4,5 and 6) are included by kind permission of the originator (Grimshaw, 1978).

1 Wyre District

2 Fylde District

3 Preston District

4 Ribble Valley District

5 South Ribble District

6 West Lancashire District

7 Chorley District

8 Blackburn District

9 Wigan Metropolitan District

10 Bolton Metropolitan District

Designated area

Figure 2. CENTRAL LANCASHIRE NEW TOWN. Constituent and Fringe area Local Authorities

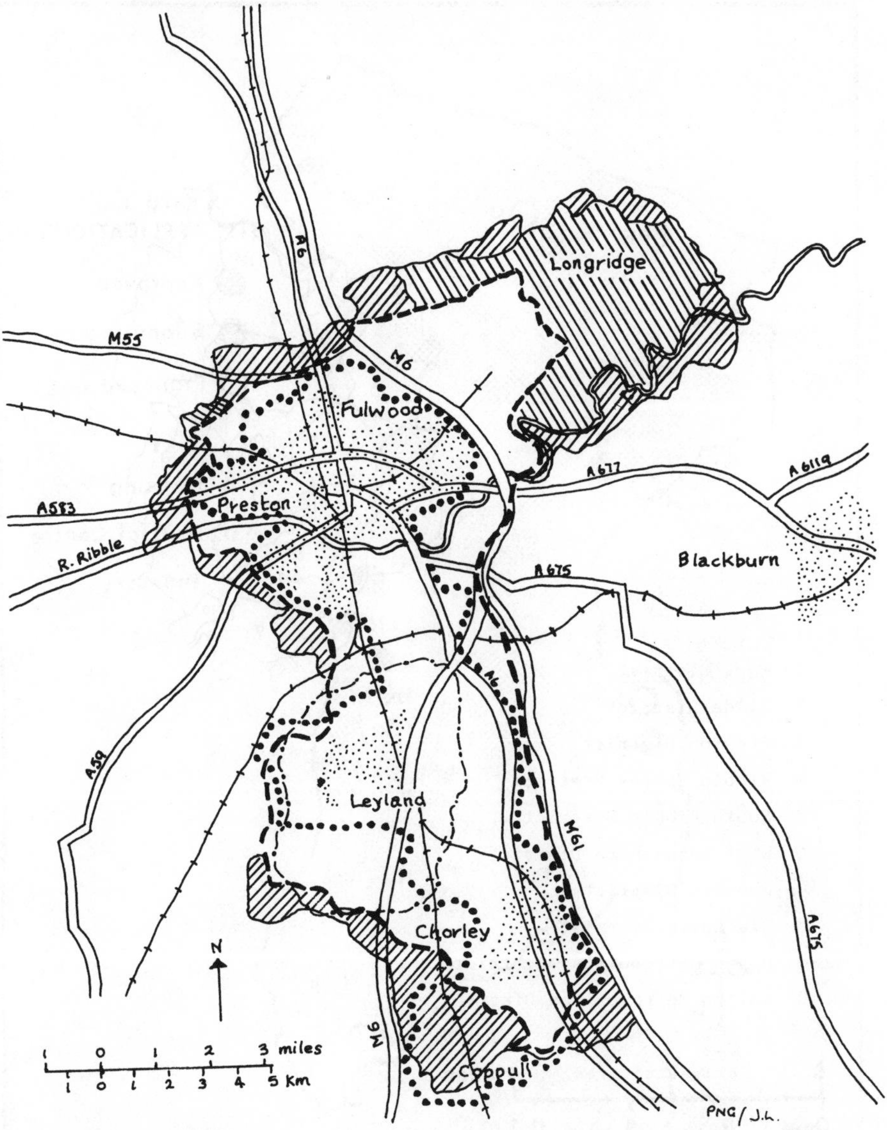

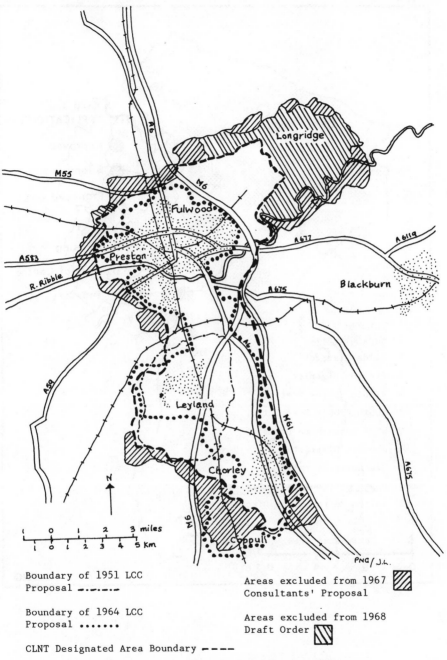

Boundary of 1951 LCC Proposal -.-.-.-

Boundary of 1964 LCC Proposal •••••••

CLNT Designated Area Boundary - - - -

Areas excluded from 1967 Consultants' Proposal

Areas excluded from 1968 Draft Order

Figure 3. Development Areas proposed for Central Lancashire 1951-76

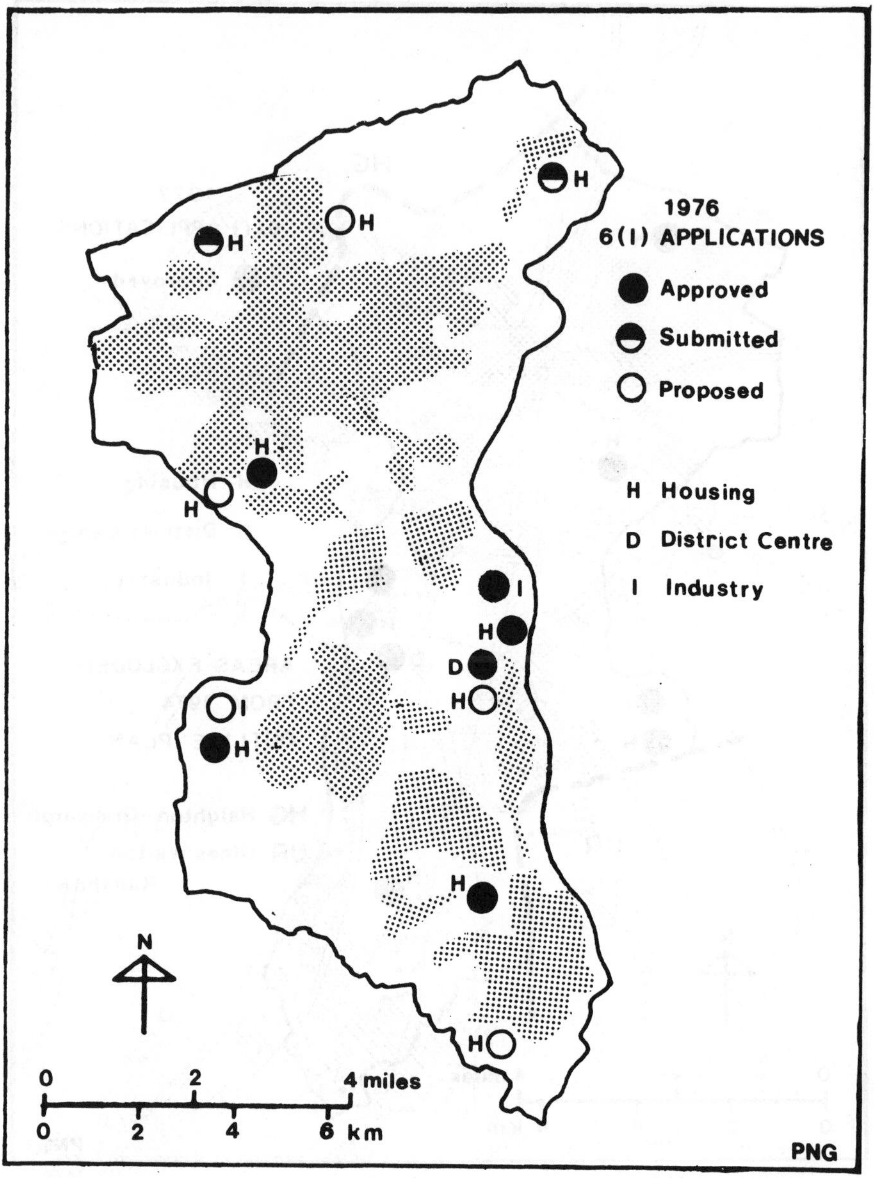

Figure 4. <u>CENTRAL LANCASHIRE NEW TOWN. Development Position in 1976</u>

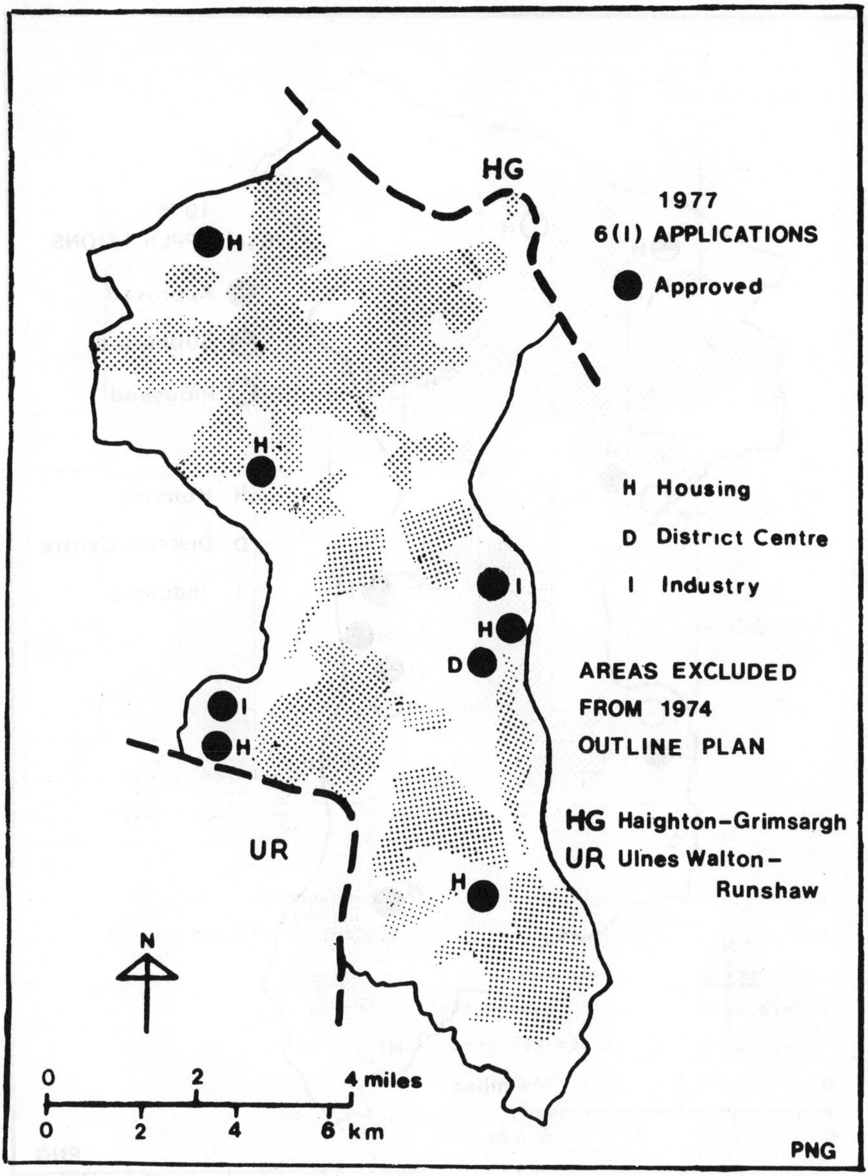

Figure 5. CENTRAL LANCASHIRE NEW TOWN. Development Position in 1977

POPULATION 000's

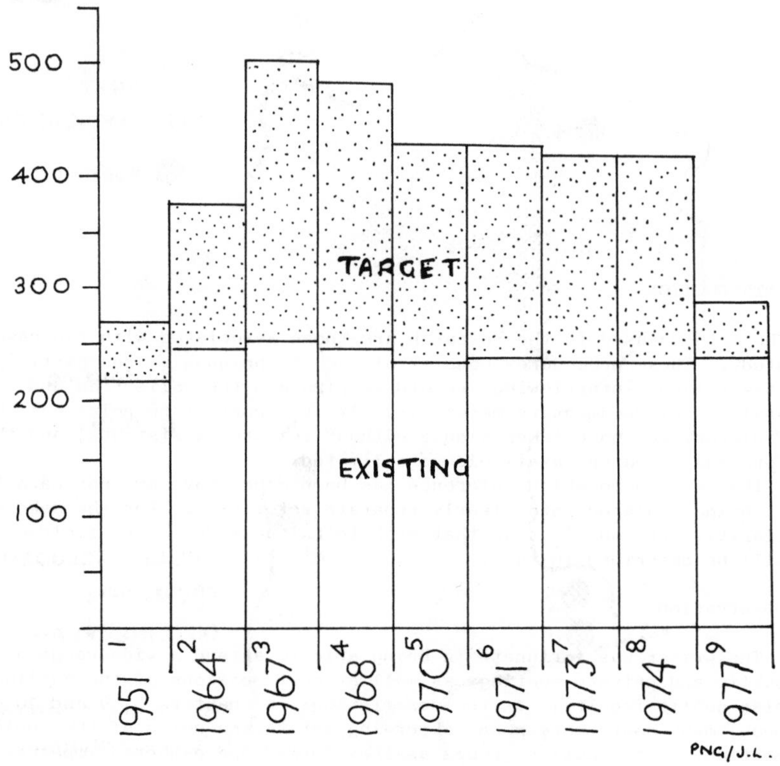

Reference 1	Preliminary plan for Lancashire
Reference 2	Future development of Central Mid-Lancashire
Reference 3	Study for a City
Reference 4	Draft Designation Order
Reference 5	Designated area decision
Reference 6	Draft Master Plan
Reference 7	Consultative document
Reference 8	Outline Plan
Reference 9	Outline Plan decision

Figure 6. POPULATION PROPOSALS FOR CENTRAL LANCASHIRE, 1951-77

3 Research methodology

INTRODUCTION

The methods used in the research are those associated with the case study. These procedures consist of such techniques as non participant observation, interviewing, record keeping and the collection and analysis of documentary materials. It is important to point out that fieldwork was undertaken alone, without research assistants, and therefore the resources available were limited.

The methods to which reference has been made above are not capable of being isolated into clearly separate activities. For the sake of clarity, the contribution that each technique made to the fieldwork will be described in turn.

Observation

The writer was fortunate in being able to attend a wide range of public and private meetings as well as most sessions of the outline plan public inquiry. As the descriptions in Chapters 8, 9 and 10 will show, many hours were spent observing ant taking notes of the public meetings of the action groups as they formed and gathered impetus. Almost every public meeting held by the development corporation on the outline plan, road appraisal reports and the transport network was witnessed and as many sessions of the outline plan public inquiry as practicable were attended (See Chapter 11).

Just as important were the numerous private meetings to which the writer was fortunate to be permitted entrance. These included many committee meetings, working party meetings and, most important of all, negotiations. First, there were the negotiations between action groups and the CLDC officers and a second, crucial category there were bargaining sessions between action groups attempting to achieve joint policies and strategies. (See Chapters 5 and 7).

Interviews

In depth interviews were conducted with a large number of key individuals involved in varying capacities with the CLNT designated area. Officals interviewed included the general manager of the development corporation, Mr. Richard Phelps and his personal assistant, dealing with press and public relations, Col. Carl Barras. Although wider contact with CLDC staff was common, circumstances made it impossible for lengthy formal discussions to take place, though this restriction was more than compensated for by the generous time afforded the writer by the inspector to discuss the inspectorate, the public inquiry and his general impressions of those involved.

Officers of the local action groups, the secretary of CPRE (Lancashire Branch), key local councillors and as many prominent individuals that could be identified, either by position, reputation or by publishing in the local press, were contacted and interviewed during 1973 and 1974. The initial link was often maintained through the various public and private meetings attended by the writer as an observer, or in some cases through correspondence. Many of the most prominent informants' activities were also capable of being monitored through the press coverage of their statements or letters.

Interviews were also conducted with members of local press lobby and regular contact subsequently maintained with Peter Dugdale of the Lancashire Evening Post (LEP) and Jeff Barnes and his staff at the news agency in Preston.

Record keeping and documentary materials

Whenever feasible, full notes were taken of all interviews, meetings and discussions. When overt note taking would have inhibited the development of views or ideas, records were made as soon as possible after the event. Such notes were complemented by a wide array of documents and cuttings which provided either corroboration or a differing perception of events observed or interviews undertaken.

Interview notes,in the case of CLDC staff in particular, were supplemented by biographical details published in newspaper supplements or books (such as Apgar, 1976). Records of public meetings similarly were corroborated with reports in newspapers and meetings of action groups with minutes kindly made available. It is acknowledged that both forms of record to which reference has been made are partial, imperfect and selective, yet both served as essential sources of research data.

During the period of the research, press cuttings files were compiled and proved to be an invaluable adjunct to fieldwork notes. In addition to regular scrutiny of the national and local press at the news agency, the writer visited CLDCs offices and the Harris Library, Preston, to check on the selection of press cuttings which each organisation had collected and to ensure that relevant materials had not been overlooked.

Documentary materials used, other than books, newspapers and journal articles, also included official documents, varying from Hansard, as a record of parliamentary interventions, and DOE circulars to the various publications of CLDC, the inspector's reports, the proofs of evidence submitted to the public inquiries and the many briefings, press releases, copy letters and newsletters originated by action groups and national interest groups.

It was not always possible to obtain the documentation requested or required. CLDC press releases were not available and a most important document, an organisational study of the development corporation 'The Morgan Report' was restricted (Morgan, 1973). In the latter case, the writer was only able to draw upon secondary sources. Organisation charts of CLDC were circulated to members of liaison committees and the confirmation of the 'logic' for such structures was later elaborated in a chapter in a book (Apgar,1976), an article in the Financial Times and a report to the International New Towns Association, all written by the general manager of CLDC, (See Chapters 6 and 12).

Reflections on the methods employed

The concepts within social network theory proved applicable, particularly that of the action set (Mayer, 1966, p.111). This leads one to discover what might be a transitory, yet valid, personal network which is strongly instrumentally orientated. Using such notions, which are elaborated upon in Chapter 4, requires the interlocking application of all foregoing methods. Indeed, as Chapter 12 illustrates, the short comings of one method to an area of enquiry may be supplemented by employing another complementary technique. In what is termed 'triangulation' of methods, observation, documentary sources and interviews together will give a more complete impression of the events or the social institution to be studied.

One pre-eminent method which was not utilised in this study was that of the social survey questionnaire. While it would have been possible to have conducted a small scale inquiry into attitudes, social linkages etc., using the survey method, involving sampling frames, statistical tables, tests of significance and so on, it was decided to rely upon the results of the CLDCs 'Master Sample Social Survey' (CLDC, 1974a) for data when necessary (See Chapter 7).

Structured questionnaire techniques were rejected for this study for a number of additional reasons. First, experience in employing this method in previous research (fieldwork for which was based in six industrial plants) suggested that this technique would not be appropriate for what was potentially such a lengthy period of fieldwork. Second, and linked with this factor, was the realisation that structured questionnaires or panel interviews, by their very nature consist of snapshots of individual attitudes and opinions suspended in time. With a dynamic environment surrounding CLDC existing throughout this period the timing of such interviews and re-interviews would have been crucial and problematic. Third, the wealth of data becoming available did not warrant additional survey material. Indeed an important feature of the reflective case study used here is not only the collection of data but the attempt to interpret the study material in new ways. The data obtained by the method described in this chapter is often less relevant than the understanding of the social processes, interactions, networks and social institutions being observed. Fourth, and finally, survey techniques often fail to take the social process of the interview and investigation itself into account. Uncritical advocates of such methods often insist on the 'objectives' of the data collected and the neutrality of the practitioner. Although this position is commonly held by many undertaking academic research, it is a stance which appears to be regarded by many members of the general public as exceptional. A number of contacts and respondents gave the impression that they found it difficult to accept the position of the 'value neutral', 'impartial' university researcher.

Summary

This chapter has described the research methods used in the research, it has discussed some of the occasions when these were employed in the fieldwork and it has indicated the importance of employing a range of techniques in a complementary fashion. Some of the shortcomings of the survey technique for the particular study have also been summarised.

PART II
THEORETICAL ASPECTS

4 Participation in planning : processes and participants

INTRODUCTION

Participation, as a concept, has its roots in democratic theory. There have been sporadic attempts in recent history to introduce elements of a fully participatory democracy within the dominant western representative democratic tradition. The last two decades have witnessed a period of heightened interest in participation which is currently waning under recent town and country planning legislation,(1) housing policy, and the failure to implement fully the Bullock and Taylor reports, intended to affect the governance of industry and education.

Much has been written in recent years about the basis of participation (Fagence, 1977; Sewell and Coppock, 1977). Its literature has been widely documented in both British (Barker, 1979) and wider English speaking contexts (Woodcock, 1980). Within the broad definition of participation, 'being stronger than consultation but weaker than determination' (Groombridge et al, 1982, p.1), it should be viewed as a process of information and exchange; and, also within such wide limits, as a means of reducing power differences between parties.(Strauss,1963)

Reaction by those in authority has led to cynical and humorous comments (Howard, 1976; Johnson, 1979). More seriously, the main objections have been analysed and rebutted by Jowell. The categories of disapproval, 'increasing inertia', 'building in bias', 'retarding reform' and 'compelling commitment' distilled from detractors both in Britain and abroad illustrate much of the inherent opposition or disdain exhibited by the more powerful partners in the process (Jowell, 1975).

Although participation is an integral part of the debate about industrial democracy, personal social services, housing and school management in Britain, it is in the area of town and country planning that the focus of this study will be concentrated. The official basis for the concept of participation in planning in Britain derives from the Minister's Planning Advisory Group, formed in 1964, with the objective to ensure that the planning system included a means of public participation. Subsequent legislation, the 1968 Act, included a broad provision for participation in the new development plans and it was left to a committee under the then joint parliamentary secretary, Mr. Arthur Skeffington, M.P., 'to consider and report on the best methods including publicity, of securing the participation of the public at the formative stage in the making of development plans for their area'. This report produced what, in the British context, has been regarded as the official definition of participation in planning, 'the act of sharing in the formulation of policies and proposals' (Skeffington, 1969, p.1).

The report was not accepted in full, but its major recommendations were given ministerial approval through Circular 52/72. For the proponents these were days of optimism, a time of democratic endeavour. To quote the TCPA, all that was required was

> ".... central government would need the 'will'; local government and officers and members would need to adopt 'flexible attitudes'; and the public at large would have to emerge from in front of their TV sets and take advantage of the various new participatory mechanisms that were to be provided; but somehow it was only a matter of time before all this happened". (TCPA,1981)

During the 1970s the county structure plans and their constituent local plans have provided case study evidence about the effectiveness and interest of both planners and the public in participation procedures. These processes have been studied by, and have been linked with adult education agencies (Hampton and Beale, 1976; Woodcock and Emerson, 1977). Participation in certain county structure plans (Cheshire, Merseyside, North East Lancashire, Teeside) has been monitored in a linked research project funded by the DOE. (Boaden, et al, 1980). Its conclusions suggest that, while structure plans were not the easiest of levels at which to commence such public involvement, the issues being often too remote and abstract, a most important factor in the process was the professional planner's attitude to information exchange.

In this study, while professional and bureaucratic attitudes to information exchange were crucial, the special circumstances of new town participants gives rise to unfulfilled expectations of participation. Rights and precedents observed under general planning legislation only applied obliquely, and through administrative suggestion, rather than through legal obligation. These frustrations will be illuminated through an examination in the next section, when participation is related to political theory.

A THEORETICAL BASIS FOR PARTICIPATION IN PLANNING

It has been pointed out in the introductory section of this chapter that participation is grounded in political theory. In a comprehensive review of 'Theoretical Perspectives on Planning Participation', Thornley provides an overview to which it would be difficult to supplement. In this survey he asserts that all approaches and views on planning participation can be related to the range of theories described (Thornley, 1977, p.49). These are generally categorised under consensus or conflict theories of society. The former are typified by Parsons (1960), Almond and Verba (1965), the latter in two strands: that of Dahrendorf (1959) and Marx. To these theories of social order (in which the key variable is the emphasis given to stability in society) is added the dimension of 'degree of participation'. This relationship is shown diagramatically as follows:-

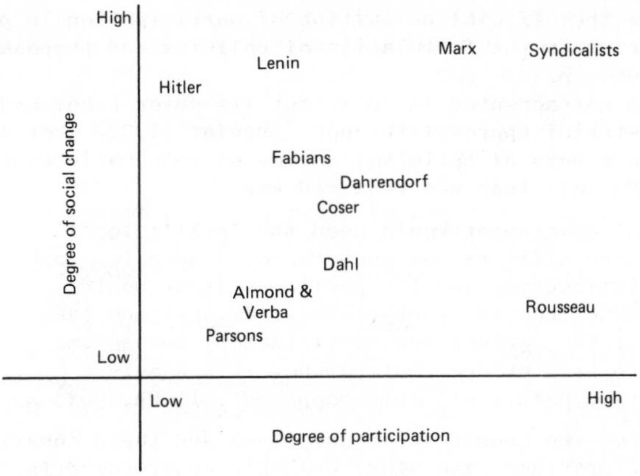

A hypothetical location of theorists (Thornley, 1977, p.8)

Thornley then provides a synthesis of the theoretical background and historical development of participation to construct three alternative perspectives which correspond to Almond and Verba and the modern theorists (Consensus and Stability), early Dahrendorf (Containment and Bargaining) and late Marx (Conflict and Increased Consciousness).

In reviewing the theoretical basis for participation in planning and some of the typologies constructed around the concept, the relevance of these notions to the focus of this study, the central Lancashire new town, requires a special assessment. The more usual locations for studies of citizen involvement or confrontation are the established communities, possibly threatened by redevelopment, or in the declining urban or inner city areas experiencing deprivation and social and economic disadvantage. In recent years, the additional examples of protests about sitings for power stations, waste disposal, airports, mineral extraction and motorway routes have become more evident, particularly as these tend to involve opposition from the more articulate and national interest groups as well as local amenity societies.

Considering the allocation of public investment which they have absorbed in post war years, and the peculiar position they hold within planning and regional policy, new towns are no less important. As such they do not conform with the regular provisions of the planning legislation for participation in development plans. Their 'special' position in this respect will be outlined briefly in the next section.

PARTICIPATION IN NEW TOWNS: A SPECIAL CASE?

The peculiar regulations defining the extent of participation in British new towns will be described more fully in Chapter 8. In brief, general managers of new town development corporations were asked in Circular 276/72 issued by the Department of Environment to use the Circular 52/72, directed at local authorities, as a guide to the implementation of the Skeffington Report.

Earlier new towns in Britain were 'greenfield' developments with small initial, generally rural, populations. The later Mark III new towns have tended to be expansions of existing urban settlements of some size (See Schaffer, 1972; Aldridge, 1979). Yet all phases possessed, as a basis for their development, an underlying ideology that new towns represented a fresh start for developing 'balanced' communities. This philosophy was outlined fully in the Reith Report (New Towns Committee, 1945). In his review of the report, Wirtz outlines these assumptions which included, not only the provision of physical amenities and a youth service, but also that the inhabitants would need 'an opportunity for participation' (Wirtz, 1975, p.6). Social development would be the vehicle to encourage such participation.

The appointment of the first social development officer was made by Lord Reith himself, as chairman of Hemel Hempstead development corporation in 1949. Yet it was 1963 before the ministry set out the role of social development officers in new towns (MHLG, 1963). Despite this circular it was stated 'few schemes have been developed that take advantage of the £4 per head of population which since 1963 it has been possible to levy for social development projects in new towns' (Broady, 1968, p.71). The relatively low priority for this function continued throughout the development of British new towns.

Despite the expectation that the later 'imposed' new town development would require an even more 'sensitive' approach, it has been conceded that the 'process of planning and development of most new towns in both Europe and the United States has been fairly autocratic' (Hanson, 1972, p.82).

New town populations, particularly since Gans' Park Forest Study (Gans, 1953), have been regarded by many commentators to be more likely to be involved in political and social activity that citizens in general and indeed, this 'heightened activity established among new town residents has lasting power', and according to Baer, it 'does extend into the second generation' (Baer, 1978, p.244). Yet Baer admits that he only concentrates his research upon the limited area of activity in social and political organisations, while ignoring 'the participation of citizens in the planning of their community' (Baer, 1978, p.238). Had he extended his inquiries he might have discovered, as MacMurray concluded from his survey of development corporations, that:

> '.... Participation by the public in the development and management of new towns is fairly limited and ineffective: the new towns' tradition of innovation and social concern has not extended to the social processes of decision taking and the exercise of power and influence' (MacMurray, 1974, p.27)

It is salutary to discover that, despite the high democratic ideals of the founders of the new towns or 'Garden Cities' movement, the concept, when taken into the public domain, is regarded more as a vehicle for efficiency than political and social change. In such settlements within Britain, which potentially might have been pace making examples in participatory practices and collective decision making, we find the anomalous situation that even the minimal provisions of the Town and Country Planning Acts do not apply. New towns are, indeed, a special case.

THE CATEGORISATION OF INDIVIDUAL PARTICIPANTS

As outlined in Chapter 3, the fieldwork for this study consisted of a considerable amount of observation, discussion and interviewing with the main actors involved in the promotion, opposition or scrutiny of the central Lancashire new town. The Participants which were so identified should be viewed as individuals, as leaders or activists, and many additional as members of formal or informal political institutions, ranging from the bureaucracy of the development corporation, a government agency and members of residents' and amenity groups. A review of theories of community leadership and of the articulation of interests, through the activities of informal political institutions such as political parties, chambers of commerce, trades councils and action groups, is a useful precursor to the actual description of the main organisations and groups involved in the political environment of the central Lancashire new town (CLNT).

Apart from the very important classification of members of society into classes or socio-economic groups, a number of studies have attempted to refine such blocks, usually defined by occupation, income or education, into descriptive categories which more accurately describe life style or attitudes. In British industrial sociology the work of Goldthorpe and Lockwood has provided an insight into a possible differentiation within shop floor workers (Goldthorpe and Lockwood, et al, 1968) and similarly the terms 'cosmopolitan' and 'local' and 'spiralist' and 'burgess' provide 'labels' for group norms and attitudes in communities (Merton, 1957, pp.387-436; Watson, 1964). While such classifications tend to be too simplistic to be applicable in anything more than an initial description of a community, provided such concepts are treated as 'ideal types', (2) they are useful in affording the basis for further analysis.

Lowry has provided further refinement in his study of 'Micro City' leaders by isolating two major variables which he believes to be crucial in understanding the range of leadership types arising through community conflict. These variables are 'the cultural or ideological orientation of the leaders' and 'their place and role in the community and political structure as determined by their participation in daily group life'. The ideological orientation is described as 'conservative' and 'non conservative' (or 'Utopian') and the type of participation is recategorised by the addition of a further category of 'Mediator'. Thus:

> 'According to their participation in the group life of Micro City, leaders may be designated as 'Locals' (those who play significant roles in groups which are predominantly oriented towards the community, per se, in origin and interests), 'Cosmopolitans' (those who give a majority of their time and interests to groups which transcend the local community), and 'Mediators' (those who participate within areas of both local and larger societal activity)' (Lowry, 1962, p.131)

As a conceptual aid in visualising the structure and general nature of the Micro City community leadership, Lowry shows this typology in diagrammatic form:-

A Typology of Community Leadership

Participation in the structure of group life	Cultural Orientation Conservation	Utopian
Local	C-L	U-L
Mediating	C-M	U-M
Cosmopolitan	C-C	U-C

(Lowry, 1962, p.131)

Lowry points out that the above categories, as in any typology, are ideal categorisations and are not intended to be mutually exclusive and, indeed, deviant cases are discussed. The diagram however, should not be interpreted 'as merely a static picture of power and influence' for, 'not only do the six types of community leaders exhibit common beliefs and patterns of social activity but also particular lines of influence and responsibility can also be observed between the types'. (Lowry, 1962, p.131) (my emphasis). This particular analysis forms a basis for classifications to be introduced later in Chapter 6.

It is generally recognised that the number of persons involving themselves in voluntary organisations and community activity is but a small proportion of the total active and eligible population. (3) A comparison of the social characteristics of participants in different kinds of issues, and the population at large, in Syracuse showed that the leaders were, in general, of

> '.... higher social level (or status), and more often they were males, in middle years, from high status families . . . surprisingly enough however, they were less apt to be long term residents of the community' (Freeman, 1962, p.8)

The Syracuse study does find, however, that the tendency to possess such characteristics was not equal for all issues. 'Different issues involved participants with different sets of social characteristics'. In addition, this study showed that those endowed with formal authority differed from influentials and that a refined treatment of the data suggested three distinct types of leadership roles: 'Institutional leaders', 'Effectors' and 'Activists'. (4) (Freeman, 1962, p.26). A similar treatment of the group activities in central Lancashire will be developed in Chapter 6.

In addition to the general patterns of leadership discussed above, this research has been concerned with the role of the individuals involved in the mass media and special attention has been given to the activities and attitudes of the 'gatekeepers' in the channels of mass communication, most specifically journalists associated with the local press (See Chapter 7).

INFORMAL POLITICAL INSTITUTIONS

These may be defined as groups and organisations which are formed to affect the way in which the power of the state is exercised, which though they may have a formal structure of their own internal regulation, are not a formal part of the constitutional framework of government. Political parties and interest groups fall within this category, and though the distinction between them is somewhat blurred, (Rose, 1974, p.245), political scientists appear to be in favour of an attempt at delineation. Murray, for example, characterises political parties as 'institutions which are declaredly concerned to control power', while he sees interest groups as 'institutions which directly or indirectly seek to, or just do, influence the way the power of government is exercised . . . Both political parties and interest groups play a part in affecting what governments do and how they do it, but there is a difference in the way in which the two act' (Murray, 1971, p.50).

Although this study relates some of the activity of the political parties at the local level, it is primarily concerned with the action within a number of interest groups in central Lancashire, groups which essentially differ from the parties by having limited objects. The narrow objectives of the groups provide an easier procedure in obtaining local consensus and party or class differences are able to be set aside, temporarily at least,in the furtherance of a particular cause. As Dilys Hill puts it

> '.... Individuals no longer think of themselves as just voters, or as members of the working or middle classes, when they approach these areas of local interest. New forces are at work which encourage individuals to pursue their interests in fresh ways' (Hill, 1970, p.198)

This fragile harmony can be destroyed by attempts to widen the objectives of the group, which then permits differences in 'cultural orinetation' to be aired and made explicit. The potentially disruptive effects of the anti new town groups at Grimsargh and Walton Summit in forming an umbrella organisation, SCRAP, upon the other action groups, which consist of both members against and broadly in favour of the new town concept, will be described later in Chapter 10.

The action groups studied do not conveniently fall within Finer's categories of interest groups, apart from somewhat loosely within his eighth 'omnibus' category of 'educatoral, recreational and cultural groups' (Finer, 1958, pp.8-17). More aptly they may be analysed in relation to Blondel's dichotomy of 'protective' and 'promotional' groups (Blondel, 1969, p.160) the local action groups, specifically protective in their concerted action against road proposals; Planwatch and SCRAP, in their different ways, promotional - the former in relation to 'better planning' and participation in planning, the latter to promote the long term abolition of the development corporation.

Interest groups, in general terms, can operate in three ways:

> .... First, an interest group can seek to <u>influence indirectly</u> those who determine public policy by arousing public interest and support for action for a particular cause, thus trusting to general lines of communication between the public and the government to convey a demand. (Murray, 1971, p.67)

Murray cites Martin Luther King's effective use of the media in this connection.

The various groups' use of the media and the development corporation's 'special relationship' will be fully explored and described in Chapter 7.

.... A second way in which interest groups operate is through <u>political parties</u> . . . the variety of methods is considerable. The objective however, is to secrue the adoption of an interest group's cause as the policy of the party as a whole, or at least as an aim of a section of the party. (Murray, 1971, p.67)

This mode of operation is particularly relevant in describing certain action groups. The Preston North action group used its ready access to the local M.P. and ward labour party, Planwatch sought all party support to its requests for better public participation and SCRAP lobbied parliamentary candidates and threatened to promote the candidature of anti new town candidates in three marginal seats prior to an expected general election. (See Chapter 8)

.... Finally, the most pervasive and important method is by <u>direct action</u> on the government. It is a general characteristic of interest groups that they focus their attention on those parts of government whe power relevant to their objective lies. In Britain, where much of the relevant power is concentrated in the executive, activity is directed towards the executive ministries. (Murray, 1971, p.67)

In the context of this study, the relevant power is concentrated within the Department of the Environment. Either through the local M.P.s or directly by letter, as described in Chapter 10, the department was lobbied to postpone the date of the public inquiry into the outline plan. The ministry's inspector is a central figure in the decision making machinery and a public inquiry provides indirect access to the department for local groups, though this procedure was later perceived to be inadequate, and caused the formation of a concerted lobby - the joint groups Working Party. The circumstances of its founding are covered in Chapter 12.

LEADERS, INTEREST GROUPS AND THE COMMUNITY POWER STRUCTURE

If we view power as the ability to influence decision making in a specific context, information on decision making could provide useful indicators about the locus of power. Three areas have been suggested which often provide indices of the power of individuals or groups: '(1) who participates in decision making, (2) who gains and who loses from alternative possible outcomes, and (3) who prevails in decision making'. (Polsby, 1963, p.40)

The arguments relating to who actually prevails and the place and relevance of interest groups provide a key to divergent theoretical and ideological orientations towards power in both communities, and in society, generally. These basically are divided into monolithic or pluralistic models of power. The monolithic model views power as being centralised in either a ruling class or an elite. The ruling class model is based on a Marxist analysis of class conflict where one class, which includes a wide range of business interests, exercises power over another coherent group, the working class; while the elite model represents the organised minority in power as dominating an unorganised majority. (Mosca, 1939). Studies which have used this model in investigations of community power in the United States have been given the general category of 'stratification studies'. It has been suggested that these studies make five common assertions. There are: first, that 'the upper class rules in local community life'; second, that 'political and civic leaders are subordinate to the upper class'; third, "a single 'power elite' rules in the community"; fourth, 'the upper class power elite rules in its own interests'; and fifth, that 'social conflict takes place between the upper and lower classes'. (Polsby, 1963, pp.8-110.)

In contrast, the pluralistic model 'posits a society in which power is widely shared and influenced by an electorate organised into voluntary organisations'. (Bollans and Schmandt, 1970, p.146; see also Laski, 1975; Nicholls, 1975; Dahl, 1961, 1980).

The dialogue between these two positions has largely been concentrated upon the study of Atlanta, Georgia, by Floyd Hunter (Hunter, 1953) which concluded that key decisions were made by handfuls of influentials who formed a stable locus of power; and that of New Haven, Connecticut, by Robert Dahl (Dahl, 1961) which found a diffused system of community power with different elites dominant in separate issues.

A wider interpretation of studies of community power has, however, been evolved by Jennings, a political scientist, who partly replicated and reinvestigated the Atlanta Study by Hunter. He suggests that five non mutually exclusive groups of studies can be delineated which emphasise different orientations. These are: 'traditional political science, traditional sociology, interpersonal influence processes, case studies, and power structure'. (Jennings, 1964, p.3). Traditional political science studies are described as generally focussing upon formal government and political party variables, and those within the traditional sociology upon latent and manifest social structures, the processes and functions of the community analysed through a wide range of sociological institutions: the family, the churches and economic organisations.

Jennings' success in providing a synthesis of the different approaches is summarised in the following passage which describes the relative contributions of the five approaches which he identified:

> .... From the traditional political science comes an interest in the impact of the formal government structure on community decision making, the roles of government officials, and the importance of the electoral process. The older community sociology leads to examining the social and economic bases, characteristics, and concomitants of political decision making and status. The lessons of interpersonal influence studies direct attention to the interpersonal relations of select actors in the decision making structure. Case studies offer a way of determining different types of decision making roles and variations in process. Finally, the power structure approach suggests that we should try to assess the major dimensions of community influence and influentials over extended substantive areas. (Jennings, 1964, p.14)

This last approach is regarded by Jennings as likely to be the most useful in providing a body of knowledge about patterns of influence in the community since its

> .... scope of attention is larger than that of traditional political science, more specific than the traditional

> sociological approach, both more inclusive and exclusive than the focus on interpersonal influence, and more expansive than the single issue or case study analysis. (Jennings, 1964, p.13)

The attitude taken towards these various perspectives provides a balanced and multi-disciplinary approach to community decision making; an open sensitive and adaptable orientation to research which this particular study of central Lancashire will attempt to emulate. It is important, however, that separate generalisations are reached about community power and decision making a British context. One possible approach is to examine interest groups in their urban context, their successes, relationships and the position of the 'non participant' citizen, through the consideration of 'urban social movements'.

URBAN SOCIAL MOVEMENTS

The study of pressure groups may imply that ultimately the ballot box will act as a feedback mechanism for the inarticulate. Ryan suggests that the problem of the unorganised in a pressure group democracy, 'can only be effectively overcome by hopeful appeals to conservative metaphysics' (Ryan, 1978, p.14).

In contrast, the study of urban social movements, in its broadest interpretation, tends to take as its central theme the partiality of urban relations. By accepting the existence of anomie in society it highlights political activity as well as over action. The lack of urban protest in Britain, in contrast to that experienced in some European and North American cities, is a useful starting point for a comparison of cultural and economic differences in urban life (See Saunders, 1979, pp.132-6). In parallel with the more radical analysis of pressure groups, the study of urban social movements in the British context, directs the interpreter to the major dilemma of those engaged in political protest, whether to be 'acceptable'; to abide by the rules, and use the permitted machinery of representation; or to challenge the 'authorities' by direct action or the disregard of imposed norms. An appreciation of this dilemma, Saunders points out, is in many ways central to the sociological analysis of urban politics and can also provide an insight into the lack of involvement of the majority of citizens. The two major explanations are as follows:

> .... On the one hand, there are those whose interests are generally safeguarded by the policy making process and who therefore do not need to act; on the other, there are those whose interests are routinely neglected or sacrificed by government but who feel they can do little about it. Political inaction may therefore be the result of the prior satisfaction of people's interests, or of their inability to make their interests heard, and it is an important task for any empirical study to be able to distinguish between these two explanations. (Saunders, 1979, p.19)

It is also important to stress the effectiveness of organisations and the degree to which resignation is masquerading as latent protest inarticulated either by unrepresentative leaders, (See Hindess, 1971) or lack of organisational ability and therefore political muscle.

As Olson puts it:

> .... The smaller groups, the privileged and intermediate groups, can often defeat the large groups, the latent groups, which are normally supposed to prevail in democracy. The privileged and intermediate groups often triumph over the numerically superior forces in the latent or large groups because the former are generally organised and active while the latter are normally unorganised and inactive. (Olson, 1965, p.128)

Much of the study of urban social movements derives from the Althusserian Marxist formulations of Manuel Castells which have been redefined and reformulated by Pickvance, Saunders and others within the British context. To Castells, the types of political action practised by urban organisations, residents' groups and so on, are valid only if they tend to shift the balance of power in society. In a strict Castellsian interpretation, 'successful' urban social movements effect radical, even revolutionary change. A second broader definition of success incorporates the possibility of including the construing of action in the groups' own terms. This activity could, in the light of pressure group categorisation, be reactionary, support the status quo through 'tactical protest', (Saunders, 1979, p.262) or, at best, be reformist.

In a classic British study of urban pressure groups in the London Borough of Kensington and Chelsea, Dearlove shows how councillors' perceptions of the 'successful' pressure groups relates to their'helpfullness', that is their demands conform to council policy, and their 'acceptable' modes of action in representing their point of view, (Dearlove, 1973). Certain methods of protest such as demonstrations being frowned upon and counter productive, (See Miller, 1970, p.42). As Saunders in his Croydon case study signifies: 'Quiet discussions and informal meetings were much preferred to loud demands and highly visible public demonstrations', (Saunders, 1979, p.232). This preference translates into acceptability which, in turn, determines the extent of access.

The rules of access based either on acceptability or, more rarely on 'naked'power, are seen as the key to action or inaction in urban social movements. This factor is influential in the assessment of British urban social movements. Tenants' associations, perhaps the most 'pure' form of urban working class organisation, may start their life as militant bodies campaigning against rent increases, housing policies or planning proposals, but tend to retreat into 'acceptable'negotiating bodies and their influence depends on their powers of persuasion and ability to seek a hearing (See Richardson, 1977), or become largely social and fundraising organisations (See Stacey, et al, 1975). These and other more issue specific urban movements ('sit ins', etc,), apart from a common readership of 'Community Action', have little impact through national coordinating bodies. Indeed, in the British context, planning and housing issues tend to be place specific and are more likely to be conducive to individual or small group protest rather than the catalyst for an emerging wider urban social movement. As Pahl summarises:

> .... Since different groups benefit at different times indifferent parts of the same city, common city or nationwide situations of deprivation rarely occur. Those

who claim they can see the development of 'urban social movements' leading to radical changes in the nature of urban society would find difficulty in getting empirical support from British evidence. (Pahl, 1975, p.273)

Apart from the brief flowering of suburban ratepayers as a national movement in the later 1970s (NARAG), with threats of civil disobedience over rapidly rising rate demands, the most consistent and loosely co-ordinated urban social movement in Britain is that of the civic societies. The Civic Trust, formed in 1957, is the national coordinator of an urban amenity movement which in Britain has its roots in mid nineteenth century concern for public open spaces and historic buildings, though 85 per cent of its currently responding societies have begun since 1957 (Civic Trust, 1976, p.21). Consistent with the public image, as being middle class dominated, Barker, in a survey, found that most societies admitted, 'most of our members are white collar or professional-managerial people and their spouses', and four-fifths went so far as to concede that they lacked so much as one-third of members from manual occupational groups (Civic Trust, 1976, p.25).

The approach adopted in this study, while stressing the effects or outcomes of urban social movements, and thus their degree of success as broadly defined above, also focuses upon the study of organisations themselves, their internal structures and external relationships and their environments. (See Chapter 5). The importance of this multi faceted approach is exemplified by Ferris's case study of Barnsbury in Islington, (Ferris, 1972). Here the conservation, traffic management orientated amenity society, the Barnsbury Association, after considerable effort, was able to defeat the Barnsbury Action Group. The association, by organising an effective minority, which was a predominantly middle class owner-occupier membership, was able to employ its greater expertise, political knowledge and social networks to achieve its aims. It is important to note, however, that the association might also have been assisted by a favourable central government 'policy environment', based on Buchanan and thus "the 'urban effect' obtained was the result of the movement organisation <u>and factors internal to the authority</u>", (Pickvance, 1975, p.35). The association, accused of displacement of working class tenants by promoting a policy of gradual gentrification, is seen as an example of a typical civic society, whose officers, as Barker showed, were predominantly 'anti road' in outlook (Civic Trust, 1976, p. 27). This case caused Cowley and his colleagues to proclaim, in line with Anthony Crosland:

> .... The amenity movement with its blatantly elitist approach to planning can still count on support from middle class socialists because it appears to challenge the brutal planning activities of the large commercial and state developers. This is a mistake because middle class amenity groups are nearly always willing to impose what they regard as disastrous proposals for their own districts on 'soft' working class areas elsewhere. (Cowley, et al, 1977, p.181)

Why are some urban groups more 'successful' than others? Pickvance argues that organisational resources affect the ability of the group to survive and succeed, and he stresses the importance of the degree of community (horizontal) integration, or national (vertical) integration, (Pickvance, 1975, p.41).

These factors are fundamental in the assessment of the activities of the groups and organisations to be described in Part 3 of this study. The variability of horizontal integration, the extent of social networks and the relationships of members which arise from it, form an integral part of the analysis of groups in central Lancashire. In addition, it is also significant to note the delay in understanding the need for vertical integration displayed by the local groups, which forms an important element of Part 4.

This brief survey of the theory of interest groups, the variaous approaches to local community power structures and urban social movements, is intended to provide a basis for the subsequent interpretation of the research investigating the dynamics of the political environment of a new town.

NOTES

1. The Local Government, Planning and Land Act 1981, according to the Town and Country Planning Association, dilutes the public participation process through 'removal of the requirement for local authorities to make local plan survey material available for the public to see and comment on; removal of the power for the Secretary of State for the environment to prescribe locations for displaying information relating to local plans, and to prescribe the contents of public participation statements provided by local planning authorities' (TCPA, 1981).

2. An ideal type may be defined as a descriptive model constructed for analytical purposes which need not necessarily exist in its exact form in the real world. It is based on Max Weber's concept (See Gerth and Mills, 1948).

3. This has been estimated as being 15-20 per cent in the United States of America, (See Bollens and Schmandt, 1970. See also for comparative figures, Almond and Verba, 1965).

4. These are defined as 'institutional leaders who direct the large organisations of the community, who enjoy the reputation for influence, but who participate very little in decision making in terms of personal action on specific issues: Effectors, who are usually either employees of institutional leaders or governmental personnel, and who constitute the bulk of participants in decision making; Activists who seem to gain access to decision making through their motivation and drive in the activities of voluntary associations (Freeman, 1962, p.26).

5 Organisations : their analysis, their environments and their networks

The central Lancashire development corporation is the dominant formal organisation of this study. In order to interpret its activities internally and its relationships with its environment, it will be useful to review a number of theories of organisations; first by employing organisational analysis, and second more specifically by analysing external relationships with other organisations, both formal and informal, since the main focus of the study is concerned with CLDC interaction with its 'public in contact' and the 'public at large'. (Blau and Scott, 1963, pp.42-3).

ORGANISATION THEORY

Organisations have been studied from various disciplinary viewpoints, and the state of organisation theory may still be 'fragmented and disorganised', (Perrow, 1974, p.18). Despite this disparateness, it would seem most appropriate here that the organisation theories which have been derived from such studies should be interpreted primarily from the approaches of social psychological theories and within socio-political perspectives. That is, first, they should be described both with regard to the individual in his organisational role and also the types of communication flows and social influences which are implied within each theory; and second, with an awareness of the wider influences of society as a whole, its power structure, culture and values.

Three of the seminal theories, bureaucracy, scientific management and human relations may be criticised for having expressed an over simplified view of man in his organisational role. Yet it will be useful to review these theories briefly before turning to more recent formulations of organisational theories.

Weber referred to organisations as bureaucracies and his theory was mainly constructed from a wide historical comparative analysis of administrative systems. (Weber, 1964).

The 'ideal type' of the bureaucratic typology was shown by Weber to be a highly rational structure and the subjects within it were seen to accept its rulings as justified, because they accorded with a set of rules which they considered to be legitimate. Later commentators have used Weber's groundwork for further development (Blau, 1956; Albrow, 1970; Gouldner, 1954; Perrow, 1972).

By focussing on the prescriptions of a role within an organisation, this approach generally disregarded the human characteristics of the individual who filled the position. This criticism is important in the context of this study since it is contended that the influence of individual personality and the consequent 'management style' will be a key factor in the types of organisational behaviour exhibited in the development corporation.

Some argue that 'the theory of bureaucracy has still not been given the sustained attention it deserves', (Meyer, 1978, p.11), yet, as this can direct organisational theory towards the dynamics of power, Weber's work as a whole may be seen as guiding the researcher, as McNeill puts it 'to incorporate a societal perspective in which organisational action is part of a larger set of market and political dynamics', (McNeill in Zey-Ferrell, 1981, p.65). The wider implications deriving from this framework may thus be regarded as a basis for other socio-political approaches described later.

Unlike bureaucracy, scientific management theories as developed by Taylor were not so much concerned with the organisational problems of society's power structure, but rather with the practical problem of efficiency, (Taylor, 1911). Taylor's main unit of analysis was not society as a whole, but the individual in the workplace. The emphasis of this approach was on the detailed study of the physical operations which were relevant to the performance of the task. The organisation member was thus conceived of as an instrument of production who could be handled as easily as any other tool, given knowledge of the 'laws' of scientific management. These 'laws' neglected the psychological and sociological variables of organisational behaviour. No allowances were made for the feelings and attitudes of the individual,of the culture and norms of the work group,or of the influence of the wider social structure. It will be useful again to bear these shortcomings in mind when considering the attitudes of members of the development corporation.

Deriving from these theories of bureaucracy and scientifc management, 'universalistic theories' of organisation were developed. (For example, Gulick and Urwick, 1937). In addition to the rigid delineation and the grouping of roles associated with this approach, a formally structured information and communication system was laid down. This system was designed to be generally vertical in form and 'messages' generally flowed down the organisational hierarchy. Little horizontal communication was expected at the lower organisational levels and communication flows up the hierarchy would be minimal. This view of organisations is enshrined in the development corporation's dichotomous design for its 'executive' functions, the implications of which will be developed in Chapter 6.

Perhaps in reaction to the scientific management approach which has been attacked for its concentration upon physical capabilities and needs and for ignoring the emotional aspects of human nature, Mayo's organisational approach started with a study of man's motives and behaviour. (Mayo, 1949). In what became known as the human relations school, criteria were developed which would create an organisation designed to stimulate employees to cooperate in achieving its aims. It has been stated that a fundamental weakness in human relations theory was that it tried to solve major organisational problems by reference to the individual or group level and it was thereby not paying much attention to the organisation as a whole. (Mouzelis, 1967, p.113). Human relations theorists have further been accused of neglecting the presence of organisational conflict.

The three foundation schools of organisation theory, whilst to some extent coexisting with each other, have had their assumptions repeatedly dissected by the industrial social sciences. As a result, certain reformulations and changes in emphasis and dogmatism have taken place. These include 'organisation theory', together with an associated development termed the 'systems approach', 'organisational psychology', which includes within its wide parameters the neo human relations school and the 'structuralist/action theory', which may be seen as a return to a more strictly sociological perspective.

This third development in organisational analysis has arisen from the growing results of social science analysis and research where organisational behaviour is generally the product of a complex system of interaction between a wide variety of internal and external psychological and socio-economic determinants. The meshing of organisational and individual needs is regarded as being never complete, and thus the success of an organisation is largely dependent on its ability to maintain control of its participants. Etzioni attempts a classification of means of control, and of its correlate, compliance. (Etzioni, 1961). This typology facilitates a greater understanding of a full range of organisations. The nature of power typically employed by the organisation is determined; whether coercive, normative or utilitarian and to what degree. The typical orientation of the group of participants is then established; the degree of alienation or commitment this orientation involves.

It is important to point out that many of the approaches to the study of organisations need not necessarily be treated as being mutually exclusive. It has been argued, however, that the foregoing approaches represent strands of a hitherto 'dominant perspective' of organisations which is 'asociological' (Zey-Ferrell and Aiken, 1981, p.3). Insufficient emphasis has been placed upon the non rational features of organisations and studies have focussed upon the goals and concerns of the dominant administration. There has been a low priority given to the historical dimension and the dynamic aspects of organisation, but above all there has been a neglect of power relations and their analysis. This omission, critics of the 'dominant perspective' contend, is a crucial element ......

> .... The subject power is of interest primarily because of its importance for <u>understanding</u> what occurs in organisations. Power has consequences in organisations for resource allocations, administrative succession, structures and strategic choices. (Pfeffer, 1981, p.231) (my emphasis)

The increasing importance of this dimension as a factor in organisational analysis has been evident during the 1970s (Pettigrew, 1972; Handy, 1976, pp.111-4; Hunt, 1981, pp.60-79), but it is most marked in a 'critical organisations' approach (Colignon and Cray, 1981) and advocates a 'genuine sociology of orgamisational structure' whose major elements are traced to the work of Weber and Marx (Salaman, 1978, p.519). This perspective is typified most markedly in a dialectical approach to organisations. This critical view of organisations seeks to challenge the theoretical orthodoxies dominant in their analysis and study. In contrast to a concern with 'the interests of administrative elites', and while incorporating phenomena as 'political economy, negotiated order, and cooptive mechanisms', the dialectical analysis is a general perspective 'expressed through Marx's analyses of capitalism but not locked into the specific categories and arguments of that analysis' (Benson, 1981, pp.264-5).

This view stresses the fundamental importance of change and dynamics and the need to view organisations within the context of the wider social structure and the multiple inter connections of members.

The official authority structure may also be seen as a means of enforcing power on its lower members. Instead of analysing organisational structure as a measure of an organisation's effectiveness, a dialectical, or political perspective, 'looks at the structure as being the outcome of a political context for control within the organisation' (Pfeffer, 1981, p.286). This comment is most apposite when one considers the organisational design of CLDC and its well documented rationale (See Chapter 6).

In other approaches the power base of the leadership is not considered since Benson argues, such an examination would probably extend beyond the boundaries of the organisation. The dialectical approach, however, sees the importance of 'the grounding of organisational authority in larger systems, inter organisational networks, political/economic power blocks, legal systems and the like' (Benson, 1981, p.269).

The organisation itself, if it is possible to conceive it as such a totality within this framework, is not seen as an integrated system but rather characterised by schisms or distinct semi autonomous occupational groups. The range of inconsistencies within organisations are termed 'contradictions', which may lead to the production of change. The focus on the role of powerful individuals and dominant coalitions within organisations as developed by Karpik (Karpik, 1972, p.300) is of particular relevance to this study. It is from this approach that the organisation and its members may be seen 'as a window through which the observer can discern general societal level processes' (Weiss, 1981, p.395). The relevance of this perspective to this study is not only in the way in which it indicates possibilities of relating the study of organisations to wider society, but also in its congruence with the socio-political framework developed through the research.

In this short review of approaches to organisations, it is notably the social action model which owes its main emphasis to Weber and the dialectical approach, in which the influence of Marx predominates, which indicate a greater emphasis on the wider environment. It is this particular aspect which will be explored in the second part of this chapter.

THE PLACE OF ENVIRONMENT IN ORGANISATION THEORY

Many of the organisational theories reviewed place little emphasis on the importance of environmental factors in the analysis of organisational behaviour. The schools derived from the bureaucratic, scientific management and human relations traditions tend to view the organisation as a closed entity. This criticism also applies to some branches of systems theory.

The 'open systems' approach postulated by such writers as Katz and Kahn, and Thompson, however, provides some useful insights into the organisation/environment relationship (Katz and Kahn, 1966; Thompson, 1967). This is particularly evident where the existence of conflict is taken into account.

> .... The open systems perspective . . . alerts us to the fact that the source of many organisational problems lies outside the organisation, in the organisation's environments.

> The organisational theorist is thus forced to concentrate his attention on variation both in the organisation and in the environment, since the organisation/environment perspective requires one to look at both sides of a relationship to predict an outcome. This implies that a theorist cannot make accurate predictions about the effect of organisational variables without some knowledge of the organisation's environment. (Aldrich, 1971, p.281)

The structuralist, broadly sociological, approaches to organisations also provide for environmental influences in analysis. While Etzioni's structuralist formulation is 'highly tentative', (Etzioni, 1964, p.110), Perrow's sociological view of organisations makes the environment one of the key concepts in his analysis. (Perrow, 1971, pp.92-132).

The environments of organisations are complex and varied, but the degree to which external influences take effect depends upon the 'openness' of the organisation or, indeed, its defensiveness or vulnerability. Here the concept of 'permeability' developed by Aiken 'to measure the degree to which the focal organisation is open to influences from its environment', (Aiken, 1974, p.4), is most constructive. This notion is linked with the implication that organisations have roles and procedures which perform the functions of filtering and negotiating with the environment, and also positions which link the organisation and its environment, described by Thompson as 'boundary spanning jobs'. (Thompson, 1967, pp.110-2).

The environments of organisations have been classified by a number of academic investigators. Perhaps the most often quoted is that proposed by Emery and Trist who utilise the systems perspective to develop their model (Emery and Trist, 1965). They focus upon the 'casual texture' of the environment using a 'placid turbulent' continuum as a dimension and have isolated four 'ideal types' of casual texture. These are the 'placid, randomised environment' which equates broadly to conditions conducive to the 'perfect competition' model of classical economics; the 'placid, clustered environment' which describes more groupings, which is similar to the conditions surrounding 'imperfect competition'; the 'disturbed reactive environment', in which 'the existence of a number of similar organisations now becomes the dominant characteristic of the environmental field', the economists' 'oligopolistic market'. The fourth and final classification, unlike types one and two, is dynamic and is far more complex than type three. This 'ideal type' environment is described as a 'turbulent field'.

> ..... Unlike type 3, the dynamic properties arise not simply from the interaction of the component organisations, but also from the field itself. The 'ground' is in motion. (Emery and Trist, 1965, p.26)

The attempts by an organisation, particularly a relatively dominant one, to influence and shape its environment is a relatively neglected area. In the terms of this study this aspect of organisational behaviour is most important.

The study of this area, as Aiken points out, should follow logically from a discussion of organisation as 'open systems'.

> .... If one begins to pose questions about the impact of the environment on organisation, one becomes sensitised to the importance of many factors not previously recognised. More important there follows the logical question

of how an organisation affects or attempts to shape its environment. (Aiken, 1974, p.24)

Perrow's sociological view of organisations is particularly valuable since it reminds us of aspects of the organisation which are apt to be taken for granted. Following Parson's lead, Perrow explores the organisation's legitimacy within its environment. (Perrow, 1971, p.98). Such legitimisation comes from individual groups and organisations, such as 'consumers, suppliers, regulatory agencies, the investigating public and, tax payers'. Legitimacy, he argues, is not quite so easy to achieve, industrial organisations need to prove the need for their products, and for non profit organisations, it is sometimes an even greater problem. He points out, admittedly in the United States, that 'government agencies die more frequently than we realise because their legitimacy is questioned, and other agencies expend great resources to stay alive'. (Perrow, 1971, p.99).

An organisation may accommodate environmental influences either with ease or through lack of subtlety and political skill be in conflict with various elements. The environment is basically both a threat and a resource and how the organisation copes with pressures will depend upon how its skills in external, or 'public' relations, and its strategies in neutralising the opposition are employed, as well as bearing in mind the nature of the environment.

Both Perrow and Thompson provide interesting descriptions of methods used by organisations to 'control' their environments. They may try to increase their power by 'competitive' or 'cooperative' strategies. Competitive strategies include the dispersal of dependence to avoid suppliers gaining power through concentration, and the gaining of power through prestige. Cooperative strategies, on the other hand, with the exchange of commitments provide the effective achievement of power. The three strategies described are directly relevant to the organisational behaviour of the CLDC. They are contracting 'the negotiation of an agreement for the exchange of performances in the future',(Thompson, 1967, p.35) coopting , which is derived from Selznick's notion and is defined as 'the process of absorbing new elements into the leadership or policy determining structure of an organisation as a means of averting threats to the stability or existence', and finally, coalescing, which 'refers to a combination or joint venture with another organisation or organisations in the environment'. (Thompson, 1967, pp.35-6).

Environments, as described in this chapter, consist of other organisations. As Perrow points out, 'Each organisation is itself the environment of some other entity'. (Perrow, 1971, p.131). It is thus important to focus in the next section of this chapter upon a developing area of study, that of inter organisational behaviour.

INTER ORGANISATIONAL BEHAVIOUR

This relatively under developed aspect of organisation theory is likely to become a major area of analysis, particularly in the study of environment since, as Terreberry points out, 'other formal organisations are increasingly important components of organisational environments'. (Terreberry, 1968, p.606).

There are distinct advantages in focussing upon inter organisational relationships. First, the tendency in much organisational analysis to ignore or undervalue the place of conflict is diminished; second, this approach leads to an increasing importance of the concepts of power within and between organisations; third, organisations and their networks provide an intermediate unit of analysis and an insight into the workings of advanced industrial societies; and finally, a link is forged between organisations and communities and by so doing there is the possibility of effecting a synthesis between some of the traditional concerns of industrial and urban sociology.

Reference has already been made to the fact that many traditional approaches to the study of organisations have a tendency to neglect the occurrence of conflict. Inter organisational analysis has provided additional support to alternative sociological/structuralist and some open systems perspectives, (Aldrich, 1971) by stressing the importance of conflict. As Aiken and Hage point out:

> .... The study of inter organisational relationships appears to be one area which can appropriately incorporate the processes of both conflict and cooperation. Therefore the concept of organisational interdependence becomes a critical analytical tool for understanding this process. (Aiken and Hage, 1968, p.913)

So it is important to stress that both cooperation and conflict are likely to exist in inter organisational relationships and 'good communications' and frequency of interaction are just as likely to be based upon a conflict situationas well as a cooperative one.

Closely associated with the examination of conflict is the concept of power and the possibility of interpreting organisational networks as political economies. (Zald, 1970; Benson, 1974).

In some sociological approaches to organisation theory generally the importance of power has been increasingly stressed. (Etzioni, 1964; Crozier, M. 1972; Aldrich, 1971, pp.282-3). Crozier, for example, takes the view that:

> .... no system of organisation can be constructed without power relationships, and all organisation is built around power relationships which afford the necessary link between the desired objective and the human means that are indispensible to their realisation. (Crozier, 1972, p.241)

This emphasis on power, and the need for an'integrated approach' to organisation, has led to the development of what has been termed the 'political economy approach to the study of organisations'. This approach has been defined by Zald as 'the study of the interplay of power, the goals of power wielders and productive exchange system'. (Zald, 1970, p.223). Within a specifically inter organisational focus, Benson has evolved an approach which interprets a network of organisations as a political economy. The network is the basic unit of analysis and consists of 'a number of distinguishable organisations engaged in a significant amount of interaction with each other'. (Benson, 1974, p.2). It will be noted that it is the network which is analysed and not, as in some approaches, a focal organisation and its environment. Benson argues that there are two basic types of resources which are central to the political economy of inter organisational networks: money and authority. It thus follows that the bases of inter organisational power lie in the control of resources and in processes of negotiation between organisations. (See diagram on p.41)

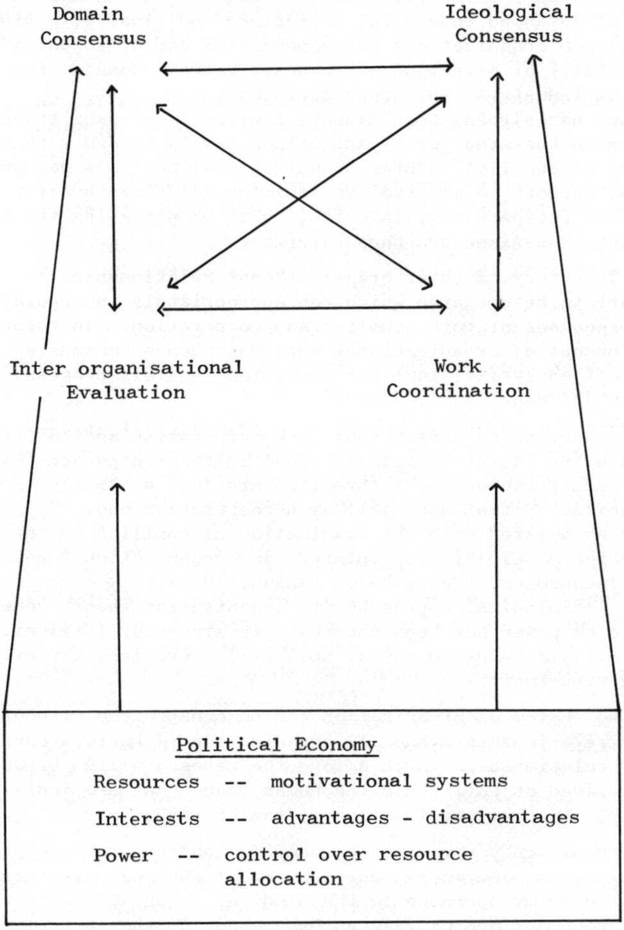

From: Benson, 1974, 6a

The political economy of inter organisational networks

The wider environment of this network 'relevant to resource transactions and power differentials is an organised structured entity even though its structure is sometimes difficult to discern'. In describing the structure of this environment by which he refers to patterned relationships among and between 'participants', such as organisations and publics and the network, Benson has isolated some important dimensions. These are:

1. Resource concentration/dispersion: the extent to which control over resource disbursements to the network resides finally in one or a few participants.
2. Power concentration/dispersion: the extent to which some participants in the environment dominate others.
3. Network autonomy/dependence: the extent to which the network is controlled by environmental forces.
4. Environmental dominance patterns: the types of participants exercising power in the environment.
5. Resource abundance/scarcity: the amounts of resources at the disposal of the environment.
6. Control mechanisms, incentive versus authoritative: the means of control by the environment over networks may be formal and authoritative, involving the delegation of authority in bureaucratic fashion to agencies in a network.

The organisation of the environment

> .... consists of a number of organisations (e.g. lobbies, government bureaus, foundations), officials (e.g. legislators), and publics (e.g. advocates of government reform, recipients of agency services). These 'participants' (organisations, officials and publics) are linked together in interaction patterns centring about the governance of a given network, i.e. the distribution of resources and power within the network. The environment relevant to a given network is to some extent unique. (Benson, 1974, p.14)

Of course a number of inter organisational networks are themselves part of the environment of the major organisation's environment. In this study the CLDC will be studied with this perspective and knowledge in mind. Both the focal organisation and the network are themselves subject to a yet wider environment. This setting involves aspects of the socio-economic world which are the most influential in changing events within the network, such as changes in economic conditions. Inter organisational power relations and environments cannot therefore be fully analysed without reference to influence and power structures in wider society.

The study of organisations and their networks thus provides a useful intermediate level of study, a 'middle range' between primary groups and society as a whole. It has also been a force towards comparability and integration in sociology between its industrial and urban specialisms since inter organisational networks have involved studies of business, public authority and community organisations (See Tuite, et al (Eds), 1972; Litwak and Hylton, 1962; Zald, 1966).

Inter organisational relations thus provide a link for sociologists who wish to study organisations and communities.

ORGANISATIONAL ENVIRONMENTS AND NETWORKS

The adoption of an analytical framework of inter organisational relations based on power and resources provides a fresh insight into organisational environments and networks. The contributions of the alternatives, however, should not be completely discarded since their perceptions may also be employed selectively in the development of this important area of organisational behaviour. The hitherto dominance of, what Perrow terms, the institutional approach, is linked to the 'enfeebling assumption of structural/functional theory' and is unlikely to face up squarely to 'the fact of organisational power in an organisation society' (Perrow, 1972, p.190). Yet he acknowledges its contribution to the emphasis on organisational environments. Similarly, another alternative, the 'information perspective' (See Aldrich and Mindlin, 1978, p.151) leads one fruitfully to the incorporation of the mass media organisations into the network. Yet it is power relations within, and between organisations which are seen as a basic and permanent feature of collective relations and organisational behaviour. As Crozier and Friedberg put it:

> .... power, and its hidden counterpart, manipulation and blackmail is an unavoidable input into any kind of collective endeavour, an input that raises concrete problems of its own that have to be handled. (Crozier and Friedberg, 1977, p.94)

Traditionally, environment has been seen as influencing organisations and, indeed, environmental models have been described and organisational responses postulated (See Emery and Trist, 1965 and Aldrich, 1979, pp.70-4). Yet, according to Perrow, this approach does not describe the situation experienced between many large organisations and their environments:

> .... To see these organisations as adaptive to a 'turbulent', dynamic, ever changing environment is to indulge in fantasy. The environment of most powerful organisations is well controlled by them, quite stable and made up of other organisations with similar interests, or ones they control. (Perrow, 1972, p.199)

Both interpretations may have overstated their case. Organisations with the power to influence their environments may largely be limited to those which are economically dominant or politically unaware. Yet, on the other hand, in keeping with the assumption of a competitive capitalist economy, too much stress can be placed on the small and medium sized industrial organisation existing in a presumed combative environment without acknowledging the factor of environmental dominance by many organisations, both public and private. The power perspective, or as Aldrich prefers to define it, the dependence perspective, may be developed to include the possibility of organisation's 'managing' environments or at least their seeking to buffer themselves from environmental pressures rather than changing its condition. Above all, an organisation will find its decision making less fraught, and even its continued existence less unsure, by adopting strategies to cope with environmental uncertainty.

Through the political economic approach and that pursued at the University of Minnesota, (Hall, et al, 1973) inter organisational research has inevitably led to the discussion and analysis of power structures both at local and national levels, yet these forms of analysis should not obscure the uniqueness of many organisations and this distinctiveness certainly applies to the CLDC. Neither should such such theories be just strictly applied to 'formal organisations' since, as Crozier points out, this kind of analysis can be fruitfully applied to much looser 'groups which are in some manner organised', (Crozier, 1964, p.242) nor, finally, should such emphasis on organisations divert us from the importance of the individual.

It is necessary, therefore, to make allowance for the factor of individual differences among organisational members and for the personalities and interests of the dominant and most powerful officers. Some observers, almost in a return to a psychological orientation, see the organisation as only consisting of individuals and there is some merit in this. As Silverman put it, 'Organisations do not react to their environment, their members do'. (Silverman, 1970, p.37)

A research focus for the observation and analysis of inter organisational behaviour is provided by a major public inquiry. This type of public hearing brings together representatives of major public bodies, voluntary organisations and individuals. Each participant's perception of the function of the public inquiry procedures and processes will tend to differ. In the final sections of this chapter we will examine public inquiries, their place in the administrative process and how they perform as a microcosm of inter organisational behaviour.

THE PUBLIC INQUIRY IN THE ADMINISTRATIVE PROCESS

The 7,000 or more public inquiries held each year in Britain are convened to inquire into an aspect of administration and are overtly intended to 'establish facts and to make recommendations', (Wraith and Lamb, 1971, p.13).

Planning appeals account for the majority of public inquiries. They are usually concerned with a dispute over an interpretation of development control and the inspector hears the case of the local planning authority and that of the appellant. The Secretary of State is somewhat distanced from the protagonists in these inquiries. The public inquiries held under the provisions of the New Towns Act, 1965, however, are concerned with observations, objections and indeed, intense criticism towards a project which, by its very nature, is a creature of the minister himself. (1) There are three broad categories of public inquiry which may occur during the establishment and development of a new town. The first is to hear objections to the area designated by the minister/secretary of state defined in the draft designation order. Section 1 of the New Towns Act, 1965, obliges the minister to consult the local authorities and by the time the draft designation order is published in the London Gazette and elsewhere in the press, most of the public authorities will normally have agreed to the proposals, at least in principle if not in detail.

A major criticism of designation inquiries relates to the controversial question of evidence from government departments. A minister's representative may be questioned on fact but not on policy. As the Franks Report put it,

> (Policy is something) which is the function of Ministers to discuss and defend. It is further argued that the collective responsibility of Ministers makes in constitutionally inappropriate for witnesses from one Department to give evidence at inquiries conducted by another department, (Franks, 1957, para 315)

In all types of public inquiry hearing objections into new town proposals, there is the recurring criticism that it is the same minister (or his successor) who makes the final decision on an aspect of his own scheme; that is, he is 'judge in his own cause'. By convention, a minister, when the initiator of a scheme, such as a new town, will normally appoint as inspector someone from outside his permanent staff, such as a clerk to a county council. Although, potentially, this ploy may be seen as a possible tactic for minimising criticism about independence, in recent years some such inspectors have commented infavourably about procedural shortcomings. The minister is not a party to a designation inquiry and he does not therefore call witnesses nor is he normally represented by counsel. A great deal of resentment is caused by the inability of objectors to question the consultants since they are not called as witnesses. The Clerk to the Nottinghamshire County Council, the inspector at the designation inquiry for Ipswich, in his report made the point that a number of questions could have been 'more easily and simply answered had the consultants been called as witnesses'.

Levin recalls

> .... a memorable event at the Warrington inquiry was the attempt by the clerk of an objecting local authority, on spotting in the public gallery, a senior partner of the firm of consultants, to have him called down to give evidence .... The attempt was unsuccessful. (Levin, 1969, p.17)

The inspector, in his report, commented on this shortcoming unequivocally:

> .... Other criticisms were on firmer ground, being directed to the absence of the consultants . . . and to the fact that the consultants were known to have made considerable progress with . . . the production of the master plan in advance of the minister's decision on the inquiry . . . The administrative decisions taken by the minister to proceed with the master plan and not to offer the consultants as witnesses . . . lent support to the contention of a number of objectors that the minister was acting as judge in his own cause; and moreover had given judgement in the cause before hearing the evidence.

The anomaly between most planning inquiries and new towns and motorway inquiries, where the minister is a party to the proceedings, was commented upon by Sir Andrew Wheatley in his report on the designation of CLNT. Objectors' criticisms of the published consultants' reports, which could not be confirmed or denied through the absence of the consultants as witnesses, apparently made a considerable impression on Sir Andrew who, in his report, admitted that 'as the proceedings progressed doubts were raised in my mind that remained unanswered'. Had the minister been a normal part of the inquiry and represented by counsel it would have been 'a far more effective method of ascertaining the truth of the matter, and would be a much more satisfactory way of making the case for, and countering opposition to, a project....'.

The minister/secretary of state is within his legal rights in not calling witnesses, since his position was tested in the courts from the very first designation inquiry at Stevenage in 1946. Taken to the House of Lords, the ruling stated that it was not the minister's duty to call evidence in support of the designation order, his sole obligation was genuinely to consider the report and the objections, (2) though as Levin points out:

> .... Clearly he is within his legal rights in not calling witnesses. But it must be pointed out that the judgement does not prevent him from doing so. Thus it is the result of an administrative decision (as the inspector at Warrington pointed out), and not of the House of Lords judgement, that the minister's case at these inquiries was not supported by witnesses and that there was no one present to cross examine the objector's witnesses. (Levin, 1969, p.17)

There would be less cause for disquiet, however, if the inquiry included a thorough examination of the arguments. The dissatisfaction is manifested repeatedly in the subsequent inquiries when some objectors persist in attempting to bring arguments before the inspector which they regard to be unresolved. The inspectors, in their turn, somewhat disingenuously state that 'arguments about designation were settled at the designation inquiry'.

Two further categories to which these 'restrictive presumptions' apply are the inquiries held to receive representation about the 'master' or 'outline' plan and into developments under Section 6(i) of the New Towns Act, 1965, together with inquiries into associated or other compulsory purchase orders such as 'land banking'. The outline plan public inquiry is not provided for under legislation, but a non statutory inquiry has been held for each new town designated so far, in Britain. In contrast, the compulsory purchase provisions of the New Towns Act, 1965, in schedule 3, lay down that the minister must provide an objector to compulsory purchase orders with an opportunity of being heard, 'or, if it appears to him that the matters to which the objection relates are such to require an investigation by public local inquiry, he shall cause such an inquiry to be held ....'.

Many of these associated public inquiries formed an important element in stimulating the involvement of the public and local groups in the development of CLNT, but it was the principal event, the outline plan inquiry, that provided the forum for the arguments about the extent and form, and by implication, the continued need for CLNT.

THE PUBLIC INQUIRY AS A SYMBOLIC ASPECT OF INTER ORGANISATIONAL RELATIONS

Inter organisational analysis has provided an insight into the often conflicting relationships which can exist between organisations of many categories. The political economy of organisational networks (Zald, 1970; Benson, 1974) is provided with an observable veneer through many aspects of the public inquiry procedures and transactions. Through the formal and informal aspects of the public inquiry process, it is possible to construct evidence of the structure of the organisational environment, the extent of organisational permeability (Aiken, 1974,p.4) the relative importance of various boundary spanning roles (Thompson, 1967, pp.110-2; Aldrich, 1978-79, pp.248-365) and assess the internal power structure, its authority and membership compliance, (Aldrich, 1978-79, p.244) and strategies adopted for organisational survival.

The focal organisation, CLDC, in its relationship within its major network in the public and commercial sectors, gives some indication of its perception of the power hierarchy of the organisations in its organisational network in various ways. The dominant objectors in the outline plan public inquiry to be more fully described in Chapter 9 were the adjoining local authorities. Local commercial and industrial interests appeared less important, perhaps because they had a generally favourable attitude towards the development. The local pressure groups were regarded with circumspection, but less priority, and individuals with uncertainty. Taking the ordering of the inquiry agenda may be interpreted as an implied 'pecking order', indicating a crude measure of the relative influence of these organisations and whether they are within the relevant CLDC 'task environment' (Dill, 1958; Thompson, 1967) at that time. Within this environment the major local authorities sought to command resources and favour for their arguments with CLDC and ultimately before the department of the environment and its ministers. The public inquiry may thus represent a public demonstration of the theatre of inter organisational power, within which the main rivals sought ascendancy for their respective organisational goals, and the less prominent members of the cast discerned their subordinate roles.

The structure of the CLDC network environment may be described bearing in mind certain dimensions (See Benson, 1974) and correlated with public inquiry behaviour. It is an environment with a tendency towards resource concentration rather than dispersion. The goal of the CLDC is to channel public and private resources into a specified sub region in the North-west; its opponents support more scattered investment or a diversion of priorities towards the Mersey belt and other older urban areas. Power is concentrated in few organisations in the planning field; CLDC, through the role in the public inquiry sought to confirm its continued pre-eminence in central Lancashire and within the future of new town policies nationally.

The degree of flexibility of an organisation and its propensity to bargain and adjust goals can be shown by the extent of concessions made to others in the network. This adjustment is normally a dynamic process but it may be particularly accentuated prior to major decisions. Such adjustments in policy goals, or in their practical realisation, may not be viewed simply as a measure of inter organisational power or of the degree of organisational permeability (Aiken, 1974, p.4). In addition, it may be interpreted somewhat negatively as an instance of a more powerful member of a network showing magnanimity, or patronising weaker organisations. More positively, by applying the concept of permeability organisations can be assessed for their sensitivity to environmental influences. The degree to which an organisation's propensity to bargain is apparent or real will be indicated from other dimensions of organisational behaviour described in this section. Concessions and compromises negotiated by CLDC prior to the public inquiry were often documented by the local press. Major concessions were reported to be gained by local authorities following severe criticism of proposals for a hypermarket in Hollins Brook by South Ribble District Council ('New attack on town's plans', LEP, 4 January, 1974). Lancashire County Council's major objections were reported, together with its differences of opinion with Preston Borough (LEP, 25 July, 1974) as well as Fylde Borough Council's objections to fringe area policies (LEP, 30 July, 1974). The CLDCs 'reassessment' was published as a supplement to the outline plan in July 1974, and included some minor amendments to the road proposals, but the most significant adjustments were acknowledged at the public inquiry itself by the circulation of a CLDC statement indicating a number of more substantial changes 'some of which are the result of comments by L.A.s'.

A significant indicator of an organisation's 'openness' to its environment is the degree of importance placed upon specialist boundary spanning roles. While to a lesser degree some roles are a response to environmental influences and stimulation, as Aldrich points out, their existence can serve as 'an important guide to environmental contingencies perceived as significant by authorities', (Aldrich, 1979, p.243) (my emphasis). In the case of CLDC a hierarchy of boundary spanning roles may be identified. The legal and liaison officer, Mr. Cudworth, held a pivotal position in its structure with a strong emphasis on liaison with local authorities. Less prominent was the work of the principal officers responsible for industrial liaison and social facilities, which reflects the non controversial relationship with industry and the underdeveloped status of social development (See Chapter 6).

The central and crucial coordinating function of the general manager should be recognised, who with the aid of his personal assistant and press officer, also performed a dominant and near monopolistic information filtering and negotiating oversight with the press and 'public in contact'. The public inquiry procedures and organisation confirmed the pre-eminence of the boundary spanning roles of the general manager and the legal and liaison officer and some insight into the internal political structure of CLDC.

The public inquiry process can place great strain upon some organisational loyalties since uncertainty can be generated by such inter organisational conflict. Some officers were not in as much prominence in the proceedings as some network members expected, (2) and this omission could be viewed as evidence of boundary control and the need for achieving maximum membership compliance at this time.

In its assessment of its task environment and its awareness of its more vulnerable position in the wider administrative and political system, the CLDC, in its quest for organisational survival, adopted an active pre inquiry strategy of maximum dispersed commitments through the Section 6(i) provisions, (See Chapter 7). Though dominant in its task environment, CLDC was less certain of achieving its goal; that of full development of the designated area in the context of national decision making.

SUMMARY

This chapter has outlined a number of theories of organisations giving special emphasis to the place of 'environment'. Such a comprehensive range of influencing factors which embodies the term environment was

was examined in terms of organisation - environment interaction which led into a consideration of inter organisational behaviour and an emphasis upon a political economy approach.

The public inquiry was described in this chapter as an administrative procedure and further was analysed in terms of inter organisational relations with specific reference to the public inquiry into the CLNT outline plan, the proceedings of which will be fully related in Chapter 9.

NOTES

1. Although designation inquiries are not governed by statutory rules, a pattern of procedure has been established. The minister has considered the options and is convinced that there is a case for the order he is proposing. He puts them forward in an explanatory memorandum which may be supplemented at the public inquiry. As Wraith and Lamb point out, 'he is holding the inquiry not to defend (his) case, but to hear objections to it', (Wraith and Lamb, 1971, p.70). There may be an opportunity to question his representative, a senior official, on factual aspects but not on policy. In central Lancashire, therefore, the principal of a new town's development was not in question, what was open to objection was its location, exact size and form. There may be a great deal of potential adjustment possible, and as Telling, in encouragement, points out: 'Although the minister will be considering objections to his own scheme, it should not be assumed that it is futile to object; such objections have in fact resulted in a reduction of the designated area', (Telling (4th ed.) 1973, p.20). This was borne out in practice, since as a consequence of some of the 670 objections received, the controversial Longridge Spur was deleted with other minor contractions of the proposed designated area.
2. See Franklin v. Minister of Town and Country Planning (1948) A.C.87.

PART III
THE CONTEXT OF THE STUDY

6 Central Lancashire New Town : regional planning and new town policy

REGIONAL PLANNING

Regional planning can be separated into three strands which are often viewed in isolation by the 'planning disciplines'. The economic strand is concerned with regional imbalance and the distribution of resources between regions; this element is closely linked with the public administrative dimension which focuses upon the devolution of power and the institutions, real or proposed, which perform the functions of administration and accountability at the regional level. Finally, there is the physical or spatial element, the concern of town and country planners, from which three chief policy areas have been distinguished: urban containment, protection of rural land and the creation of self contained and balanced communities. (Hall, et al., 1973, p.39). When considered in conjunction with national population policy based on the Barlow report (Barlow Report, 1940) and the influence of the idealist, even utopian, movement based on Howard's Garden City concept, (Howard, 1902), these objectives give rise to the very important considerations of the new towns as a means of implementation of regional planning policies.

The largest and potentially the most far reaching product of this aspect of regional planning has been the concern of this study: the central Lancashire new town (CLNT). The outline plan for the new town makes allusions to both the inter and intra regional dimensions of regional planning in paragraph 1/2 when it states:

> .... The project . . . is designed to improve the prosperity of central Lancashire and to provide for the general growth in the population of the north west region . . . This growth has been seen for some time to be too big to be catered for solely by the expansion of existing towns without serious loss of efficiency and environmental quality. The central Lancashire project thus takes its place at the largest of a series of new town developments in the north west whose creation is part and parcel of policies for controlling the growth of existing towns and cities, maintaining large tracts of unspoilt open country between them and at the same time helping to improve the competitive position of the region in relation to the Midlands and the south east. (CLDC, 1974, p.9)

The uniquely large scale nature of the central Lancashire new town led Mr. R.W. Phelps, the new town development corporation's general manager, to concede that 'It is, in planning terms, more of a sub region and the term 'new town' has a technical rather than a physical or sociological meaning'. (Phelps, 1973, p.11).

It is necessary to emphasise that, to date, sub regional plans have been indicative and advisory in nature, and that CLNT, even in a truncated form, constitutes a significant departure from previous tradition and practice. In effect it became the first imperative quasi sub regional plan, since it had at its disposal the very wide powers of action vested in its development corporation under the New Towns Act, 1965.

REGIONAL PLANNING IN NORTH WEST ENGLAND

By coincidence both standard texts on town planning and regional planning have taken this region as a case study (Hall, et al., 1973, vol.I, pp.566-610; Glasson, 1974, pp.247-56), and central government also chose this area as the subject of its second major regional study. (SPNW, 1974). The north west is a microcosm of Britain comprising great sub regional variety within the compact geographical area as defined by the planning region. Whereas it covers less than 5 per cent of the United Kingdom by area it does contain 14 per cent of the population (6.7 million), which is settled in two major cities and a number of major towns as well as in small settlements and remote rural areas. It has suffered a general decline in the traditional industrial base which provided the source of its prosperity during the industrial revolution; the economic problems caused by this blight being predominantly concentrated in the north east Lancashire and Merseyside sub regions.

Under the stimulus of the 1947 Town and Country Planning Act, regional advisory plans were introduced which were intended to provide an indicative framework to the planning authorities, the counties and county boroughs, in their detailed planning , but much groundwork had already been undertaken during the later years of the second World War. Not only was the Abercrombie plan produced for London in 1944, but a City of Manchester and Manchester regional plan were produced in 1945, and with Longstreth Thompson's Merseyside plan, also in that year. (Hall, et al., 1973, vol.I, pp.575-81). These plans were inevitably focussed upon the problems of housing and of population movement to the surrounding areas, predominantly towards Lancashire and Cheshire.

In 1974, the north west economic planning council did produce a document comparable with the south east study, the strategic plan for the north west (SPNW). The government's reactions to this plan, published in a Green Paper, were generally favourable (1975). The strategy envisaged that the region's resources should be largely concentrated upon the two major conurbations and the existing new towns lying between them, 'the Mersey Belt', and that the CLNT should, perhaps, be expected to develop at a slower rate than had originally been proposed. As Hall points out, by the beginning of the 1970s:

> .... the new towns programme appeared to be more than ample to deal with any public sector housing overspill from the two major conurbations, without the need for a continuing programme of additional new town designations throughout the 1970s. (Hall, et al., 1973, p.609)

The tightness of the conurbation boundaries introduced in 1974 does mean, however, that the population in new centres tend to be beyond normal commuting distances and this feature, in turn, requires attracting enough new industry in the new towns to match projected population growth. This factor has been particularly critical in the case of CLNT since the two Merseyside new towns of Skelmersdale and Runcorn have through the past years been treated as part of the special development area, while Preston-Leyland-Chorley has had to attract industry without any additional special government incentives over and above those provided for the region as a whole.

The reasons for the anticipated success of the CLNT, despite the lack of preferential financial incentives, lay in the belief in the attraction of the 'natural advantages' of the area. (CLDC, 1974, p.12). This optimism was based upon theories of the location of industry and in the efficacy of the growth centre theory as a cure for sub regional and regional deficiencies.

INDUSTRIAL LOCATION THEORY AND GROWTH CENTRE THEORY

Theories of industrial location have been proposed by economic geographers and economists, and by using the tools of economic and spatial analysis, they have attemted to provide rules which indicate the optimum location for a particular firm. Three general theoretical areas have been identified: first, the least cost approach, based on the work of Alfred Weber (Weber, 1929) and his followers, which focusses upon factor costs; second, market area analysis which concentrates more on demand factors and market variables which has been developed, in particular, by Lösch; (Lösch, 1954) and finally, the profit maximisation approach which attempts a synthesis of the other two, which tend to regard either the market demand or the input supply as constants.

Glasson has provided a most useful five point critique of locational theory. (Glasson, 1974, pp.111-8). He points out that first, local interdependence with market rivals is difficult to incorporate into a theory; second, that is difficult to evaluate the relevant variables; third, the difficulty of incorporating the decisions of large, modern corporations into the theories; fourth, whether firms do seek to maximise their profits rather than just seek a 'satisfactory' level of profits or growth; (March and Simon, 1958, pp.140-1) and finally, the behavioural and attitudinal factors must be an important consideration, particularly, say the unwillingness of the families of industrialists or key workers to move to 'obvious growth points'. In all, these arguments form a neat parallel with the criticisms of certain economists of many traditional theories of 'market economics'. (Galbraith, 1969; Donaldson, 1973, pp.143-6)

Several surveys have been undertaken, notably those for the Hunt report, of mobile firms which seek to identify the major location factors as seen by the firms themselves. The major categories which they suggested were: labour, its availability and quality; transport and communications; site and premises; government aid; and in the widest sense, environmental factors such as climate, landscape and 'social amenity'. In the end, it seems that largely 'irrational' pressures influence the location chosen by firms which have decided to move either for internal or external reasons, and it is most probable that most firms do not consider fully and dispassionately all the relevant factors. As the Hunt report commented rather guardedly: '...we are concerned that the quality of many firms' investment decisions is not as sophisticated and thorough as would be desirable'. (Hunt Report, para 358). Undoubtedly the locational, urbanisation and financial economies available in the north west lie within the new towns and special development areas of the Mersey Belt. In comparison, central Lancashire has had to rely heavily upon the 'quality of labour' and 'quality of life' selling points in its 'prospectus', since it has been unable to match its rival new towns' other advantages.

Growth centre theory and the associated notion of 'economic spin off' form a central argument in the justification of the CLNT and its defence against its critics from other areas of the north west, particularly north east Lancashire. The official view was given by the minister responsible for the designation, the late Richard Crossman, when he stated:

> .... this new town . . . should contribute to the industrial revival of the whole region, and form a new focus for urban renewal . . . The importance we attach to it is that we see it as a point for the industrial revivalof the whole region, which I think will inspire the region to feel that the south does not get it all. (Quoted in Levin, 1976, p.192) (my emphasis)

Sir Frank Pearson, chairman of the development corporation also stressed the importance of the growth centre concept when he wrote:

> .... I very much hope that the area will be regarded not so much as a town but rather as a focal city region stimulating growth over a wide area. For too long now central and north east Lancashire have missed out, and the creation of the corporation now provides an opportunity for them to prosper . . . I take the broad and positive view that prosperity spreads out and that our success will have valuable 'spin off' for the rest of the region. (Pearson, 1973) (my emphasis)

Thus it can be seen that great weight is placed at official level upon the concept of the regional growth centre and in particular upon the so called 'spread effects'. Reference has already been made to the commissioning of an impact study in response to the widespread political opposition to the CLNT in north east Lancashire. This report applied the Garin-Lowry model of spatial interaction, (Garin, 1966) and its findings were able to mollify the opposition from that area when linked with proposals of 'intermediate area status' and the projected Calder Valley motorway. Primary emphasis tended to be placed upon the 'spin off' effects from manufacturing investment , yet the CLNT project was also seen as a centre for concentrated infrastructure investment and such provision of economic overhead capital, in the form of roads, sewers and drainage, and public utilities.

Although supporters of the project confidently expected that such expenditure would stimulate growth, it has been pointed out that there is little empirical evidence to support the contention that superior infrastructure attracts new industry, indeed as Gwilliam suggests, improved inter regional roads may open up a problem region to dangerous competition rather than encouraging new development. (Gwilliam, 1970). This possible consequence intra regionally, between the central Lancashire sub region and the north east Lancashire sub region, has been of constant concern to leaders of the north east towns, evidence of which was clearly articulated at the outline plan public inquiry (See Chapter 12).

Donnison contends that recent research 'shows that even when such enterprises succeed, their multiplier effects often 'leak' to the more prosperous regions, and generate little further growth'. (Donnison, 1974). The experience of some of the country's large employers with labour problems, the temporary excursions into the development areas to obtain short term financial incentives, and the doubts about the cost effectiveness of some forms of regional investment, Donnison insists 'are now the common places of debate about regional economics . . . But they seem unfamilar to those concerned with regional politics who are engaged in a different debate'.

Following this suggestion, it will be useful to place the new towns policy, as a whole, into a regional prespective.

NEW TOWNS IN THE REGIONAL CONTEXT

Traditionally, the propagandists for new towns advocated the ideals of balanced communities, in terms of social classes, and self contained, in terms of job opportunities and population. The reality of CLNTs policies has proved to be markedly different. The outline plan and the evidence at the public inquiry demonstrated the new aims. The importance of attracting, if not the captains of industry, certainly management and professional groups, by housing, superbly landscaped, and sometimes integrated into golf courses, and the expectation of substantial in and out flows of the working population stress <u>economic</u> rather than <u>social</u> goals. Better class housing will encourage entrepreneurs; 'labour markets' are more in evidence than 'communities'. As discussed earlier in this chapter, CLNT was viewed at designation by Richard Crossman and later reiterated by others, including Sir Frank Pearson, that the development would serve as a point for the industrial revival of the whole region. The 'spin off' from economic activity in the designated area would, it was argued, benefit the surrounding areas and particularly north east Lancashire.

Comments from Roger Stott, M.P., in the Commons, which will be quoted in full in Chapter 13, underline the doubts expressed by the adjacent areas that, particularly in periods of economic stagnation or decline, the concentration of resources is more likely to have a 'creaming off' effect and to heighten the differences in economic activity, environmental standards and social amenities between the new town and its hinterland. Whether or not the application of growth point theory would have been valid within the region at a time of economic buoyancy remains to be demonstrated, but as Levin asserts, it was a key theory entering into the cabinet's 'action scheme' on designation. (Levin, 1976, p.142) So it was, as Aldridgepoints out:

> .... in the 1960s many parties to new towns policy assumed that a combination of development corporation powers to assemble land and to supply infrastructure and the cash incentives available in the development and special development areas could not fail to rejuvenate declining areas. (Aldridge,1979, p.141)

CLNT, of course, did not have the benefits of special development area status. It was argued, as indicated earlier in this chapter that the special advantages of location, its existing and economic base and labour force, together with its growing social facilities, would be sufficient incentives to provide a basis for a growth centre. The concept is regarded by many as, not only having utility in providing links between economic theories of development and decline, but also, in a sociological sense, forming a bridge between economic and physical planning and hence bolstering the prestige and mystique of members of the planning profession. The growth point theory, it is argued, potentially offers a method of reconciling regional and urban economics. Yet Richardson contends:

> .... Unfortunately, it has never lived up to this promise. Despite a voluminous interpretative literature, it remains cloudy and ill defined. Moreover and even worse, there has been about a decade and a half of operational planning experience and growth poles have failed to work as the theory predicted. (Richardson, 1978, p.164)

Thus a theory which requires a deliberate stimulation of industry and its spin off, employing the notion of high technology, leading industries which will require local suppliers and services, has been criticised for being based on an outmoded assumption of the theory of the firm. Holland, indeed, goes so far as to assert that the 'intellectual and economic foundations' of the theory 'range from slim to false'. (Holland, 1976, p.48). International experience has shown an increasing disillusionment with growth pole strategies and this setback is primarily because 'they have failed to generate the anticipated spill over effects over their surrounding hinterlands'. (Richardson, 1978, p.167)

It is evident that apologists may point out that the failure of the theory is based upon national economic conditions, and that, as a result, the anticipated incentives to encourage inter regional distribution and intra regional spin off failed to materialise. This unproven basis for a regional role for new town policy is compounded by the lack of evaluation of the new town programme itself. The report of the expenditure committee on new towns pointed out that there was no suggestion of an analysis 'in order to establish the social and economic opportunity costs of undertaking the programme, or the policies themselves'. (1974, p.34)

From purely descriptive or case study examples, it would appear that the infrastructure and comprehensive site planning can add a strong incentive to employers to locate their factories or offices in new towns, though some would argue that direct financial incentives would be less costly in inducing job movement or job creation (See, Hunt Report, 1969). The extent of beneficial effect upon the surrounding area for either method, however, is unproven. Indeed there is the fear that improved transport networks could accelerate decline, not only from the hinterland and the so called growth point, but also from the growth point in the region to the main centre of economic activity.

One reason postulated for the perpetuation of the growth centre as a central justification of new towns is the professional interest of the planners. The Royal Town Planning Institute has an institutional interest in claiming autonomy and 'mastery of a field of knowledge'. This assertion had led them to 'claim jurisdiction over regional questions' and 'to define regional problems in physical planning terms despite an inability to render those problems solvable without employing over simple theories and structural concepts'. (Levin, 1976, p.306)

Traditionally, the majority of planners have regarded new town policies with favour since they serve the interests of the wider community in the implementation of slum clearance programmes and overspill agreements, so that, as Thomas and Creswell put it: 'in the face of local opposition their actions are likely to be justified by the argument they are serving the needs of the 'community' outside the local area'. (Thomas and Creswell, 1973, p.45). Thus the planning profession are steeped in the ideological basis for the new towns (Foley, 1960) deriving largely from a critique of the city and an anti urban stand, motiviating many early town planners and social reformers. This stance in turn, some would argue, had its origins in a basic fear of the large industrial city as a breeding ground for working class insurrection and disorder. By the time Howard's idea for garden cities had been promoted as Heraud observes, most of Britain's population was already predominantly urban.

> .... Given this situation, it is something of a puzzle that the idea of the movement of big city population to small towns and suburbs came to be so readily adopted as a solution to city problems, by comparison to a direct concentration on the problems of the cities themselves. (Heraud, 1975, p.42)

That this approach had dominated the decision makers thinking for so long should be credited to the Town and Country Planning Association's influence. Yet this body, too, has adjusted its policies away from the continued need for a large programme of self-contained new towns, promoted on the basis of population densities, living conditions and a sense of community, to that of a regional decanting strategy, coupled with the idea of growth points. The TCPA's more recent position on regionalism has been typified by Aldridge as the 'jug and bottle model':

> .... From this perspective, city problems remain essentially problems of scale: too many people for the roads and houses, too much employment for the roads, the trains, the drains, etc . . . The excess in the jug should be poured into other bottles . . . (Aldridge, 1979, p.136).

This approach was challenged by the Shore initiative on the Inner Cities, which attempted to grapple with the paradox identified by Heraud, by focussing resources and attention on the cities themselves, rather than indirectly through new or expanded towns. The emphasis, tacitly, would now be on arresting decline in the selected metropolitan areas, rather than expecting statements about growth points to mollify opposition within the regions. New towns may thus be regarded as a decaying example of the centre's control over the periphery.

New forms of direction have emerged through the inner cities partnerships initiated by the Labour government, and the legislative proposals on housing and local government finance from the Conservatives. The centre is thus extending influence at the institutional level in the local government system, yet ironically this change does not mean the demise of the direct arm of the government in physical planning, the development corporation. The urban development corporations now starting their operations in such places as the London docklands and Merseyside, often in the face of initial local political opposition, have provided a replacement. It remains to be seen whether this latest attempt at central control, albeit directed at the source of the deprivation, is based upon valid theoretical criteria. One also has to reflect whether such policy decisions have their origins in non rational elements of decision making which serve to bolster the greater power of the centre over the peripheral regions.

7 The Development Corporation and amenity groups

The complexity of inter organisational relationships has been described in Chapter 5. In order to provide the background information to the activities in central Lancashire it will be useful to give a brief account of the key organisations involved in the political, communication and interaction processes in the development of the new town.

THE CENTRAL LANCASHIRE DEVELOPMENT CORPORATION

The chosen instrument of new towns policy is the development corporation which is created by central government under the appropriate legislation. The Central Lancashire New Town Development Corporation was brought into being by the Central Lancashire designation order, under the New Towns Act, 1965, on 14 April 1970. It is, as such, an agency of government and responsible to the government through the appropriate section of the Department of the Environment, the junior minister responsible for the running of the section, and ultimately the Secretary of State for the Environment. The corporation consists of a board selected by the secretary of state which comprises a chairman, deputy chairman and a maximum of seven members. The responsibility for executing the corporation's policy is that of the general manager who is appointed by the board. The general manager then selects and appoints his senior officers and staff.

The casual observer might be forgiven for assuming that all new town development corporations are basically similar in structure and operation. Admittedly, certain variations might be expected but these, it is assumed, would be derived from the personalities and 'managerial style' of key officials. A closer examination of development corporations shows considerable differences to exist, a point to be discussed in more detail in Chapter 14. This variation is most marked in the status and organisation of social development in new towns. This activity, unlike most of the constituent departments of the corporation, is not related to legislatively defined goals. It has developed from early ad hoc appointments and among other things, guidelines laid down by the department of the environment in the new towns handbook. (See Chapter 14 for a further detailed consideration of this function).

In essence, the main activities of social development include community development, arrivals work, social planning and research, liaison with voluntary and statutory bodies and planning and public relations and information. It is possible for these functions to be encompassed within one comprehensive social development department with a chief officer in charge, perhaps combined with the housing department as in Runcorn, or to be dispersed between other sections entirely. Ranged between these extremes some of the functions might be incorporated within other departments; for example, social planning within planning, social research in planning or finance and arrivals in housing. The residual functions are then grouped into a social development section or, as in the case of the CLDC, the 'social facilities' section.

As Meryl Horrocks has reported:

> .... the research team were often told that the existence of social development at all and certainly its relative power, depended upon the attitudes of the general manager. In places where there was no SDO, the reasons given were almost uniformly that either the general manager positively did not approve of social development, or more moderately, did not see its usefulness at that stage or scale of development. (Horrocks, 1972, p.554)

The example of social development provides an important indicator of the power, overt or potential, which is enshrined in the role of the general manager. He can decide whether the social aspects of planning are to be coordinated under a strong principal officer, as in Runcorn, whether they are to be dispersed or, at least, severely limited in scope, as in central Lancashire. Even more remarkable is the fact that the general manager either directly, or nominally through his board, can shape his own organisation and select his senior staff. The general manager of the CLDC, during the course of interviews, has indicated his reservations about the functions of social development and his pride in the uniqueness of his organisation's structure.

THE ORGANISATIONAL STRUCTURE OF THE CLDC

Richard Phelps, the general manager of the CLDC, decided that since the new town with its sub regional scope was 'unique in its scale and concept', it reinforced the need for innovation in building up a new organisation. The separation of 'thinking' and 'doing' or 'planning' and 'execution' provide the cornerstone of the organisational design. In the first of a series of articles or publications, this philosophy was clearly articulated as follows:

> .... real delegation . . . of routine work seemed essential if the ongoing tasks of planning, marketing and implementation, which involve all professions, were to be handled in the depth required. The board, therefore, decided to hive off staff responsible for the executive functions of providing works or services in whatever field they lay from those who engage on forward planning and marketing functions.
> . . . Staff on this (executive side of the fence will be organised on fairly conventional and hierarchical lines to reflect well established practices and responsibilities. On the other (planning) side, however, my main concern will be to coordinate the work of a fully multi professional planning and implementation group which will contain all except one of the corporation's chief officers (he being responsible for the executive

services). Here the structure will be much more flexible and organic in nature. (Phelps, 1972; See also Phelps, 1976; 1977)

The general manager, who has only a small personal staff, provides the only formal link between these two groups of the organisation. The organisation chart representing the organisation as planned at its inception in 1972 is shown below.

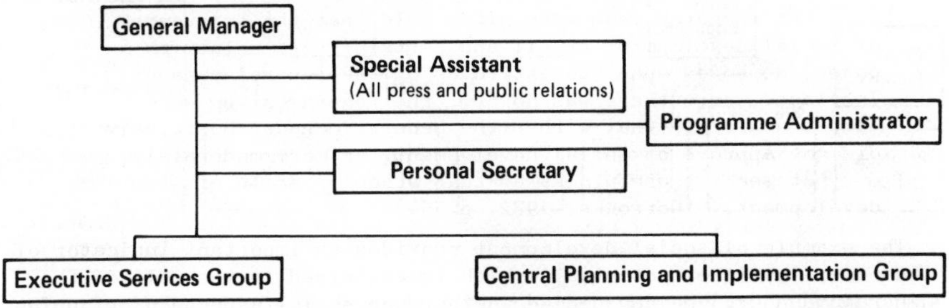

The executive services group is divided into five sections under the chief officer for executive services. Some of these have planning equivalents, for example Finance and Surveying. An abbreviated version of the organisation chart for this group is shown below.

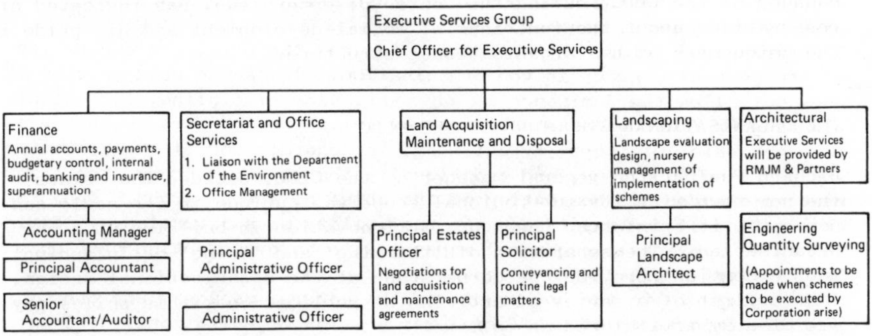

In addition to coordinating the executive and planning functions, the general manager also acts as the coordinator of the various branches of the central planning and coordination group. This also has five sections but, in this case, led by a chief officer. A simplified version of the organisation chart of the group, (p.64) shows how the social development functions, which have been adopted, are allocated to the departments of the chief officer, legal and liaison (social facilities) and the chief officer, financial planning and research (research). Community development as such does not have a place in the organisation but some of this work will be included in the housing department, added later.

The official reasoning to support this organisational structure has been clearly stated by the general manager in an article in the Financial Times. (Phelps, 1972). It is illuminating to explore the unofficial reasons for such a structure and the practical effect upon the staff. Mr. Phelps' recent job history includes a post as an

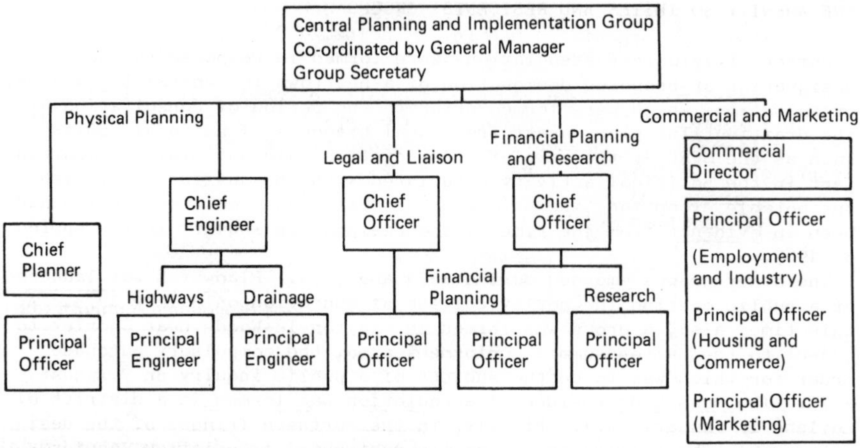

administrator in Hampshire county council, and as the general manager of Skelmersdale new town development corporation. (1) In both cases, the structure of the organisation was well defined and, in the latter case, although the position gave nominal overall control of the organisation, the pattern had been set by his predecessor. The new organisational design for the CLNT development corporation might be viewed as eliminating some possible frustrations experienced in the past by the general manager.

In practical terms, the new design ensures the effective centrality of the general manager in the organisation. It can be used so that it does not allow the dominance of any particular discipline, for example planning or finance, or a sub focus of influence to emerge with the relevant chief officer. By acting as the coordinator of the executive and planning functions, and additionally the planning group, the general manager ensures his domination of the chief officers' group. The combination of centrality and the possibility of a situation of 'divide and rule' provides the general manager with an organisation over which he can exert a great deal of power and control.

The reference to the background of the general manager, and the possible importance of unofficial reasons for organisational design, provides an indication of the importance of exploring informal aspects of the organisation and its officers. At a rudimentary level this information may be obtained by studying published documentary sources, particularly a special new town supplement of the Chorley Guardian. In this, brief life histories of 'the management' of the new town are described. There are a number of interesting features. The chief officer for executive services was Mr. Phelps' successor as senior administrator to Hampshire county council. Both he and Mr. Phelps had been in the colonial civil service in Africa and had become deputy permanent secretaries. The chief engineer previously worked for Mr. Phelps at Skelmersdale, as did the current chief planner. The life histories also give account of the military service of the chief officers. With only the briefest published evidence it is possible to infer that, with a number of chief officers, the additional informal links could serve to reinforce the strong formal position of the general manager. In short, the organisation is constructed formally, and its officers selected informally, in order to achieve the most effective and 'efficient' personal direction from a strong general manager.

THE AMENITY SOCIETIES AND RESIDENTS' GROUPS

A number of voluntary associations were formed in response to the designation or proposed designation of a new town in central Lancashire. Organisations which were formed prior to the period of consultation of the draft outline plan, apart from local branches of national bodies such as the CPRE or the Ramblers' Association, did not play an important part in the political activity associated with the outline plan, with one notable exception, the Grimsargh and Haighton committees, which had been in evidence from the time of the designation inquiry in the spring of 1969.

The other groups emerged during 1973 and 1974. Planwatch was launched at a public meeting in Chorley college of education on 3 July 1973. At this time, also, a group was formed in Clayton-le-Woods near Chorley to object to the Walton summit employment area, the compulsory purchase order for which was to be the subject of a public inquiry on 7 August 1973. The Moss Side residents' association was formed in a district of Leyland in January 1974. Finally, in the northern fringes of the designated area, the Fulwood and Broughton residents' association was formalised following a public meeting on 22 July 1974.

In such a large designated area it was not expected that opposition should be diffuse and, potentially, disjointed. Attempts were made by Planwatch to act as a coordinator for the action groups but, as the 'political' stance towards the new town adopted by Planwatch was not sufficiently strong for some activists, a rival 'umbrella' organisation was formed by key members of the Grimsargh and Walton summit groups which became known as SCRAP (the society for the coordination and reaffirmation of anti new town policies). The eventual cooperation between these groups, and their concerted programme of lobbying, will be described in Chapter 13.

Planwatch

This organisation was set up as a 'watchdog organisation to monitor all planning developments in the area'. It evolved from an adult class held in Chorley college of education during Lent term 1973. The class included a number of people whose concern about planning issues and the effect of the new town on the area apparently went beyond receiving information. Towards the end of the ten week course, Keith Williams, who was later to become the secretary of Planwatch, suggested the formation of a planning action group. There was an enthusiastic response to this proposition by a number of the class and a small steering group was convened. It was suggested that the, yet unnamed, group should be launched at a public meeting at which there would be a guest speaker. A planner sympathetic to the cause of public participation was approached from the Liverpool city planning department and the meeting arranged. 500 leaflets were distributed in the Chorley area through the personal contacts of the founder members. Forty people attended the inaugural meeting. The discussion following the speech by the guest speaker, Susan Cartledge, was lively, and stimulated a response from a chief officer of the development corporation who was present 'as an observer'. Keith Williams circulated all those who had expressed an interest and the first formal meeting of the group took place, the week following the public meeting, at the Seaview Inn, Whittle-le-Woods, on 10 July 1973.

The group were concerned that their membership and sphere of activity should not be concentrated upon Chorley only and attempts were made to involve known activists in Preston and Leyland. To that end a meeting place was sought which was more convenient for members, in the wider catchment area for potential membership. The area of Lostock Hall was chosen for this purpose.

The Planwatch was suggested and the constitution and objects were formalised to permit affiliation to the Civic Trust for the North West and meetings, open to all members, continued for a period in members' homes.

In the spring of 1974, despite the distractions of a general election, the group started to make initial preparations for the presentation of its evidence for the public inquiry into the outline plan for the new town. A number of working parties were set up to focus on certain aspects of the plan, most active of which was the transport working party under the chairmanship of Alan Howard, a Ramblers' Association activist from Preston. General meetings of the organisation came to be regularly held at the Bridge Inn, Penwortham: the first annual general meeting being held there on 17 April 1974. Executive meetings came to be held on a regular basis at the treasurer's house at Samlesbury, Preston. These executive committee meetings were open to all members to attend.

John Hagarty, the chairman of Planwatch, invited a neighbour, a town planner, to advise the group on its evidence. He was Chris Turner who had been formerly employed in the Lancashire county planning department and was now with the Greater Manchester county planning department. Under Chris Turner's guidance the outline plan was discussed paragraph by paragraph in executive committee meetings and, in the transport working party, he also acted as advisor. The evidence was finally drawn together and agreed at a one day conference held on the Sunday prior to the commencement of the public inquiry on 5 November 1974.

From the outset, Planwatch sought all party support for its activities. Soon after its formation a letter was drafted which gained signatures from members of the local Conservative, Labour and Liberal parties. Such a balance was thought to be desirable by the leading members but it was inevitable that a bias should unwittingly develop. During the months when the group was primarily Chorley orientated, support had been forthcoming from a college lecturer and Labour councillor, Mike Pearson, and one of the early activists was the chairman of the Chorley Liberal party, Frank Wilson. The first chairman of Planwatch, John Hagarty was a Labour parish councillor and chairman of his local Labour party. Despite the fact that known members of the Conservative party were recruited as members, such as the chairman of Whittle parish council, Councillor John Livesey, the composition of leading officials and members gave the impression that the group was Lib/Lab in political outlook. This apparent orientation was important in the early relationships with other groups, notable Walton Summit and Grimsargh and Haighton, at a time of a general election when political tensions were evident.

Moss Side Residents' Association

This group was formed into the Moss Side district of Leyland to represent the residents of the area in their objections to the development of Moss Side and in particular the routing of the western primary road of the new town which was regarded as a potential physical barrier between 'the village' and the rest of Leyland.

The first meeting in the area in December 1973 was initiated by a founder member of Planwatch, and a member at the time of the new town social development advisory committee, Bernard Davies. (See Chapter 9). A second public meeting was held on 10 January 1974, at which a committee was formed and the association founded. The groups' initial objective was to gather material for the submission of evidence to an expected public inquiry into the proposals under Section 6(i) of the New Towns Act. The proposals for a village development at Moss Side were thus in advance of the outline plan inquiry. Committee meetings were held weekly, usually at the home of the chairman, Bernard Casey. The group members were inexperienced in this type of activity and a number appeared to be doubtful at the very outset of their formation whether their efforts were worthwhile. Evidence of this scepticism was shown during the public meeting held by the development corporation following the exhibition of the Moss Side proposals on 2 May 1974. There were some searching questions asked about public participation in this meeting and doubts were strongly expressed about 'taking notice of Moss Side' and whether 'our views will make any difference'. Despite a spirited defence of new town participation policies by Col. Carl Barras, it was evident from comments that the memory of a recently screened television programme about the extension of a runway at Edinburgh had made a more significant impact. (2)

The initial spark which had been provided by Bernard Davies was not available to the group as a continuing stimulation, as he was shortly to leave the area for a new post. This, a friendly, quite well integrated group, perhaps lacked the fighting cutting edge of some of the other groups. The length of time which they had available to present their case was short and, in the view of the officers, the experience of the 6(i) inquiry was to lead to a sense of disillusionment with the planning process. The group submitted evidence to the public inquiry into the outline plan in a low key, somewhat dispirited way. They appeared to be certain that, at least as far as their own area was concerned, they were fighting a losing battle.

Walton Summit Protest Committee

The Walton summit group was formed following a public meeting on 25 June 1973. The name of the committee indicates that the focus of its protest was the planned employment area and associated housing at Walton summit. Like Moss Side, Leyland, this development was scheduled to proceed before the general approval of the outline plan and was to be the subject of a Section 6(i) application by the development corporation and, should objections warrant, a public inquiry. This inquiry took place on 7 August 1973. The committee distributed a leaflet advertising an eve of inquiry protest meeting and this publicity resulted in a well attended meeting at St. Bede's Hall, Clayton. The meeting ended with appeals to attend the inquiry so that the inspector, the corporation and the general public would be aware of the strength of feeling against the development. This request was successful and the original venue for the inquiry in the Walton-le-Dale U.D.C.s council chamber was so overcrowded that the inquiry moved to a school hall nearby. Banners had been organised and the chairman of the committee, Mr. Jim Pilkington and the general manager, Mr. Richard

Phelps were both interviewed by a BBC film crew for the regional news bulletin that day. The Walton summit protest committee's objection was led by Mr. Pilkington with vigour, and some emotion.

This group, unlike Moss Side, found the experience of a prior public inquiry had affected members differently. Some lost their enthusiasm, but other leading members, by joining in an alliance with Grimsargh and Haighton to form SCRAP, found additional moral support. At the outline plan public inquiry, Mr. Pilkington, supported by one witness, a local general practitioner, conducted the case for the committee. Such was the personality of Mr. Pilkington that his experience of the earlier public inquiry and other 'felt grievances' spurred him on to be more determined, wilder, and more indignant in his accusations of 'maladministration', 'collusion' and 'insensitivity' against the development corporation. To an extent this emotional approach alienated Mr. Pilkington from his local support and from members of some of the other action groups and Planwatch. His manner of presentation seemed to have been counter productive with the inspector at the outline plan public inquiry. It had little effect upon the Walton summit employment area; the buildings have since been constructed and the associated housing has been built.

Ashton Action Group

As with the other Preston area groups, the Ashton action group was principally concerned about the effect of the road proposals contained in the outline plan. Alan Howard, a key activist, commented upon the proposed line of a new eastern primary route through the Ashton-on-Ribble area of Preston in a bus queue in the hearing of Leslie Jacobs, a senior employee of a local authority. He was appalled at the prospect and immediately set about forming an action group during March/April 1974. (3)

The nucleus of the group started their public activities by judicious use of the local evening press. They commenced their campaign by alerting the Lancashire Evening Post about the human and environmental impact of the 'favoured' route 4 in the road appraisal reports, which by this time were receiving their first publicity. (Leyland Guardian, 28 March 1974). The result was a large report, with suitable photographs, by a staff reporter, Roger Beam with the headline '£1 million plan which is threatening paradise'.

> .... 'Hands off paradise' and 'don't destroy heaven' is the cry of residents determined to stop concrete and cars ruining their local beauty spots.
>
> And if they lose their battle, a main road, besides demolishing 140 houses and uprooting more than 100 mature lime trees, will be built on land specifically given as a park.
>
> The residents of the Haslam park area of Preston are to fight the central Lancashire development corporation's plan for a 'primary' road to serve the expanding area of Ingol in Preston.
>
> Two notable beauty spots would be victims of the road . . . (LEP, 3 April 1974)

The following day a more 'considered' article appeared written by the Post chief planning writer, Peter Dugdale, giving the reasoning behind the preferred route for a section of the western primary road. The headline 'Homes before trees?', 'Dilemma on future of a smart suburb' was an apparent attempt to redress the balance from the previous day. The general effect, particularly with the sketchmap provided on 4 April 1974, was to alert opinion formers in the Ashton area, and assist the action group in its publicity campaign.

In reaction to this press publicity, the Member of Parliament for the Preston North constituency, Mr. Ron Atkins, gave Peter Dugdale an interview which was published on 5 April. The headline was 'Fight for your home' - MP.

> .... Hundreds of houses will have to be demolished in Preston to make way for new town roads, claims one of Preston's MPs, Mr. Ron Atkins. And he has urged the public to form their own campaign committee to resist the plans before they are too late . . .

Although Mr. Atkins' interview goes on to relate more specifically to the effects on north central, and north eastern Preston (which was soon to become the concern of another group, the Preston north action group) the three days of publicity served to place the new town roads issue before the interested public, to the advantage of the embryo Ashton group.

The formation of the group was fomally announced in the press on 30 April and the first public meeting was arranged for Thursday, 2 May 1974. This meeting was very well attended and supported by the MP, in whose constituency Ashton is a part, Mr Stan Thorne. At the close of the meeting volunteers were sought, and about fifty notified their willingness to work for the group. This group was convened and from their number a committee of ten was elected. The remaining activists continued in existence, forming working groups for fund raising, social activities, petitions and research and became known as 'the forty'.

One of the first tasks which the committee discussed was the handling of the meeting held by the development corporation as part of its 'participation' programme on the road proposals for the area. This was to be held on Tuesday, 21 May 1974 at St. Cuthbert's church hall, Fulwood: a location on the peripheryof the activities of the action group. 'The forty' were provided with a full briefing of questions to ask at this meeting. The meeting was the first occasion that the development corporation experienced the indignation and strong feeling aroused in Preston by their proposals. The meeting ended with a speaker quoting Oliver Cromwell 'In the name of God, go', which was accompanied by sustained applause.

As the result of the objections made at this meeting about the inconvenient location, a second meeting was arranged to explain the road proposals. As the Ashton action group information leaflet No.2 explained:

> This meeting in Ashton would not have been held if the action group had not taken the line at the Fulwood meeting that Ashton matters must be discussed in Ashton and thereby forced the new town development corporation to hold a meeting here which clearly they did not want.

This second road appraisal meeting took place in a crowded St Andrew's school on 18 June. The tone was set by the initial exchange between Mr Jacobs and Mr Phelps, when the meeting was informed that the development corporation had charged the group £5 for a copy of the tape recording of the previous meeting. After the usual formal statements and some prepared questions the meeting reached its climax when Mr Stan Thorne made a speech in support of the action group. This was fully reported in the Lancashire Evening Post the following day:

> New town anger grows - I'll take fight to commons - MP.
>
> .... none attacked the corporation more than Mr Stan Thorne, MP for Preston south, who told the meeting he would ask the secretary of state to set back the date of the public inquiry due to be heard on 17 September (LEP, 19 June 1974)

Mr Thorne asked a commons question a few days later, pressing for a postponement of the public inquiry. The secretary of state for the environment, in reply, stated:

> .... The publication of the central Lancashire development corporation of their outline plan on 31 May gives sufficient time for it to be considered by the public before the public inquiry on September 17. Mr Thorne was reported to say that he was bitterly disappointed at the government's attitude and that he would seek an early adjournment debate (4) in the commons on the whole question of planning and the new town. (LEP, 21 June 1974)

Ashton action group, though largely drawn from an area which tends to have more anti Labour voters, valued the efforts on their behalf by their MP and continued to have close liaison with him over a long period. In this respect, it is interesting to note throughout the study the relative involvement of the MPs whose constituencies covered the designated area of the new town at this time: Mr Ron Atkins, Mr Stan Thorne (Preston north and south), Mr George Rodgers (Chorley) and Mr Edward Gardner (South Fylde).

The first large scale event organised by the group was a coffee morning on Saturday, 29 June 1974. The Ashton area was leafleted and St Andrew's school was filled to capacity. It was one of the group's most successful fund raising efforts raising £289 for the group. (LEP, 17 July 1974) Its ability in this direction was unequalled by other groups.

Preston North Action Group

This group was formed to cover the north and north eastern districts of Preston which were believed to be threatened by a proposed eastern primary road and the possible impact of upgrading of a cross town route, St George's Road/Aqueduct Street. A moving force behind this group was a local comprehensive school headmaster, Bryan Hughes. The group was launched at a public meeting in April 1974, and by June a meeting with some 150 attending, was held at which an all party platform was presented. This meeting and its noteworthy final speech by Mr Ron Atkins, MP are fully described in Chapter 9.

This group, under the chairmanship of the then councillor, Dick Evans, met regularly to prepare its evidence for the outline plan public inquiry. Of all the groups emerging, it had a most difficult period of early growth, becoming unwittingly involved in local Labour party politics. Local ward councillors were discouraged from becoming members after its initial months, and only the chairman and Mr Atkins remained committee members.

Despite this apparent setback, the group maintained its momentum, and with a wide delegation of tasks, a number of members presented linked evidence at the public inquiry concentrating upon objections to the eastern primary road and its likely social effects. (See Chapter 12)

Grimsargh and Haighton Action Committee and SCRAP

The area to the north east of the designated area had long been one of the most contentious and controversial aspects of the new town's designated area. The original proposals had been strongly resisted earlier and, following the public inquiry into designation in 1969, much of the Longridge Spur was excluded (See Figure 3).

The Grimsargh action committee originally formed in 1969 to oppose designation became active once more, in opposing the compulsory purchase orders for 2,686 acres of land in their sphere of influence. Objections to the CPO were made at a public inquiry in August 1973 by this group.

The interest in the committee temporarily waned after this inquiry and when the chairman, Mr George Jepson, was succeeded by Mr Ray Johnson the group was revitalised as the Grimsargh and Haighton action committee to prepare for the task of submitting an objection to the outline plan inquiry. It became a detailed document of some 103 pages.

The consistent and vehement anti new town stance of this group was mirrored by that of the Walton summit protest committee. Following public meetings in their respective centres of Grimsargh and Whittle-le-Woods in mid August 1974 (See Chapter 11) and an attempt was made to form an umbrella organisation. It was to be, unlike Planwatch, a grouping unequivocally committed to the dismantling of CLNT in its entirety - the 'Society for the coordination and reaffirmation of anti new town policies' - SCRAP. Its formation was largely stimulated by the desire to influence the major parties' candidates at the forthcoming general election. The organisation was launched officially at a public meeting in Preston in early September 1974, but lack of funds caused the withdrawal of the threat to nominate anti new town candidates later that month.

SCRAP and its allied constitutent groups would all later submit objections to the outline plan public inquiry (See Chapter 12). Despite the rivalry for the adherence to their policies, as distinct to those of Planwatch towards the other local action groups, it is important to note that these groups would later sink their differences (See Chapter 12). Ray Johnson, for example, was to become a member of the drafting committee of the local groups joint working party formed in 1976 to request a reappraisal of the new town.

Fulwood and Broughton Residents' Association

This association, the last of the major action groups to be formed in central Lancashire, was given its initial prompting through a letter in the <u>Lancashire Evening Post</u> in July 1974. Unlike the other groups, which were convened prior to the meetings on the outline plan, the need for this group's existence was derived from material and information gained from such meetings. Some of its leading members had already made contact with the Ashton, Preston north, and Planwatch groups, and had noted the procedures and best methods of inauguration. The group's initial activities are described in Chapter 10. Like the other 'local' groups, a prime concern was the impact of the proposed roads which were intended to serve projected developments for the area. Its main differentiating feature was its ability to draw members from relevant professions to advise in the collection and presentation of its objections at the outline plan public inquiry. Being based in the suburbs of north Preston and beyond its boundaries, it was perhaps the most middle class area in the new town.

GROUP ACTIVISTS - A TYPOLOGY

From the many months close observation of committee meetings, public meetings and the public inquiry, it has been possible to place the main 'actors' into broad categories, based upon individual attitudes and ideologies. The majority of each category within the individual groups would, of course, tend to produce an action group of a similar overt orinetation, though, as in all organisations, the 'dominant coalitions' ideology will prevail.

In Lowry's terms (Lowry, 1962) most activists in central Lancashire were predominantly local in orientation, but having some members also who are occupationally mobile (e.g. teachers, planners) and had some cosmopolitan influences. It is suggested that three 'ideal types' may be distinguished: the 'Skeffington idealists', the 'anti new town militants', and the 'local protestors'. If these are linked with Lowry's 'conservative' and 'utopian' ideological orientations, the following diagram may be suggested:

	'C'	'U'
Skeffington idealists	-	X
Anti-new town militants	X	X
Local protestors	X	-

<u>A typology of group activists</u>

The Skeffington idealists possessed a belief in participatory democracy, one which, in de Tocqueville's phrase, should be 'active'. The spirit of Skeffington, as they interpreted it, invited them to become involved in a partnership with the authorities with a right to involvement in planning matters. With Burgess and Travers they would argue that:

> .... It is not enough . . . that the people should, once every five years or so, elect a central government. For

a real democracy the people must continue to take
a share in the management of affairs. (Burgess and
Travers, 1980, p.5)

This ideology produced ambivalent attitudes to new towns as such. Most Skeffington idealists were concentrated within the leadership of Planwatch, and there was much goodwill towards the concept of integrated planning and schemes produced by multi-disciplinary teams. The idealism became soured over time, through the experience of development corporation relationships and procedures.

Both the Skeffington idealists and the anti new town militants gave indications of a utopian, or anti establishment bias, which was independent from party political allegiances. The anti new town militants, of which SCRAP is the evident example, took their broader remit to be that of complete opposition to CLNT, as a concept.

The local protestors tended to avoid the wider issues: for example, whether a new town should proceed or be curtailed. Their prime concern was the effect upon the area they were formed to protect. As such, the Moss Side and Ashton leaderships were generally within this category; the other groups, because of multiple memberships or links with SCRAP or Planwatch less so. Preston north, Fulwood and Broughton had their strong affiliations to Planwatch; Walton summit and the Grimsargh and Haighton groups were closely allied to SCRAP.

The studies of other areas of either urban planning or strategic planning (Dearlove, 1973; McKie, 1973) have demonstrated that it is unusual for a united or monolithic opposition to be in operation. They too, tend to exhibit either different class, ideological or interest variations. With each case study there will be the likelihood that these differences will be place and issue specific.

The observation and study of interest and local action groups, whether in North America or Britain, has thus tended to demonstrate a range of approaches and ideologies towards a common cause. Reactions to CLNT were consistent with these findings. More unusual, however, is the subsequent joint action of the groups following the outline plan public inquiry, which will be described in Chapter 12. This gives an indication of the possible transient nature of the typology and the need to appreciate the dynamic of external events or 'non events', which may stimulate the temporary subsuming of differences at a time of 'local crisis'.

8 The mass media — with particular emphasis on the role of the press

INTRODUCTION

This chapter analyses and describes the central role of the mass media in British society and in particular the importance of the local press to this study. In relation to the CLNT the press is viewed in its function as 'an observer and filter of events' as 'a promoter of dialogue' and as 'an opinion former'. The relationship between the press and the local political system is explored.

Much has been written about the relationship between national media organisations, their employees and central governments (for example Deutsch, 1963; Seymour-Ure, 1974; Tunstall, 1971; Curran and Seaton, 1981). The linkages between the local media and local political and economic institutions have been less widely documented, but their importance have increasingly been recognised by recent studies (Murphy, 1976; Jackson, 1971; Cox and Morgan, 1973). It has also been demonstrated that both at local and national level the press can have an important influence upon planning decisions (See Jenkins, 1973). The direct link, through the Hartwell family to the Daily Telegraph (1) was useful to the campaigners against the siting of the Third London Airport at Cublington (McKie, 1973, p.182). The Central Lancashire New Town, though hardly as emotional and newsworthy a planning issue as the third London airport, was covered comprehensively by the local newspapers serving the designated area and also by the national and many local newspapers circulating in the north west.

The chapter will focus not only upon the press as an active current element in the local political system, but also upon its function as a record for the contemporary historian, however partial or selective a source these organs are acknowledged to be.

A BRIEF DESCRIPTION OF THE LOCAL PRESS AND RADIO

Preston, Leyland and Chorley are served by editions of the provincial evening paper the Lancashire Evening Post (LEP), a member of the United Newspapers group with current circulation of 70,000 (Willing's, 1982, p.985). Leyland and Chorley have a weekly newspaper owned by the same group which in different editions appears as the Chorley Guardian (CG), or the Leyland Guardian (LG) (now the Leyland and South Ribble Guardian). These publications have a joint circulation currently of 22,001.

Preston itself was not served by a regular weekly newspaper at the time of the research fieldwork though sporadic efforts have been made to revive or launch a weekly newspaper for Preston, this aspect was not an important feature during the period of this study. A free weekly, the Preston Citizen, with a self proclaimed circulation of 63,000 was launched in 1981. The only other significant local newspapers circulating within the designated area are United Newspapers Farmer's Guardian and the small independent Longridge News which is read mainly in the Grimsargh and Haighton areas of the new town.

Unlike some industrial towns in the north west (such as Liverpool, Rochdale, Leigh) there is no 'alternative press' and new town developments or activity did not stimulate the formation of community newspapers similar to those in Milton Keynes (City Limits) or Birchwood, Warrington (The Birchwood Pioneer). The CLNT is within the transmission area of BBC Radio Blackburn, (now BBC Radio Lancashire) and, though an increasing emphasis has been given to Preston items in the years following its inception, it was not until 1975 that Preston offered temporary studio facilities for a local reporter and a more consistent coverage of mid Lancashire items was achieved.

The Lancashire Evening Post

This Preston based newspaper serves an area of Lancashire straddling the M6 motorway from the extent of the of its Wigan based sister paper the Post and Chronicle in the south to the Lancaster/Carnforth district in the north of the country. It is owned by one of the five national groups which by 1969 owned 55 per cent of English and Welsh provincial evening newspapers. (Jackson, 1971, p.24). The United Newspapers group, owners of the LEP, is best known as the proprietor of the Yorkshire Post, but has evening papers based in Sheffield, Leeds, Doncaster and Blackpool as well as weekly newspapers and printing subsidiaries. (2)

In recent years the paper has made a reputation as a campaigning publication. Barry Askew, then the editor, was given a journalist of the year award for the newspaper's contribution to the disclosure of malpractices at the Whittington mental hospital and the paper was instrumental in advocating the investigations which led to the suspension and eventual dismissal of the chief constable of Lancashire, Mr Stanley Parr in 1978.

As one of the ten largest of the forty-eight members of the evening newspaper advertising bureau, with a circulation of 138,000 in 1969, Jackson calculated that in the central urban areas its percentage household coverage in 1969 was as high as 93.28 per cent, (Jackson, 1971, p.34). Although many new town items were reported by non specialist journalists, the main reports were written either by the local government correspondent, at that time, Colin Damp, or more frequently by Peter Dugdale, the chief planning correspondent.

The Chorley and Leyland Guardians

These two weekly newspapers, also owned by United Newspapers, were edited during the period of this study by a forceful and highly individualistic managing editor, George Birtill. With a distinctly less cosmopolitan style than its sister, LEP, the Guardian Series at this time was strongly moulded by the editor who himself contributed a great deal of copy each week. In addition to his regular column,

'Leaves from a Rural Diary', Mr Birtill took full advantage of his position to write frequent front page leading articles, often on new town issues. With a reputation as a popular local historian and author of walkers' handbooks, Mr Birtill was unusually prominent for an editor in the social life of the Chorley and Leyland communities. This status and self appointed role appears to be more in accordance with United States' practice (Janowitz, 1967).

The new town was regarded as an issue of pre eminence and was given comprehensive coverage particularly at the time when plans were published. Photographs of locations to be affected and sketchmaps of layouts were prominent in such reports, with the use of limited colour printing on occasions. Although public meetings were reported upon by a number of staff journalists, unlike the LEP, it appears that none of them, apart from the managing editor, specialised in CLNT items.

BBC Radio Blackburn (now Radio Lancashire)

As the description of the station suggests, this BBC local radio organisation tended to focus primarily upon north east Lancashire in the immediate environment of its main studio, and perhaps it was inevitable that, for historical reasons, less emphasis was given to CLNT than might have been anticipated. Much of the designated area was officially excluded from the original 'sphere of influence', if not the transmission area, of the then infant station when it opened in 1971. Consequently there was little tradition of CLNT coverage when the Radio Blackburn remit was adjusted to include Preston in 1972 with the opening of the medium wave transmitter nearby.

During the period of the most concentrated activity by new town groups the station had not opened its permanent Preston studio (1978) nor allocated a regular local reporter (1975). Apart from the processing of news releases, some follow up interviews and phone in items, the station itself did not noticeably initiate coverage of new town issues.

SOME THEORETICAL CONSIDERATIONS

Ownership and management

Newspapers are viewed by many commentators as having a symbiotic relationship with the state, a vehicle for elite control and a means of legitimation of current orthodoxies. This perspective is the view taken by Marxist interpreters who take as their starting point the often quoted passage in 'The German Ideology':

> .... The class which has the means of material production at its disposal has control at the same time over the means of mental production . . . thus their ideas are the ruling ideas of the epoch. (Marx and Engels, 1938, p.39)

The ideological domination of the owners of the 'means of production' is thus buttressed by the main channels of dissemination of information. The press is seen to be part of the 'central power cluster constituted by big business and the conservative party' (Westergaard and Resler, 1976, p.261), and the concentration of press ownership has been fully documented (See Murdock and Golding, 1974).

In his survey of the provincial press, Jackson maintained that approximately 40 per cent of the evening newspapers sampled, and 90 per cent of the weeklies, were politically neutral. (Jackson, 1971, p.20). Demonstrating the demise of the local radical press during the inter war years, Jackson points out that a further 40 per cent of the evening newspapers were 'conservative leaning' and up to 10 per cent of the weeklies, but that

> .... only in a minority of conservative supporting newspapers is the advocacy at all vigorous, so that Williams' charge that the provincial press opts for a 'Circumspect Neutrality in many matters where the clash of opinion is desirable' is largely a valid generalisation. (Jackson, 1971, p.20)

Both the LEP and the Guardians belong to the group which contains the strongly conservative Yorkshire Evening Post, but it would be fair to state that both central Lancashire papers made an effort to appear politically balanced. The LEP even going so far as to attack a conservative candidate for his anti CLNT views (See Chapter 11).

Many political theorists, however, point out that the stance and the content of media outlets are constrained by more subtle and covert influences through power relations. (Lukes, 1974). In Bachrach and Baratz's terms, the 'second face' of power is that which places barriers in the way of the public airing of issues which could be disadvantageous to the dominant interests. (Bachrach and Baratz, 1962). This view is very much consistent with the 'agenda setting functions' of media organisations, which is derived from the pluralist tradition (McLeod, Becker and Byrnes, 1974). This notion implies that the readers or audience members will tend to structure their perceptions of the importance of political issues to correspond with the order of priority given to these items by the media organisations.

This field of media effects research has proved to be an interesting area of convergence between Marxists and pluralists. Those in the pluralist tradition, when taking a more macro sociological stance, have admitted that the media serve to bolster and maintain the existing social and political structures of societies, be they capitalist or communist, (Janowitz, 1968; Seymour-Ure, 1974) which is not too distant from more recent Marxist interpretations which encapsulate other agencies of civic culture within their model (Miliband, 1973; Murdock and Golding, 1974).

The effects of economic control and cultural influence are manifested in the behaviour within media organisations of their managements. Case studies, usually researched by participant or non participant observation of workplace conditions, have shown the crucial role of management in the selections of news. As Warren Breed in his article 'Social Control in the Newsroom' points out, executives have the task of ensuring conformity by the staff to the owner's policy. (Breed, W. in Schramm, 1960). Often this policy is incompletely articulated but management has a view on most issues, whether admitted or not, and once established, these signals are usually followed. Socialisation within the profession requires that journalists submit, not only to group norms, but are present with models of output by their regular, and sometimes required, reading of their newspaper. In terms of behaviour, those who wish to advance themselves in a journalistic career would be reluctant to question policy significantly. In smaller offices, 'cub reporters' are treated as a member of 'staff' and there is thus the greater likelihood that the journalist becomes identified with management and supervision, the attitudes they hold, and policies they represent.

This explanation does not mean that the reporter is completely impotent or conformist. Apart from the 'twilight zones permitting a range of deviation', the journalist is able to manipulate his fieldwork by the selection of materials and interviews. He can achieve autonomy through specialising and using his particular expertise and contacts within his 'beat' or network and some may trade off the prestige accorded them through 'star' status as a specialist correspondent (Breed, 1960, p.192). The latter may be disruptive since personal antagonism between members of a newsroom can easily be generated within a personality newspaper, as Murphy's case study of the 'Blackville Examiner' illustrates (Murphy, 1976, p.113).

In spite of these modifications to absolute managerial control, journalists, in the collective, are not the paper and do not decide its policies. There is thus no evidence, as far as the provincial press is concerned, to support Brian Roberts' assertion that editorial prerogative is being threatened from employees 'who believe they could edit a newspaper better than any single editor' (quoted in Bergin, 1976, p.126). In reality, the pressure of news and printing deadlines are likely to leave the journalist little time for reflection on ethics and when necessary it is more likely that values will be redefined pragmatically so that internal consistency and balance are achieved (Heider, 1946) and cognitive dissonance minimised (Festinger, 1962). This process, which occurs throughout the long experience of career developments, has been likened to the chemical process of 'osmosis' (Warner, 1969, p.178).

Many provincial newspapers provide the training ground for the larger regional newspapers, the nationals and, of course, radio and television journalism (Cox and Morgan, 1973, pp.7-8). The Guardians were reputed to be useful springboards for young reporters. This combination of a young staff with a strong editorial control would provide ideal conditions for tight managerial direction on the basis of the foregoing discussion. The LEP, more prestigious and outward looking, had developed some 'personalised' staff and would appear to allow more of Breed's 'range of deviation' within its policy.

Sources of revenue

As much as three quarters of the revenue of the 'quality' or serious press is derived from advertising (Golding, 1974, p.45). With specific reference to the local press, Cox and Morgan estimate that 'revenue comes roughly in the proportion of one third sales, two thirds advertising' (Cox and Morgan, 1973, p.9). This estimate places pressure upon the editors in their marketing function, since the mix of news and advertising requires careful monitoring. They are required to know their market, or in the case of CLDC their potential market, and their estimates of balance between news and features ensuring sales and advertising as a major source of revenue are crucial.

To maintain that the commerical pressures implicit from the development of a new town would be likely to affect newspaper policy, it is not necessary to refute arguments cited elsewhere. The reports of the 1949 and 1961 Royal Commissions on the press found that there was little evidence of advertisers' pressure causing the suppression of reports. Beith's research revealed that advertisers were likely to have only a marginal influence on newspaper policy because of their nature, mostly 'small ads'. There was also the fact that local newspapers are likely to be in a monopolistic position for local advertising. (Beith, 1968). It is not necessary, even, to contradict Jackson's findings that the provincial press does not appear to yield to direct pressure from advertising. (Jackson, 1971, p.226).

These accounts of the British provincial press involved discussing the empirical end of the equation by examining the atomised and varied advertising pressures. An alternative perspective requires a consideration of the values, ideology and, above all, the interests of the newspaper management. These interests are translated into the policies which are likely to be in the long term commercial benefit of the organisation. It is argued that there is manifest advantage to the United Newspapers to be derived from the growth of CLNT, both in terms of its projected increase in members of higher socio-economic groups, and by the expansion of commercial purchasing power through industrial development.

The motives of the LEP in its support for CLNT were challenged in a letter published on 25 July 1974. Mr J. Canfield in a letter questioning the need for any further urbanisation in the north west makes the point that the LEP is 'the only organ by which we can make even a negligibly effective protest, even though you, having a monopoly of the local newspaper daily press are totally for the new town'. He continued:

> .... This is perhaps understandable since, at least, your purse strings are controlled by United Newspapers in London, who obviously would like to see a doubling of population in central Lancashire, and this would likely mean a doubling of your circulation. I'm a great believer in the old saying 'he who pays the piper calls the tune'.

These accusations were firmly rebutted in an editorial placed alongside in the same edition. That the paper's 'dominating motive' in supporting the new town concept is increased circulation is called a 'smart allegation'. Their views are based upon what they believe to be best for the area.

> .... It is true that we would like to double our circulation, just as British Leyland would like to double its sales, and just as Preston North End would like to double its attendances. and it is one of the justifications of the new town that it will be good for business. If it were going to be bad for business, it would be a bad thing. But we are to be accused of being commercially motivated every time we advocate a policy that is good for business? Let all our readers be aware that editorial policy on this paper is decided locally, not dictated by London but by the interests of the local community as we see them, and it is not decided by the yardstick of what may be commercially advantageous to United Newspapers.

'Good for business', the editorial asserts, also means better job opportunities, a better total environment and 'a more prosperous community generally'. Those who oppose the new town, in principle, were 'biting the hand that feeds them' and turning away the 'opportunity of massive investment over the next twenty or thirty years'.

Finally, by employing the tactic of the salesman's 'fear close' coupled with envy, the editorial resembles its anti SPNW vituperations with the question: 'Do the people of central Lancashire really want to drive that money elsewhere to those communities who look at our good fortune with green eyes?' (my emphasis). Clearly the Canfield letter and similar accusations had struck a raw nerve with the editor who, despite changing circumstances and evidence, appeared unwavering in the support of the concept. Not so, the Guardians, whose managing editor seemed acutely aware of the fine balance of the arguments and appeared to blow 'hot and cold' depending on the type of development proposed. With Mr Birtill there was evidence of a greater acceptance of CLNT in his columns when the emphasis was less upon rented development and more upon owner occupation, a reflection no doubt upon the electoral as well as the commercial effects of social class within the marginal Chorley constituency. His attitudes were also tempered by a deep affection for the surrounding countryside and its historical associations, which evidently modified his personal commitment to CLNT.

Advertising as the predominant source of revenue of local newspapers, it is argued, has a significant influence on editorial policy. The need to improve readership and advertising revenue is essential for commercial survival and profitability, yet it appears that the logic of openly linking this requirement to a project likely to fill this need is editorially unacceptable. This stance is not attributable to a high minded ideological adherence to C.P. Scott's dictum that 'a newspaper . . . is much more than a business; it is an institution' but rather to a realisation that, by admitting the overriding commercial interest, this concurrence would lessen its credibility as an 'objective' source of information and hence its power to influence and shape local opinion would be devalued. (Hovland and Weiss, 1951). It would strike at the 'psychological root of media power' which has been developed over time between the media organisation and the audience or readers, and undermine the bond built up and based upon 'the fulfilment of audience expectations and the validation of past trust relationships'. (Gurevitch and Blumler in Curran, Gurevitch and Woollacott, 1977, p.275).

The press and the local political system

'News is part of the political process in a community' (Warner, 1969, p.169) and the media organisations provide the channel for its dissemination. The local press is in a central position between the political elites and the citizens and, as such, to function effectively it needs to cultivate new sources in local government, commerce and industry for news gathering. There is some dispute whether the local press should be regarded as a 'fourth estate' with an independent power base within a pluralist society, or as part of the political system, in either Parsonian or Marxist interpretations. Even those within the liberal-pluralist tradition, such as Gurevitch and Blumler, admit that the independent power base is 'perhaps less obvious' but stress that sources of media power can be identified (Gurevitch and Blumler in Curran et al, 1977, p.274). Reference has already been made to what they term the 'psychological root'. The structural root of the power of the mass media, they argue, arises from their ability to deliver a large audience to the politician which is otherwise not available.

This development of the 'media effects' approach to mass media studies may be compared with the social structural approach, which takes as the main point of reference for the study of the mass media the structure of society as a whole, rather than individual members of the 'audience' somehow abstracted from the social structure. This approach thus requires the placing of media institutions and their publics in the social structure and demands and analysis of interests, overt and covert - a perspective which is congruent with the arguments articulated in the previous sections on ownership and sources of revenue.

Whichever frame of analysis is employed, in practical terms it can be shown that there is a dynamic and often symbiotic relationship between the press and the political system at national and local levels. These mutual dependancies are evident in the operation of the Westminster lobby (Tunstall, 1970), and in the reporting of local government with its obligation to cultivate sources of information (Murphy, 1976, pp.15-6). This interaction is required despite the fact that since the Thatcher Act (Public bodies' (admissions to meetings) Act, 1960) full council meetings should not be held privately. This legislation, as Murphy points out, 'relies heavily on the good nature of local authorities to implement the spirit as well as the letter of the act' (Murphy, 1976, p.26).

There has been a traditional view that local authorities do not require active publicity with the implications and expense of a mistrusted public relations operation. Some councillors, Hill argues, 'consider that publicity is disguised propaganda for the party in power rather than impartial information about local services'. (Hill, 1970, p.56). The social survey found that local papers were the major source of information on the activities of the local council (HMSO, 1967) but this prominence was expected to have been undermined by the expansion of local radio (Broadcasting, 1966; Annan, 1977) though recent research on local radio emphatically questions this assumption. (Wright, 1981).

The weekly newspapers themselves would argue that their most important function was the reporting of local government (W.G. Ridd quoted in Jackson, 1971, p.109), and this category amounts to 16 per cent of coverage (Beith, 1968) though the quality and presentation of the items appear likely to vary widely according to house style, from a bland regurgitation of council minutes, in short paragraphs scattered throughout a paper, to the more rare attempts to treat public issues in depth. Certainly the local press was accorded a vital role in providing 'a first essential step' towards greater participation in planning by the Skeffington committee. (HMSO, 1969).

Communication and the interplay of the media, groups and organisations thus constitute a vital element in the local political arena. It is argued that the media inevitably legitimate the activities of local decision makers and give publicity disproportionately to their 'positive' activities. Others suggest that the media can be a valuable counter to local elites giving publicity and respectability to opposition groups and community organisations and questioning the efficiency or even the ethics of decisions. The most insidious is the view that information itself could be regarded as a substitute for political involvement, anaesthetising the general public into acquiescence.

While both local government officials and councillors are justified in their main criticism of trivialisation of news, and a focus upon conflict rather than constructive decisions in the local press, ultimately it would seem that the balance of influence is tipped towards the local political elite. If a newspaper is overzealous it can be 'punished' by restriction of news sources or even the denial of advertisements, (3) and the journalist has still to be most wary of the laws of libel. Above all, power is related to information or communication control. It is apposite that the central Lancashire development corporation, an even more closed organisation than local government, and an important element in the local political system, should have a highly organised approach to information dissemination and collection. The next section of this chapter will concentrate primarily upon this aspect of the activities of the CLDC.

THE PRESS AND THE NEW TOWN

The local lobby at CLDC

The chairman of CLDC, Sir Frank Pearson, developed the practice of giving a press briefing after the board meetings to a select number of journalists. These were representatives of the local press: George Birtill (CG), Peter Dugdale of the LEP, and the main link with the nationals, Jeff Barnes, the principal of the local news agency based on Wigan and Preston. Sir Frank, a former MP for Clitheroe, appeared to have modelled this briefing upon the practices of the Westminster lobby. This arrangement involves the regular meetings with a closed group of journalists, such as Downing Street briefings. (See Tunstall, 1970), and the expectation that members will be specialist newsgatherers, with expertise and knowledge of the chosen field (Tunstall, 1972 in McQuail (Ed)). On occasion there was a prepared press statement of background information and this bulletin was sometimes accompanied by a personal written comment by Sir Frank. There would then be an opportunity to have a short discussion 'on or off the record'. This role was obviously one which Sir Frank relished and the information function was regarded as important enough to be serviced by the general manager's personal assistant, Col. Barras (See Chapter 6).

It should be noted that it was not possible to gain access to the lobby briefings as part of this research, despite requests to attend.(4)

These decisions to exclude access effectively limited the extent of the research's focus upon information flows and filtering and the emphasis transferred towards inter organisational behaviour and features of power relationships. The exclusion from the local briefing group also had implications for methodological and ethical aspects of the study.

The organisation of the complex, highly interdependent arrangements which have evolved for the group of parliamentary journalists licensed by the Commons Serjeant at Arms known as the lobby depends on a degree of mutual trust and a respect for press embargos and the confidentiality of sources. (Whale, 1977, pp.123-4; Tunstall, 1970). Similarly, on an admittedly microscopic scale, the CLDC arrangements involved a degree of mutuality and therefore inevitably a certain implied restrictiveness. The deprivation to this study of the experience and inclusion of the CLDC briefings can, it is argued, be more than adequately compensated for in the lack of restraints in other areas and in the maintenance of the trust and confidence of the various community groups.

When the local lobby arrangements are coupled with the influence of ownership, control and the local political system a useful interpretive foundation is laid for the greater understanding of the role of the local press as a medium of transmission and possible distortion of information.

The press as an observer and filter of events

Journalists have been subjected to professional analysis most influential of which has been the editorial selection of news based on the notion of the 'gatekeeper'. (White, 1950). The influence of personal preference and prejudices in the earmarking of items for publication is likely to be more marked in the multiple overload experienced in the choice of agency copy. This is less likely in the local press office on the occasions where scarce staff resources are committed covering specific events. This position is reinforced by the role of the journalist as a 'fellow observer'. This circumstance applied to the public meetings held by both the CLDC and the various action groups. An 'inaccurate' report is likely to be subjected to adverse comment (See LEP, 4 June 1974), a loss of credibility and a possible souring of relationships with any contacts. Public meetings associated with CLDC developments on participation programmes were often covered by general staff reporters rather than planning or local government specialists. With such a dispersed and tenuous development personal relationships with 'spokesmen' would be less important, as a check, than the knowledge that published copy would be scrutinised carefully. The Harris Library, Preston, CLDC and the newspapers themselves maintained cuttings libraries on CLNT and many local activists kept cuttings files to serve as a means of feedback and record. Many of them expressed the view to the writer that the LEP's coverage of events was quite satisfactory.

The journalists' role as a filter and interpreter of information, however, is not subject to such controls. Only the privileged, who are in possession of the original material or witnessed the event, can judge whether the reports or summaries are what they regard as a reasonable distillation. Still less amenable to inquiry and observation are the activities of the headline writers and, above all, of those who make the editorial decisions on newspaper layout which give the various items an implied order of importance.

The instances where original sources of information could be monitored and observed through the journalistic process in this research were limited but perhaps the most important events were observed and analysed: the coverage of the publication of the outline plan and the reporting of the public inquiry.

Members of 'the lobby' had been provided with advance copies of the outline plan and a full press conference was organised by CLDC to launch its publication. The CLDC press office provided a two page press release advancing the reasons for the continued requirement for CLNT. It pointed out that 'an intensive period of public involvement and participation' was now taking place, mentioned some forty public meetings and the fact that 'various specialist groups' in the new town were examining the corporation's plans 'with keen and critical interest'. It conceded that transport policies were likely to be the most contentious issue but stressed that the strategy proposed in the outline plan 'will enable the environmental and economic attraction of the area of Preston, Leyland and Chorley to be fully exploited'. This press release was accompanied by two and a half pages of background information on such items as housing, transport and recreation and also a $1\frac{1}{4}$ page note by Sir Frank Pearson drawing particular attention to sections of the plan.

Jeff Barnes took the occasion of the press conference as an opportunity to interview Richard Phelps and Sir Frank and focussed discussion upon employment prospects. As a result both his daily paper and evening paper copy shows little acknowledgement to the material provided by the CLDC. It was almost entirely transformed into personal statements by Sir Frank and Mr Phelps and great emphasis was laid upon the phrase 'family opportunity town' with an eye upon the possible headlines. The copy minus one short paragraph was printed in the Daily Telegraph under the title plan for a 'Family Town' (Daily Telegraph, 31 May 1974. (5) John Hudson of the Guardian also stressed the description that CLNT was 'a place of family opportunities', but attributed the remark directly to Sir Frank Pearson. He also made little direct use of the CLDC material.

It seems the case that, given sufficient preparation time, the journalists preferred to make their own assessments of the CLNT proposals and select what they considered either to be newsworthy, or agency copy which would attract national or evening newspaper clients. In particular all three regular members of the monthly post board briefings, as befitting putative 'specialist newsgatherers', gave evidence of a personal preoccupation with CLNT and a strong professional commitment to coverage of the project. None was wishing to appear to be a 'CLNT poodle' and, in interviews, the briefings were described by one member as 'clumsy' and lacking the relative openness of local government. One journalist pointed out that information was slow to emerge from CLDC and that it was possible to supplement limited data with that which was more easily obtained by careful scrutinising of the agendas and minutes of the district councils in the area.

Apart from the items already referred to which appeared in the Daily Telegraph and The Guardian the only significant newspaper coverage deriving from this press conference was the extensive two page centre spread, New Town Special in the LEP, by Peter Dugdale its chief planning correspondent. This feature article was accompanied by an editorial describing the outline plan as 'an opportunity for new life, growth and development'. (LEP, 30 May 1974).

The publication embargo date for the outline plan inadvertently meant that the Chorley and Leyland Guardians were unable to make more than a passing reference to its iminent publication in a speech by Sir Frank to the mayoral dinner of Chorley borough council and to the fact that there was 'an embargo dated Thursday evening 30 May which precludes reference in this week's issue of The Guardian' (LG, 30 May 1974). This mistiming caused some editorial anger and resentment: the short item on the outline plan in the following edition concentrated primarily on criticising the quality of the photography in the document. (CG, 6 June 1974).

From the evidence gained from extensive monitoring of press copy, it would appear that, although the publishers and the journalists themselves were broadly in favour of a CLNT in some form, they were not willing to act as mere ciphers or 'messenger boys' for CLDC. They were however, willing to handle 'diversionary' press releases, examples of which will be described in the final section of this chapter.

The press as a promoter of dialogue

The local press, particularly through its universal feature of the correspondence column, provides obvious evidence of written dialogue both horizontally, such as between citizens, and vertically, for example between citizens and the decision makers (Rose, 1974, p.212). It may also, less obviously, stimulate unreported or unseen dialogue and social activity which can only be 'sampled' through fieldwork. Readers' correspondence had been loosely categorised as letters of 'protest' or letters of 'argument' (Jackson, 1971, pp.152-75). Analysis of local press correspondence on new town issues would suggest that there often appears to be a lack of a neat boundary between these categories, and indeed, the editorial response to a letter may be critical to its classification.

The local council and its officers are a ubiquitous focus for the letters of protest, though within new town designated areas it is not uncommon for much of the wrath intended for 'bureaucracies' to be diverted towards development corporations as promoters of rapid change. The LEP provided a regular platform for letters on new town topics, usually under the heading 'Letters extra' but sometimes more specifically 'New town letters extra' or even 'New town your views' and 'New town countdown'. Many letters of protest in the LEP's columns from individuals or officers of action groups were not directed at a specific target for reply, but it appears were performing a 'safety valve' function. On many occasions letters of protest were converted into letters of argument by the action of the newspaper itself. Letters editors may feel that it necessary to add editorial footnotes to correspondence. It may be to correct a known misquotation (as with CLNT's chief planner, Colin Beck) (LEP, 5 June 1974) or to provide some technical explanation or additions to an outburst on a planning issue (such as LEP, 4 October 1974, on housing demolition policy). The protest letter is transformed into a letter of argument when the editor responds to the temptation to add a footnote or even to compose a full contrary editorial. Many editions of both the LEP and Guardians provide instances of the provision of a 'right to simultaneous reply' by an official body, or the simultaneous or delayed editorial reposte.

By initiating the right to simultaneous reply or advance notice of the publication of a letter to an adversary, the local press is stimulating dialogue and disputation on certain issues. It may be argued that since correspondence columns are viewed by most newspapers as valuable in 'promoting reader participation' (Jackson, 1971, p.152) it is good practice to encourage counter argument; but it is also seen as a means of ensuring an image of essential fairness and balance. Within the LEP's letters it was rare to find letters in favour of CLNT policies such as that by Councillor Ken Bodfish, chairman of Preston borough's new town sub committee (LEP, 2 October 1974). It was usually left to a footnote reply from 'a spokesman', a comment from Peter Dugdale, or a full editorial to provide the pro CLNT arguments and the necessary equilibrium.

Letters of argument seek to correct felt injustices or fallacies or to encounter controversial news items, editorials or articles. They may thus be initiated by the correspondent writing these letters: there are the officers or spokesmen of groups and voluntary associations, political parties or pressure groups; the apparent isolates without obvious group affiliations; the regular correspondents; and the 'eminent' letter writers.

Contributions from irregular and individual correspondents tended to be grouped around the most emotive of new town issues, the road network, in particular the threat to the Haslam Park trees, and the undemocratic nature of a development corporation. As predicted the ever present letter writers such as 'Vox Populi' and 'Disgusted, Chorley' contributed but perhaps some of the most penetrating criticisms came from the owner of the sinister pseudonym 'The ghost of Kellet Lane'.

Fieldwork evidence indicates that newspaper correspondence columns are capable of attracting membership and support for groups,FABRA in particular, and they also prompted action such as writing to the secretary of state. It may be that the local newspapers provide a more regular exchange of views than can be arranged through formal meetings and, indeed, at some periods of intense strain in inter group relations, the press may be the principal or the only medium of dialogue (Lane and Roberts, 1971).

The press as opinion former: the influence of the editorial

The ability of the written or spoken word to persuade, to form or change attitudes or opinions, is central to much social psychological experimentation. It is also an important element of the work of 'effects researchers' in mass communication studies. In recent years concern has shifted from monitoring overt persuasion towards the mass media's effects when they purport to be a 'balanced information source'. In such a presentation they could transmit a credible and consistent interpretation of the world which, it is argued, is likely to be far more manipulative than openly persuasive communications. This 'cognitive approach' places emphasis upon information perception rather than directly upon attitudes. The cognitive effects of exposure to mass media materials, according to Kraus and Davis (1976) are to give the media the ability to 'create reality' by 'defining activities and events moulding and shaping a variety of images for us' (quoted in Blumler, 1977, p.24).

This approach, as Garnham points out, indicates that "much empirical research seems to be consonant with the study of ideology within the 'grand theory' tradition" (Garnham, 1979, p.32). Its major departure being that it limits its concern to manifestly political events whereas for example, the 'cultural studies' approach to 'grand theory' is based on the notion that the entire contents of the media carry political meanings which may have ideological effects (See Hall in Curran et al, 1977, pp.315-48).

The hitherto research orthodoxy of the 'media effects school' had contended that the social group affiliations of the audience was still very strong (e.g. Katz and Lazarsfeld, 1955) and that the direct persuasive power of the media was minimal. Indeed a major explanation of this failure was that through the mechanisms of selective exposure, selective perception and recall, the coverage of political affairs would more likely serve to confirm existing views and act rather as an 'agent of reinforcement than as an agent of change' (Klapper, 1960).

Although it appears that 'many local papers no longer run regular leaders and their appearance and style has increasingly taken on that of the impartial observer' (Murphy, 1976, p.28), most evening papers, according to Jackson's sample follow the convention of including a leading column (Jackson, 1971, p.122). The Chorley and Leyland Guardians are therefore unusual in exhibiting a lively and controversial editorial tradition as weekly newspapers, while the evening Lancashire Evening Post is more representative of its type in publishing regular comment columns.

The regular press monitoring undertaken as part of the research identified two regularly recurring planning themes in each newspaper. George Birtill of the Guardians took every opportunity to comment on aspects of the new town, portraying himself as a local expert and taking obvious delight in displaying his undoubted knowledge of the historical and spatial characteristics of the Chorley and Leyland area. During the most intense coverage of new town matters in 1974 he returned again and again, almost obsessively, to the problems associated with participation in planning.

An editorial accompanying a report on Sir Frank Pearson's remarks on public participation ('We have told the public' - Sir Frank CG, 14 February 1974), provided an opportunity for George Birtill to add his views on the subject. Sir Frank's assertion that CLDC had so far exceeded the requirements on public participation 'normally laid down by the government', . . . 'confirms what has been pointed out in these columns on a number of occasions, but whether some of the more vocal organisations will believe it is another matter' (my emphasis). He accused these bodies of seeming jealous because the consultative document had been only to local authorities.

Continuing in a near sycophantic style, Birtill stated:

> .... there must be very good reasons why at certain stages it is not expedient to make public what becomes in the end, public business. Sir Frank gave an example of the highly technical nature of planning. But there could also be an ultimate situation in which so many documents are flying around that the public, if they have time to read them, will have difficulty in getting a clear picture. (CG, 14 February 1974)

Within a month, the comment column was used as the vehicle for speculation on the effects of a change of government on CLNT, but it could not let this occasion pass without declaring: 'Besides all these considerations, the noisesome theme of public participation in planning seems relatively unimportant' ('Will labour change new town?' CG, 7 March 1974). The Bernard Davies resignation (See Chapter 9) was also seized as an occasion for an editorial on public participation. Out of sympathy with Davies's views, George Birtill advocated the channeling of participation through the elected councils who, in turn, were answerable to the electorate rather than a direct involvement by the public.

> .... Public participation is not new. We have had it ever since villagers complained to the overseer that the handle on the parish pump was too short. It is now that it has been given a job definition it has become elusive. This is not that it has been too little, but too much. (sic) . . . If the development corporation consults the local authorities concerned in such a way that the councils get the blame or the credit, participation will be much more effective than offering the direct approach as well. ('Too much not too little' CG, 24 April 1974)

A distinctive feature of the Guardians for a number of years has been the regular column contributed by the MP for the area. George Rodgers, the MP at this time, countered this Bernard Davies resignation editorial obliquely by making the point that he was 'extremely anxious that the project should go forward with the approval and goodwill of the people affected by the programme'.

After discussions with Sir Frank, he was hopeful that 'a direct avenue of communication' would be created and suggested that the 'Planwatch' organisation had 'the capacity to make a contribution to what could become the most exciting and impressive new town of the century'. (LG, 2 May 1974).

More direct comments on the editorial came from the local Liberal party. The chairman, F.S. Wilson and the prospective candidate, Neva Orrell both sought to make points about the undemocratic nature of the CLDC and the need for more direct accountability. Neva Orrell expressed the view that the public were becoming exceedingly cynical about their right to participate and protest.

> .... More and more people are forming the opinion that public enquiries and appeals are only paying lipservice to the individual's rights and interests, and that these enquiries are just a waste of everyone's time. The outcome of any appeal is just a foregone conclusion. The large body always wins ('Voices that are not heard' LG, 2 May 1974)

In his contribution, Frank Wilson aptly developed the editorial response to the parish pump which 'presupposes that all agreed there should be a pump in the first place'. Elaborating the analogy somewhat mischievously, he continued:

> .... The development corporation however, would invite us to consider in depth the intricacies of pump handle design and manufacture, while passing over and even arrogantly prohibiting discussion on the main question, which is whether to have a pump at all. ('Some planning presumes too much' LG, 2 May 1974)

A further example of George Birtill's linking of participation with derogatory remarks is contained in his comment on Granada television's presentation of 'On the spot' - 'if only because they showed the fallacy of public participation by public meeting' (CG, 13 June 1974). By far the most comprehensive editorial argument against 'excessive' participation was occasioned by the stimulus of a letter from the chairman of Planwatch, John Hagerty, in which he called for the preparation of alternative plans and participation as defined in the Skeffington report. In a direct challenge to the Guardians he wrote:

> .... Your newspaper has an important role to play in the field of public participation. In the Chorley area it is the only medium through which both sides can air their views. You have been generous in your support of the development corporation's activities. May I now ask you to be more generous towards its critics and in particular, will you publish a full and detailed account of the Skeffington committee's proposals on public participation? The public will then have both sides of the argument and be in a position to judge the development corporation's

efforts for themselves. ('Alternative plans for participation' CG, 9 May 1974)

Impatient of the delays in designation, George Birtill appeared to interpret participation as an intrusive retarding procedure to be completed at great speed. Combining fulsome defence of CLDC with his attack on public participation, he replied to John Hagerty as follows:

> .... Mr. Hagerty says that the Skeffington committee stressed that it is the planning authorities duty to prepare alternative plans for public discussion. The development corporation have already produced evidence that they are doing this particularly in relation to the local road framework. On the other hand, it is manifestly absurd to expect alternatives to be produced just for the sake of it . . . In any event, we do not treat Skeffington as Planwatch apparently do, as a set of rules which are legally binding. In our view, participation is information in two directions. It has never been accomplished to anything like the extent it has with central Lancashire new town ('Competition for Central Lancs?' CG, 9 May 1974)

The Lancashire Evening Post, in turn, was preoccupied by the threat to central Lancashire's investment and CLNT's prospects by the so called 'Mersey Belt Strategy' of the strategic plan for the north west (SPNW). Not only did this plan serve as a focus for inter regional rivalries of long standing (See Marshall (Ed), 1977) attacking its policies served as an indirect demonstration of support for CLNT.
Pre publication reports that Lancashire county council and the fourteen district councils were likely to reject the suggestion that investment should be concentrated along the 'Mersey Belt' ('Massive rebuff for Lancs. plan' LEP, 7 March 1974) was followed by a strongly phrased editorial stating that it was 'almost unthinkable that those who prepared it should have been so blind'.

> .... As a guide to decisions on public expenditure and economic and social policies for the region it is quite useless. Any sign of the concentration of resources and development in the so called 'Mersey Belt' will be resisted, and any government encouraging such concentration will pay a political price in marginal constituencies in central, northern and north east Lancashire . . . Lower and slower growth for the central Lancashire new town is not a target we can support . . . Not to put too fine a point on it, are we to pour our scarce resources into an area with such a reputation for labour trouble that industrialists shrink from it? And what is it for, a strategy that sets one part of the region against another? For a long time now central Lancashire has been held back waiting for the new town to make it, in Lancashire county council's words, 'a major focus for growth and renewal in the north west'. What we have waited for we rely upon and need. The Mersey belt strategy would be a bitter betrayal.

Later that month comments and summaries of a confidential provisional edition of the outline plan sent to local authorities written by

Peter Darling were published in the LEP. (LEP, 18 March 1974; 26 March 1974; 27 March 1974; 28 March 1974; 29 March 1974) and reports of two county council committees confirmed their opposition ("Plan 'a menace to Lancs new town' ", 22 March 1974; also in The Guardian "Strategic planning 'hits new town' ", 23 March 1974). The detailed and comprehensive series of articles culminated in one with the title 'Plan discounts positive duty to central Lancs' (LEP, 29 March 1974).

When SPNW was published on 6 May 1974, it was reported that the planners had pleaded that they had been misunderstood and that the plan would 'not have a crippling effect on the central Lancashire new town as the outgoing county council feared' (Plan 'will not cripple central Lancs' LEP, 6 May 1974). The accompanying editorial interpreted the lukewarm attitude to CLNT as a damning with faint praise the plan for central Lancashire, and returning to the theme of regional rivalry it stated:

> .... The north west has usually been a fairly united region. This newspaper, for instance, has lent its voice in support of special help for Merseyside and more recently in support of Manchester over the Piccadilly-Victoria underground. But the strategic plan for the north west, launched in in Salford today, promises to divide the region and set one part against the other. ('Creating disunity', LEP, 6 May 1974)

The above pro Merseyside sentiment was short lived, however, when Mr Eric Heffer announced that he was considering special development area status for Merseyside which generated another editorial reference to SPNW ('Hold back, Mr Heffer', LEP, 15 May 1974). Further opportunities for comment were the coverage of the Town and Country Planning Association's conference on SPNW held in Manchester that day. ('The creation of wealth', LEP, 17 May 1974) and the meeting of Lancashire MPs held in Preston on 29 June 1974. ('Shortchange', LEP, 1 July 1974).

The metropolitan bias of SPNW was reiterated when the special development area status for Merseyside was announced by Mr Benn which Peter Darling regarded as 'Both ill judged and ill timed', ('Why Lancashire's hopes must not become pipe dreams ...', LEP, 19 August 1974). Possible expectations of influence upon the government's final decision on SPNW was attached to the Lancaster University's critique of its methodology published in September 1974. Accompanying Peter Darling's assessment and summary of the Centre for North West Regional Studies' report was a commendatory editorial, 'The planners devastated', LEP, 10 September 1974). The editorial stated the LEP's position unambiguously when it stated:

> .... As severe and unshakeable critics of the proposal in the north west strategic plan to concentrate future development and resources on Greater Manchester, south Lancashire and Merseyside, we welcome the University of Lancaster's devastating indictment of the methods and conclusions of the planning team.

In supporting the need expressed in the report for high grade manufacturing industry throughout the region as a whole, the editorial stressed its agreement that 'the preferred strategy is as bad for the Mersey Belt in the long term as it is bad for the region as a whole'.

> .... It is amazing how blind Greater Manchester and Merseyside have been to this factor. They have lapped up all the dubious

> statistics about quality of life, but they grasp at what the plan offers out of sheer and indiscriminate materialism, unaware that it threatens to add to their problems rather than relieve them. As an example of misguided self interest it is probably unequalled. But if the Mersey Belt's civic leaders and industrial leaders lack vision, and can only measure their own status by size, they are hardly to be blamed since the planners whose work they welcome have lacked vision too.

It concluded, sourly,

> .... And the division in the region has been caused by the strategic planners, with their fatuous methods, their lack of vision and their predetermined bias in favour of the sectional interests of Manchester and Merseyside.

Prior to the publication of the government's reactions to SPNW, (DOE, December 1975) LEP returned to the topic suggesting that the likely decisions would 'widen still further the rift in the north west region that was opened when the strategic study team published its perverse and short sighted report' . . . 'To support the strategic plan proposals to concentrate our resources in the Mersey Belt is to strike at the healthy for the sake of the unhealthy. It will impoverish the whole region in the end'. ('Bowing to Mr Heffer', 5 December 1975). Following the reaction report the LEP verdict was that the government's emphasis on areas requiring renewal was

> .... an excuse for continuing to steal money from the region's purse . . . within the region it is prepared to pay lipservice to a strategy penalising the natural growth area of central Lancashire while in practice removing som of central Lancashire's assets into the Mersey Belt ('Political tacticians', LEP, 9 December 1975)

'How can it consider loading the dice against the central Lancashire new town thus penalising the buoyant as well as the depressed parts of Lancashire in favour of a misguided policy of congestion in the Mersey Belt? ('Time to end this farce', LEP, 6 January 1976).

To the committed, such editorial items having been subject to the filters of selective exposure, would serve to reinforce existing opinions (Klapper, 1960) or create deeper antagonisms. To the interested and uncommitted, the ability to discriminate between news items, editorials and articles is likely to decay over time. Both local newspapers gave evidence of apparent liberal policies towards the publication of anti CLNT correspondence and news items which would assist in giving an impression of impartiality. Such a blurring would assist the creation of 'cognitions' rather than 'attitudes', but what ever the ultimate individual persuasive effect,the intentions of the editorial policies were clear: to promote CLNT.

The Guardians wished to induce a scepticism of participation. If they were implemented, the policies of the 'Skeffington idealists' would only serve to delay the progress of the outline plan, and inhibit an acceptance of what was seen to be the main raison d'etre of CLDC - speed of decision making and the ability to implement comprehensive planning schemes with the minimum of delay. The LEP was attempting to place SPNW high on the agenda of the interested readers' political priorities and, by implication, linking this importance with a commitment to support CLNT. Thus it might be possible to construe antagonism to CLNT as a form of disloyalty to the central Lancashire area. The divisive elements of SPNW could thus be utilised to maintain the morale of the pro CLNT lobby.

The role of the editors

Most editors, according to Tunstall, are now in effect departmental managers, acting within strict policy objectives laid down by management (Tunstall, 1977, pp.249-321). For both commercial and legal reasons, the local press has not traditionally been a critic of local institutions, though a notable historical exception and pioneer of the right to criticise, Andrew Brice, provides a model for the investigative editor. (See Wiles, 1965, pp.291-2).

The editor of the LEP at this period, Barry Askew, although at one time an occasional BBC regional programme presenter, did not seek personal publicity on new town matters and appeared to delegate much of the CLNT comment and coverage to his staff. Peter Dugdale, chief planning correspondent, dealt not only with news coverage, but was responsible for some in depth articles and the selection of readers' letters. He saw his, and his newspaper's role "as an opinion former, otherwise 'garbled tales' result". This stance did not mean that he accepted unquestioningly all CLDC's activities, and he was prepared to criticise certain aspects such as the system of the selection of board members and the lack of press access to meetings and information (Personal interview 27 November 1973).

In sharp contrast, George Birtill, managing editor of Leyland and Chorley Guardians, had a pivoted role in the coverage of new town items. Not only was he involved in the usual editorial duties expected in a small weekly newspaper, such as the selection and layout of news items and letters, but he was also unusually active in writing articles and editorials, particularly on planning matters. As the illustrative themes in this chapter have shown, George Birtill was able to use not only the editorial as a vehicle for his views, but also his regular column 'Leaves from a rural diary'. ('What a place to build a factory!' CG, 11 July 1974, 'Green belt for village or town', CG, 18 July 1974). Mr Birtill, a magistrate, was active in community affairs and during the period of the study his eminence was clearly demonstrated when he was asked to open the new branch library at Leyland. The event as one former councillor commented to the writer, was thus sure to be given good publicity. ('Editor opens Leyland's new library', LG, 21 November 1974).

Mr Birtill was also involved in some new town meetings and public inquiries. These events were usually covered in the Guardians by a staff reporter. A full report of Mr Birtill's contribution at such a meeting ('No objections allowed on area plans?', LG, 4 July 1974) was accompanied by a supporting editorial ('Popular choice is to buy', LG, 4 July 1974). This column gave evidence of George Birtill's true political colours (6) when he attached F.S. Wilson's arguments as being 'academic rather than practical'.

Perhaps the most telling evidence of this newspaper's position in the community, and its managing editor's status, is illustrated by the report of the attendance at the Chorley Guardian dinner and dance held in March 1974. The report included highly complimentary remarks from the chairman of United Newspapers, Sir William Barnetson about the

Sir William Barnetson, Chairman of United Newspapers, says

New Councils face untried and unknown

SIR WILLIAM BARNETSON, Chairman and Managing Director, United Newspapers Ltd., chats to the Mayor of Chorley, Alderman William Wilcock, at the dinner dance arranged by the Chorley Guardian to mark the local government change-over. On Sir William's right is Sir Frank Pearson, Chairman of Central Lancs. Development Corporation and Lady Barnetson, and on his left besides the mayor, the mayoress, Mrs. Wilcock and Lady Pearson.

COUNTY ALDERMAN Tom Jackson, enjoys a joke from Alderman Wilf Rawcliffe at the Chorley Guardian dinner dance on Friday. On the left is Councillor E. G. Williams, Chairman of Chorley Rural District Council, and Mrs. Williams. Others at the table left to right are Mrs. Jackson, Mrs. Sellers and Ald. Ian Sellers.

"WHAT LIES ahead for Chorley and its new associates may be logical and convenient, and indeed inevitable. But it is also untried and unknown."

This was stated by Sir William Barnetson, Chairman and Managing Director of United Newspapers Ltd., proposing the guests at the Chorley Guardian Dinner and Dance in the Lancastrian, Chorley Town Hall, on Friday.

He went on: "Naturally enough we approach the change with some nostalgia, and a backward glance at the old arrangements and at the people who sustained them and enriched them down the long years."

So it must have been at every milestone, at every parting, at every major upheaval. A couple of centuries ago, when the township was administered by the parish vestry, no doubt the people of Chorley must have harked back to what they regarded as the 'good old days' – back to paternalistic regime of the manor house.

Again in, in the 1850's there must have been some sadness – and also some political redundancy – when the gentlemen of the vestry were supplanted by the improvement commissioners elected by the ratepayers to bring Chorley up to scratch in terms of essential amenities.

Thirty years later, significantly enough, when the time came for a further step forward, it was these same improvement commissioners who resisted the suggestion that Chorley should apply for a charter of incorporation as a borough. It was just as well they changed their minds!

NOSTALGIA

In other words, there had always been nostalgia. And so it was today, not only in Chorley, but in many other parts of the country. Understandably so, for the old system did serve well. Up to a point.

"It is now being replaced," said Sir William, "with a broader base, a stronger voice, a less fragmented structure and a more sophisticated capability."

Sir William said he was convinced that it was the right

guests Sir William said he would ask them to join in wishing Mr. Potter well in all that lay ahead.

COMPLIMENT

Responding Mr. Potter thanked Sir William on behalf of the guests for the kindness and hospitality that he had been extended that night. Sir William was an incredibly busy man who must have gone to a great deal of trouble to fit in a visit to Chorley with his many other commitments. His business and professional interests were legion and ranged from chairmanship of Reuters to membership of the council of the Open University, from the presidency of the Press Club and membership of the Press Council to chairmanship of the Commonwealth Press Union.

Sir William was attending in his capacity as Chairman and Managing Director of United Newspapers, a very large organisation which published no less than nine daily newspapers including the Yorkshire Post, several magazines including Punch and a very large number of weekly newspapers including the Chorley Guardian and Wigan Observer.

With all these interests I cannot but think that Sir William's decision to come to Chorley tonight with Lady Barnetson is a great compliment to the Editor of the Chorley Guardian, George Birtill.

Mr. Potter remarked on the

may be that it has always been my experience that leaders of rival political groups often have more in common with each other than with a lot of their own followers."

Both Councillor Corcoran and Alderman Sellers had bags of common sense and experience and that great asset – a sense of humour.

They were really needed by the new council and it was hoped that the health of both of them would continue to improve.

NEW MAYOR

Mr. Potter concluded, "Just as many of us will be denuded of our local government ranks and titles at the witching hour of midnight on March 31 at that same time Councillor Corcoran will have the right to be called mayor of the new borough of Chorley. We wish him and his wife all the best and extend those good wishes to the officers of the new councils of Chorley and South Ribble."

Attending the dinner were the Mayor of Chorley Ald. W. Wilcock and the Mayoress, Mrs. Wilcock and the chairman of the new and old county districts as well as the principal officials. The oldest members of the councils and their wives were also invited.

The event was organised by the Chorley Guardian in acknowledgement of a long association with local councils which go out of existence on March 31.

An illustration of the status of the Managing Editor and the position of the <u>Chorley Guardian</u> in its Local Community. From the <u>Chorley Guardian</u> - 28 March, 1974.

Reproduced by kind permission of the <u>Chorley Guardian</u>.

retiring town clerk for Chorley, Mr Potter, who in turn commented on the presence of many distinguished guests, including eight retiring aldermen. Accompanying photographs show the presence of at least one CLDC board member, Councillor Tom Jackson, and also Sir Frank and Lady Pearson. (CG, 28 March 1974). It is therefore probable that, within the Chorley community at least, Mr Birtill would be placed within the local power structure, according to self identification and reputational methods (See Edelstein and Schultz in Dexter and White (eds), 1964). Some British local editors may resist involvement in the local establish ment, such as in Murphy's case study, by living outside the town, 'specifically to avoid any possibility of pressure being brought . . . by local interests'. (Murphy, 1976, p.88). It would appear however, that it is not unusual for editors of community newspapers in the United States 'to be located in the community power structure'. (Olien, Donohue and Tichenor, 1968, p.247). This status appears to apply to the remarkable editorship of George Birtill.

The link with the regional and National media - the work of the press agency

The local and provincial press by their key function have a limited geographical readership and impact. CLNT, as a sub regional project of national significance, should warrant periodic coverage in the mational media. Such news items mean that the project is likely to acquire greater validity to a wider public, particularly the interested professionals, politicians, local government officers and civil servants.

Although the national press may cover major local events,(for example John Ardill, then planning correspondent of The Guardian reported the opening days of the outline plan public inquiry) most copy is transmitted through individual freelance journalists or press agencies. They provide the vital link between the local event and its wider dissemination. Freelance journalists and press agencies operate in a harsh economic marketplace. They are remunerated by the number of column inches selected for publication and must therefore have an instinct for newsworthy sources and items. There is a natural tendency for them to seek out 'sensational'items and local disasters. The Barnes news service in Preston maintained regular telephone contact with the police, fire and ambulance services which provided the sources for local accidents and disasters. Local companies with press officers offered news of strikes and industrial unrest, but above all the county and coroners' court lists and Central Office of Information sheets provided the priority diary entries. Local government at county council level was covered, but the district council's business was regarded to be 'too local'. Such items deserving wider circulation could be extracted from the daily scrutiny of each edition of the Lancashire Evening Post as it became available.

Other than considered pieces protected by time embargos, most copy for national papers and some evenings is 'phoned in'. Styles vary according to the market. The populars expect short sentences grouped into short paragraphs. A different phraseology with longer paragraphs is acceptable to the 'qualities'.

Local radio receives copy less than the daily papers in length, usually between six or ten paragraphs, and BBC and Granada television may expect as little as four paragrahps. Local newspapers are given copy by phone and by mail and the length may be unlimited.

In reporting planning issues the freelance is, in effect, restricting his 'saleable copy' to the serious newspapers and a limited number of local newspapers. Only rarely, when there is a personal interest story, will copy be published on planning matters by one of the popular dailies. During the outline plan public inquiry the only popular coverage was an item in the Daily Mirror about the threat of demolition to a pensioner's home. ('Paradise lost - but Arthur battles on', 16 December 1974). This 'story' was a truncated version of a long news item, with photograph, which had appeared a few days previously in the LEP. ('They're taking away my home', LEP, 13 December 1974).

The coverage of serious local news items by freelance agencies is made somewhat less speculative by the unique attitude of the Daily Telegraph. Both The Guardian and The Times are less interested in local government items, though all the quality newspapers covered items on CLNT at important stages in its development. The Telegraph is a regular user of agency copy, and this method is one by which it attempts a regionally based local news coverage. As Murphy points out:

> .... Short local stories from local freelances about the affairs of various town councils have been a feature of the Daily Telegraph, which in turn sensitizes local journalists to the fact that if they have a local story to sell, the Telegraph is a likely customer. (Murphy, 1976, p.70)

This relatively sound economic base for more serious local reporting is likely to be a critical factor in assessing the risk of non publication before a freelance invests time in the speculative task of writing copy.

By virtue of the regional and national importance of CLNT the hazards of freelance work would have been minimised, however, when the Barnes news agency undertook to describe the outline plans and the opening phases of the public inquiry.

The agency's role was central to the wider dissemination of the first consultative draft outline plan in November 1973 and later with the published outline plan and the consequent public inquiry. They were able to link a process with a local impact into one of potential regional and national attention.

THE CENTRALITY OF THE PRESS IN CLNT DEVELOPMENTS

This chapter has demonstrated that the local press in central Lancashire has performed a central and crucial task in transmitting knowledge and opinion, providing a forum for exchange of views, and an alternative means of dialogue between interested individuals, groups and organisations. Through the press briefing or local lobby arrangement the local press becomes the receiver, filter and transmitter of formal and 'off the record' information output. Both of these functions provide a contemporary record and source material for items to be disseminated, selected and published by a wider national and local press through the vital intermediary operation of the press agency.

By following a firm editorial policy towards an issue such as CLNT, it is inevitable that, if not in selection or copy, certainly in ordering of layout priorities, a newspaper has the ability to rank readers' agendas. There is strong evidence that editors respond to different sources in relation to their relative prestige. It appears that for anti CLNT items to receive a front page headline position these usually

Lancashire
Evening Post
No. 27,290 THURSDAY NOVEMBER 21, 1974 5p

New Town contract for Lancs

£1m FACTORY SCHEME MAY BRING 300 JOBS

MR PHELPS

By PETER DUGDALE

JOB prospects in Central Lancashire were given a big boost today, with the announcement by the New Town Development Corporation of a factory building programme, costing nearly £1 million.

The 22 advance factories on the corporation's 250-acre site at Walton Summit could provide at least 300 new jobs.

And the contract has gone to a local firm, Conlon Brothers, of Bamber Bridge, beating some of the country's largest industrial building companies for the work.

The news is even better, because firms are almost queuing up to lease them.

New Town general manager, Mr Dick Phelps, said there had been more than 100 factory inquiries recently. — "Several of these factory units are now being negotiated with companies wishing to move into the area," he said.

But no names will be announced until the negotiations are completed and the firms ready to declare their new development.

These roads must go, demands Planwatch

Alan Howard

PLANNED SITES 'THREAT TO ECOLOGY'

EIGHT sites of grade one ecological importance were affected by New Town plans, stated Mr Alan Howard, of Planwatch.

They are at Grimsargh, Cop Lane (Penwortham), Cuerden, Euxton east and west, Chorley, Bickacre and Duxbury.

Mr Howard — who is also Preston district chairman of the Ramblers' Association — said about a third to a half of the Grimsargh site was earmarked for housing or employment and was crossed by the village by-pass.

The Cop Lane site — along the old railway track — was long and narrow, and the western primary road passing along it from end to end.

The Cuerden site was comparatively untouched, apart from the eastern primary, which passed through its northern tip, the Whittle by-pass which did the same to the south, and the existing B5256 — Lancaster Lane — which passed through its middle.

Strip

At Euxton west, said Mr Howard, the site was divided by housing and employment areas, apart from a narrow strip of open space across the middle, which might also be used for a bus priority route.

Euxton east was mostly occupied by housing, the rest by a golf course, and the site at Duxbury was mostly open space, with housing and a golf course.

The Chorley site was partly open space, partly new or existing housing, and the site at Birkacre was mostly earmarked for housing apart from two strips of open space, one of which was reserved for a proposed major road.

"I am not a biologist," Mr Howard told the [illegible]

SEVEN major roads, or parts of roads, should be struck out of the New Town outline plan as "totally unacceptable," says Planwatch.

These parts of the main traffic network are "so damaging" that they should be removed from the proposals, "even if this necessitates modifying or abandoning other parts of the network, or of the plan itself."

The lengths of road in this "totally unacceptable" category are:

- the western primary from Bark Lane crossing, Penwortham, to Marsh Lane, Preston;
- the western primary from Water Lane, Preston, to Blackpool Road, Ashton (including all alternative routes);
- the western primary extension from Blackpool Road to Lancaster Canal (including all alternatives, and Haslam Park);
- the South Ribble link, from Penwortham to Walton-le-Dale;
- the eastern primary from Victoria Road, Walton-le-Dale, to the M6 at Fulwood (including the crossing of the Ribble and Fishwick Bottoms);
- the western primary from the A581 at Chorley to the proposed M6 interchange at Euxton, and
- the road across the Ribble and Avenham and Miller Parks, Preston, using an old railway bridge to Butler Street car park, near the station.

Presenting the Planwatch case on the environmental effects of the New Town as planned, Mr Alan Howard said the removal of these sections would naturally affect the rest of the network and call for the addition or deletion of further lengths.

DAMAGE

"Such changes cannot be considered in isolation from broader transportation policies, but if and when they are considered, we ask that the total environmental and social effects are also considered," he said.

"Damage to the environment means damage to the whole community, not just to those whose homes, or farms or shops are directly affected, and the paying of sums of money — however generous — to those people does not heal the scars on the landscape, or compensate those who have lost a favourite walk or had their neighbourhood changed for what they feel to be the worse."

Mr Howard, who lives at [illegible]

By PETER DUGDALE

Nor was it saying that a new road must in no circumstances be allowed to cause any environmental or social disturbance.

Planwatch, in fact, was not objecting to the New Town as a whole and was in agreement with a great deal of the plan, but there were other parts which the members felt were less satisfactory, and needed bringing up to the standard of the remainder.

Building new roads, for instance, was not necessarily the best, or only way, of reducing traffic problems.

Preoccupation with traffic flows tended to obscure the fact that the objective of any passenger transport policy was that people should have access to the facilities they needed.

Mr Howard also challenged the concept of scattering major activities over the whole New Town area.

"As our evidence elsewhere will indicate," said Mr Howard, "the development corporation's transport policy is already biased in favour of private transport, and dispersal of major facilities would serve to increase that bias."

An even distribution of traffic throughout the New Town might only be achieved at the cost of restricting the life styles of the majority of its population.

Planwatch also felt that there was no clear evidence in the outline plan of the environmental improvements some of their new roads would produce.

Some might, in fact, do the very opposite, or have no noticeable effect. They, therefore recommended caution in considering such forecasts.

Their study of the Plan had shown that:

- 26 miles of major roads or main bus priority routes would run through high quality landscape;
- although there was an apparently generous provision for linear parks, out of 50 miles, 40 were green strips along major roads or bus routes;
- valuable environmental amenities would be lost including "the desecration of Haslam Park, Preston; Blundel Brook Valley, Haighton; the disruption of Avenham and Miller Parks and the Ribble Valley"; the loss of the one green strip between Lostock Hall and Walton-le-Dale, and damage to the Lostock and Yarrow valleys;
- hundreds of homes would be lost or seriously affected.

Planwatch was also concerned, said Mr Howard, at the special provisions which were needed for pedestrians. The designated area had a considerable mileage of public footpaths. They needed to be preserved as much as possible and integrated into a proper network.

So far the comments of the development corporation had not re-assured them. The planners seemed to be concerned only for pedestrian safety, whereas there was also need for consideration of footpaths' amenity value.

The development corporation seemed to be saying: "It's too soon to be talking about footpaths now, we'll talk about them later." Mr Howard said his own experience with local authorities was it was either too soon or too late. They hoped this would not be the case with the development corporation.

NEW TOWN INQUIRY

'Beauty before homes' plea

DEVELOPMENT of a lane "of great beauty" should at least be postponed until the end of the century, a man who lives there told an inquiry.

The delights of Walker Lane, Fulwood, and the value of the area to nature lovers and farmers were described by Mr Arthur Tyldesley, a supporter of the Fulwood and Broughton Residents' Association.

"Wild flowers and birds abound and the view is constantly changing" for the many people who used it for a stroll, he said. "If [illegible]

Residents like it that way

PEOPLE like living in north Fulwood because there is no industry there, local solicitor Mr Bill Huck told the Outline Plan inquiry.

And it was for that very same reason that they opposed New Town plans to build an employment area at Midgery Lane, in the north-eastern part of the district, he said.

The people in north Fulwood like to live in "a pleasant residential area" and travel to work somewhere else. They had no desire to have the jobs brought to them, he told Ministry inspector Mr Stanley Rodison.

Mr Huck, representing Fulwood and Broughton Residents' Association, said they accepted a further residential build-up in north-east Fulwood, but could not accept the employment area.

They could not see why the industrial area at Red [illegible] elsewhere, but it was part of the plan that people coming to live in Fulwood should have work available within a reasonable distance if they wished.

Of the possible areas for such a site, Midgery Lane was the best. If they had joined it on to the Red Scar site, that would then have become the second biggest industrial site in the designated area — bigger even than Leyland.

The development corporation could accept Mr Huck's suggested alternative route across Fulwood to avoid the built-up part of Lightfoot Lane, near A6, but it would involve mixing with other traffic at the M55 junction at Broughton and would cost an extra £250,000.

They believed the Department of the Environment would not accept this, either on cost or traffic grounds.

Reproduced by kind permission of the Lancashire Evening Post.

required to be linked with someone as eminent as a local member of parliament, for example 'New town planners a sinful elite' (LEP, 15 June 1974) referred to a slightly garbled version of a speech at a PNAG public meeting by Mr Ron Atkins, MP. CLDC statements often had sufficient influence to be given front page headline position.

An outstanding example may be cited which occurred during the press coverage of the outline plan public inquiry when residents' groups failed to achieve front page status for their evidence. In the issue reporting one of the most important submissions by a residents' group, none of the lengthy reports was considered newsworthy enough to merit front page position, yet the CLDC press release giving details of a factory building programme in the Walton summit area took the prime position in the LEP ('£1 million factory scheme may bring 300 jobs', LEP, 21 November 1974).

This edition of the LEP provides the most telling evidence of that newspaper's news priorities. This pattern, given the earlier analysis of the influence exerted through sources of revenue and links into the local political system, is congruent with the foregoing description of the likely proprietorial interests of the press.

Is it possible to assess the influence of the press on public opinion? It would seem from the views expressed by many local informants, that the blatant use of the Guardians by their managing editor as a vehicle for his views served seriously to devalue the credibility of that source of information. In contrast, the LEP, by its careful coverage of both pro and anti CLNT events, and the publication of many critical letters, would seem to have constructed an entirely different image in many readers' minds: that of a trustworthy and open transmitter of information. Apart from a few instances, such as the Canfield letter to which reference was made earlier in this chapter, and Mr J. Baxendale (LEP, 4 June 1974), most comments on LEP's CLNT coverage were approving, the most complimentary of which was Mrs Crossley's congratulations to the editor and staff 'for the impressive and impartial way which they present the news to the public', ('The Post and the fight for justice', LEP, 4 June 1974).

Survey reports have shown how important a function the local press performs in disseminating local government and planning information. (HMSO, 1967). The centrality of the LEP in the diffusion of the CLNT proposals was confirmed by the sample survey conducted by CLDC in more than 1,000 households which found that the newspaper was the 'most frequently quoted' of all sources of information, (See LEP, 24 July 1974, 'The Post first for new town news').

The representation of the local press as a possible stimulus to social action and citizen improvement is problematic. There is limited evidence that letters from officers of residents' groups may attract personal support from sympathetic readers, particularly in the more articulate middle class area served by groups like FABRA. Contrary to this interpretation is the possibility that readers will interpret information about action as a substitute for their own involvement. Information is thus seen as a narcotic, a substitute for real dialogue (See Merton and Lazarsfeld in L. Bryson, 1948, p.98).

Despite this conflicting evidence, the press themselves may have a faith in their own influence. Such is the belief in the effectiveness of editorial persuasion and authority that the view was expressed to the writer from within the LEP that, if the paper had adopted an anti CLNT stance, the government's decision to permit the new town to continue in a limited form would have been different. Certainly the success of the LEP's exposure of abuses at Whittingham hospital, the attack on wasteful expenditure on the new judges' 'lodgings' and the subsequent advocacy of an investigation into allegations of corrupt administration associated with the chief constable (which subsequently led to his suspension) may be cited as evidence for such a claim. One would expect the press to have a favourable view of its own role in current affairs. Within the limits of this study, however, it would be difficult to substantiate the claim that the stance taken by the local press would have been decisive.

Summary

This chapter has sought to link together empirical and descriptive material about the local press with a theoretical discussion of ownership, management and the professed goals of these institutions. A consideration of professional autonomy, together with editorial and staff relationships with the local political system and CLDC has been included. The thrust of the previous pages has been designed to focus upon the important role of the local press in the airing of new town issues. It has been argued that there is strong evidence of the LEP's centrality on new town matters within the local political and communications system.

NOTES

1. As McKie subtly puts it, 'the presence of Lady Hartwell on the executive committee was unlikely to diminish the zeal with which the Daily Telegraph covered the Cublington resistance'.

2. These include Punch, The Countryman, Radio Fleet, Blackburn Times, 36 provincial weeklies and 6 free weekly papers (Benn's Directory, 1981).

3. In 1977 the St Helens Reporter was 'blacked' by NALGO for advertising purposes after the local government correspondent commented unfavourably on the slow re emergence of staff from local hostelries after an earth tremor had required the evacuation of the town hall.

4. At the earliest opportunity in the research, a letter was written to the general manager, Mr Phelps, requesting that the writer be permitted to attend these briefings 'in order to assist the study which I am to undertake on communications in the sub-region'. It was explained that 'the study would not be concerned with aspects of the corporation's functions, but directed towards the response of the various media and communications networks to it, in particular the forthcoming outline plan and to examine the whole filtering and reaction processes in the area'. Despite the statement that this was 'a normal piece of University research and that the general rules of confidentiality would apply', the request to attend the press conference was refused by Sir Frank. A later written request to receive any further offical written statements to the public or the press until the secretary of state's decision was also not acted upon.

5. In addition to the more insidious selection of news, and 'setting the agenda' of importance by a newspaper there is also the more

practical aspect that the space available for a given category of story varies according to the quantity of news available in a given time span. Stories can thus be squeezed out on 'busy' days or run at uncharacteristic length in their quiet periods.

6. This allegiance was later to be confirmed when on retirement Mr Birtill entered local politics as a Chorley district councillor for a safe Conservative ward.

PART IV
THE FOCUS OF THE STUDY

9 Methods and procedures of public participation — the initial phase

INTRODUCTION

This chapter describes the phases of the public participation programme and considers some of the values which underpinned the authority's officers who advocated the development (1) and those of the inspector 'arbitrating' between the objectors and the proponents of the scheme(2).

It examines the obligation of the development corporation to participate and how this 'duty' was interpreted and implemented. A prominent event during this early period in the study was a well publicised resignation from the CLDC's social development working party. This will be described within the context of early grievances about the liaison committee system, the relentless programme of land acquisition by the development corporation, the uncertainty caused by the general election in February 1974 and the assumptions being made about the contents of the emerging Strategic Plan for the North West (SPNW).

THE DEVELOPMENT CORPORATION AND ITS OBLIGATION TO 'PARTICIPATE'

The public participation programme began with the production of a draft outline plan (CLDC, 1973) with the restricted circulation to be used in the process of consultation and discussion with members of official bodies, the local authorities' officers and councillors. This publication did not involve 'the public' but limited, selected recipients who received their brown covered copies in November 1973. The public were able to obtain a folded sketch map summary, which for those without the full document or some knowledge of the consultants' report 'Study for a city' (MHLG, 1967) on which it was based, would find difficult to interpret. (3) 25,000 of these maps were issued through 75 outlets, mainly post offices, and this document was given supporting publicity through the press with a 'non attributable' press release and on the local radio station. (It was the third item on Radio Blackburn news 6.55 am and 7.30 am on 8 November 1973).

Among those to receive the initial draft were the members of the liaison committees which had been initiated by the development corporation in August 1973 at the suggestion of a member of the board, Professor Alan Mercer. The committees were based upon the three major population centres of Preston, Chorley and Leyland. They were formed 'to receive and transmit views which will create a climate of mutual understanding and enable the multiplicity of voluntary services and interest groups to operate effectively'. (CLDC, 1974, p.87) The members of the committees were selected by the CLDC to represent various voluntary bodies and interests, such as the disabled, immigrants, manual workers, welfare organisations, the churches, youth and over 60s, and rural amenity. In a frame of reference analogous to joint consultation in industry, the liaison committees were seen as 'filling in a gap' that local authorities cannot represent adequately, to 'try to ensure an adequate dialogue with small groups whose views would otherwise be missed'. (Mercer, 1973). In Professor Mercer's view 'a pyramid needs to operate' and the liaison committees were required to provide the 'social infrastructure' between the apex (the authorities) and the broad base of the general public.

Although 'independent of the organisation', the three groups met at first at the headquarters of the CLDC, Cuerden Pavilion, where they were given talks about the aims and functions of the corporation and a secretary was provided by the office to take notes. Some disappointment was expressed of the attendance at the lectures and a decision was made to double up the representation. This new departure in consultation was thought worthy of study and the social development working party set up under the chairmanship of Professor Mercer was given the task of monitoring their activities.

The liaison committees, as originally conceived, had 'freedom to criticise other bodies' and had 'the right to give evidence against the development corporation at the public inquiry'. (Mercer, 1973). This liberal attitude was first tested when the members received the consultative draft and were, in the words of a former member of the social development working party, 'barred from showing it to any of their constituent groups and were not specifically invited to comment'. (Davies, 1977). The committees were given just over six weeks to study and discuss the plan. This timespan led to reaction in two different directions: of withdrawal or anger, not only with the corporation but with fellow members. Attendances at meetings were soon to decline, a local trades council called one committee 'a talking shop', but the most significant reaction was the minority report prepared and submitted on 19 December 1973 by two members of the most active committee, based on Preston. This report, addressed to the Chairman, members of the Board, the General Manager and Chief Officers of the Corporation, aroused no response from the corporation and the accusations and counter accusations about its circulation were to become a continuing item for contention between officials and one of its drafters, Alan Howard. (4) In addition to complaining about the time available for comment the report asserts that

> .... We have been further hampered in our efforts to obtain real participation by the 'embargo' placed on the plan, and although we appreciate the reasons why the CLDC decided to impose this embargo, we consider in retrospect that the decision was an unwise one. (Ahamed and Howard, 1973, p1)

In order to assess the reasonableness of this argument it will be useful to review, at this stage, the extent to which the development corporation was obliged to consult some of the relevant background to the designation process of CLNT and the appropriate activities of the CLDC to that date.

Reference was made earlier to the official document which underpins the argument about public participation in planning in Britain, the Skeffington report (Skeffington, 1969). Its genesis derives from the

1960s, when it was evident to some planning administrators that the existing Town and County Planning Act of 1947 was not operating satisfactorily and required reviewing. The initial stage of this appraisal was the constituting of the Planning Advisory group by the Ministry of Housing and Local Government in 1964. In addition to responding to their brief to advise on the form of a new planning system, the group also strongly recommended that the public should become involved in the plan making process in a positive sense, rather than just in the usual adversary public inquiry and planning appeals procedures.

Their report was followed by a White Paper which contained the proposal to advocate the public discussion of important planning decisions while they were still at the formative stage and capable of being influenced 'by the people whose lives they affect'. This commitment to 'public participation in planning', as it was termed, was embodied in the Town and Country Planning Bill and while this legislation was being considered by Parliament, in March 1968 the Ministry set up a committee

> .... To consider and report on the best methods, including publicity, of securing the participation of the public at the formative stage in the making of development plans for their area. (Skeffington, 1969, p.1)

The committee, under the chairmanship of one of its Ministry's Joint Parliamentary Secretaries, Mr Arthur Skeffington MP, produced a report <u>People and Planning</u> whose recommendations, according to Levin and Donnison's initial reaction, 'should leave a lasting and constructive impact on our planning procedures'. (Levin and Donnison in Cullingworth (ed), 1973, p.90). The report dealing specifically with the new development (structure and local) plans to be prepared by local authorities incorporated such proposals as 'community forums' and community development officers to be appointed 'to secure the involvement of those people who do not join organisations'. (Skeffington, 1969, p.47) Levin and Donnison, with hindsight, appear to have been over optimistic in their assessment.

The report, permissive in form, and intended to supplement the consultative procedures laid down in the 1968 Act, was eventually given official status by a department of environment circular No. 52/72 issued on 12 June 1972. With the notable exception of the community development officers, who were 'unlikely to be necessary solely in the specific context of development plans' many of the proposals were endorsed, if in diluted form. Noting that the Skeffington report 'made it plain that in their view participation should not be a formalised rigid process but should be flexible enough to meet all types of local need' (<u>DOE</u>, 1972, para. 4), the circular states that the Secretaries of State have also 'adopted this approach by keeping to a minimum the provisions dealing with publicity and participation in the regulations'. There is much in the circular which indicates that more needs to be known about methods, techniques and affected areas before final views about procedures can be laid down. The basic philosophy adopted in paragraphs of the circular could initially have given rise to renewed expectations of constructive change. This document states that:

> .... If the policies to be embodied in the plans are to be understood and generally accepted, and if the proposals in them are to be implemented successfully, the authorities <u>must carry the public with them</u> by formulating, for public discussion, the aims and objectives. Giving the public the

> opportunity to participate in the formative stage will, when handled with skill and understanding, not only make the plan but also do much to improve relationships between the planning authorities and the public. Participation is a two way process. (my emphasis)

Despite these laudable sentiments, little appears to have been promulgated from the Department of the Environment to give them further practical effect. There have been a number of studies funded by the DOE undertaken by a team of university researchers under the leadership of Dr W. Hampton of the effectiveness of public participation in structure planning (See Boaden et al, 1980) and the inner cities programme, the inception of which ironically did most to curtail the growth of CLNT, saw public participation as an integral part of new policy. The spirit of Skeffington and the high intentions of circular 52/72, present in the backgorund, have not developed defined, workable guide lines. In the inner cities the DOE 'has issued no formal guidance on the processes of community involvement and scarcely any distinction has been made between agency and residents' participation'. (New Society, 1978, p.584).

For the new towns, the DOE had prepared a circular sent to General Managers, which invited them to study circular 52/72, to use it as a guide, but giving them the freedom to interpret it in their own way, bearing in mind the varying conditions found in new towns. These were seen to depend on

> .... Whether the planning of a district calls for an informal district or area plan (which could readily lend itself to a public participation exercise); whether the area or district concerned lies in green fields or is already partially developed; whether the master plan itself is rigid or flexible in nature etc. etc. (my emphasis)

On these criteria the presence of a substantial indigenous population in central Lancashire would suggest a strong indication for public participation, but this expectation may be viewed as countered somewhat by the inherent rigidities in the outline plan, based as it was upon the consultants' draft proposals for land use and transport, and the shape of the designated area (CLDC, 1974, p.136).

THE IMPLEMENTATION OF THE PARTICIPATION ARRANGEMENTS

From the above, it appears that the extent of public involvement in the CLNT developments was entirely discretionary and depended ultimately on the commitment and attitudes to the ideal by officers of the corporation their 'practical interpretation' of what the phrase meant and the unknown messages received by the General Manager on the subject through 'the usual informal channels' referred to in circular No. 276 (DOE, 1972). The expectation of those activists who understood the philosophy underlying the Skeffington report was severely tested by the restrictions placed upon the draft outline plan. A member of the social development working party, then a Chorley College of Education lecturer, Mr Bernard Davies, had set down his views and proposals on participation in January 1973. In a paper 'The public and new town development - can the planners participate?' he advocated the need for liaison committees, similar to the community forums suggested by the Skeffington report, which given the

> .... Expertise and experience they include would enable them to comment on proporals from an early stage in the planning process and even to weigh and advise on hypothetical alternatives long before these have been given concrete expression.

Though their role was not as active or as innovative as envisaged by Mr Davies, at least they were created by CLDC. The reaction to Mr Davies's other major suggestion, that of 'grass roots adult education', was far from positive. Not only did the CLDC fail to appoint 'grass roots workers, not unlike the community development workers recommended by Skeffington', it did not even allow its community or social development function to develop to the extent that currently existed in other British new towns; a feature of the organisation which will be expanded upon in Chapter 14.

With this failure of the CLDC to respond to a unique opportunity to introduce new forms of community involvement, the decision to limit the bodies and persons consulted about the draft outline plan, provided the stimulus for a number of events during the spring of 1974, which culminated in the well publicised resignation of Mr Davies from the social development working party on 18 April 1974.

An initial reaction to this disappointment had been a press statement by Planwatch issued with the support of councillors from Conservative, Labour and Liberal parties in the form of a letter to Sir Frank Pearson chairman of CLDC. (13 December 1973). This correspondence expressed deep concern about the lack of information accompanying the 'information sheet' and the exclusion of the general public from access to the full consultative document.

This event was followed by a memorandum drawn up by a group of representatives of amenity organisations covered by Planwatch commenting on the information sheet describing the draft outline plan and circulated to local councillors in January 1974. Although subjects such as transport, conservation of communities and recreation were included, the first mentioned was that of public participation. Clearly, expectations had been aroused by Skeffington and the fact that CLDC had chosen to limit its consultation to lectures, small exhibitions and the establishment of liaison committees was interpreted as a one way flow of information and with 'no evidence of any effort to secure a meaningful and informal <u>dialogue</u> in the spirit of the Skeffington report'. (Planwatch, 1974 - their emphasis).

A further event was the circulation of a letter to all liaison committee members by the chairman of the Ramblers' Association (Preston and Fylde group), Mr Alan Howard. In this letter Alan Howard attacked the development corporation's approach to public participation and quoted examples of practices which he regarded as hampering effective public reaction.

> .... In other words, they are quite happy for us to be watch dogs, on condition that we are toothless watch dogs, able to wag our tails and bark a little, but never, in any circumstances likely to growl or bite . . . I believe that in order to achieve the 'enhanced environment' the corporation has promised us, there must be a real exchange of views between them and us, with a genuine desire <u>on both sides</u> to understand and take note of the other's point of view. (Howard, 1974)

These and other criticisms prompted the Chairman of the Development Corporation, Sir Frank Pearson, to call a press conference on 8 February 1974, to announce that 'significant changes' had already been made in the , still unpublished, draft outline plan. In answering critics who had complained that the public had not been given enough opportunity to participate in planning the new town, Sir Frank was reported to state: 'Everything we have done up to now in the way of consultation has been a bonus. We still have all the normal procedures of new town planning approvals to follow'. He believed that they had started 'participation' with a major exhibition at the time of the 1972 Preston Guild, they had continued it with a series of press conferences and public lectures, they had had regular meetings with all the local authorities and the offices of the corporation had dealt with 'literally hundreds of enquiries'. (LEP, 11 February 1974).

The following meetings of the liaison committees provided a forum and an opportunity to discuss these statements and Alan Howard's letter. Two members of the social development working party, Carol Sheppard and Bernard Davies, were present at a meeting of the South Ribble (Leyland area) liaison committee held on the 12 March 1974 at which Mr Howard's letter and the role of the liaison committees formed the main items for discussion. Doubts were expressed by Mr Davies about the independence of liaison committees whilst they involved themselves primarily in activities determined by the Corporation and relied upon Corporation officers to act as their respective secretaries; they were in danger of being overtaken by other more active groups: and no member of the committee had attended any meetings of the newly formed Moss Side residents' association active within their sphere of influence.

A number of events were to follow in quick succession. Controversy and mid Lancashire rivalry with the Mersey Belt were associated with the indications of the likely findings of the Strategic Plan for the North West (SPNW). (See Guardian, 22 March 1974). The government agreement for the Walton Summit Employment Area, prior to the endorsement of the outline plan, was announced; and a campaign against housing demolition for new town roads was launched by Mr Ron Atkins, MP (LEP, 5 April 1974), following the press publicity for the road appraisal reports. In addition, the 45 minute Central Lancashire new town film with many public showings, was promoted. Above all, the event which stood out in the local participation debate at this time was the self publicised resignation of Mr Bernard Davies from the social development working party on 18 April 1974.

FURTHER DEVELOPMENTS: THE RESIGNATION OF BERNARD DAVIES

Mr. Davies had written his letter of resignation to Professor Mercer with copies to the Chairman and General Manager of CLDC. He then used this letter as a basis of a press release which received national coverage in the serious dailies on 23 April 1974 and the local press that evening. This statement prompted such headlines as 'Planners are accused of ignoring the public' (Times), "public 'not given fair say on new towns'" (Daily Telegraph) and "Public's views 'ignored'" (Guardian). All newspapers led their coverage with the allegation made that the development corporation of the largest new town in Britain had failed to keep its promises to encourage public participation. Distinguishing between consultation and participation, the statement complained of the serious weaknesses of the methods of consultation employed to date, social surveys, public meetings, exhibitions and liaison committees. These techniques Davies argued, need to be used in combination with other forms of machinery and 'ways of monitoring grass roots opinion and knowledge'. To achieve participation elected community councils should be set up, residents' groups should be officially encouraged and more professional staff should be in regular and direct contact with the public and headed by a chief officer with status and power.

This organisational point was supported by Mr Davies's own private survey of other development corporations, all of which at that time had smaller population targets on completion that CLNT had initially. The survey showed that all but one of the eleven corporations had a chief officer responsible for social development and that eight employed twelve or more staff on social development work and six of them employ more than twenty. Yet, Mr Davies revealed, the officer most directly responsible for social development had to report to the General Manager through the chief legal and liaison officer; and his staff comprised only four professionals and two non professionals.

> .... With a staff commitment of this sort, and with an initial population of 250,000 and a planned increase of 180,000, how can anyone take seriously the corporation's claims that it intends to seek public opinion and cooperation on every occasion.

In a concluding point from his resignation letter (reported only in the local press) Mr Davies stated:

> .... I have of course no exact understanding of why or by whom the development of fuller public participation is being blocked within the Corporation, but this is happening, I am now convinced. As I am particularly resistant to being used as part of a face lift operation, and as this seems to be all that the Corporation's present efforts in this field are designed to achieve, I must admit to you that I offer my resignation with some relief. (LEP, 23 April 1974)

Mr. Davies had been a founder member of Planwatch and this independent action was quite understandably fully discussed at its executive meeting that evening, 23 April, and a decision was made to endorse the views expressed by him on public participation and to issue a supporting press release. Considering the views expressed by Planwatch it may be reasonably assumed that this action was not that of an isolated and disgruntled individual. Why were relationships so soured? Their source lay within the formal and informal relationships between the CLDC and its publics, evidenced from correspondence between officers of the Corporation and activists within the liaison committees and other groups from stresses in the loyalty to its goals and methods from within the Corporation, but above all from the growing experience of a number of individuals and groups of the procedures and public inquiries associated with the schemes initiated before the outline plan approval using powers under Section 6(i) of the New Towns Act 1965. These instances will be described later in this chapter.

SPURNING THE SKEFFINGTON IDEAL

Not only was defensiveness and lack of openness perceived by some of the public in contact, there were difficulties surrounding the differences in interpretation and definition of the principles and practices of participation. Given the explanations of the differnt frames of reference possessed by the parties, to which reference has been made in Chapter 4, this misunderstanding could have been predicted. Sir Frank Pearson, in his reply to Mr Davies's letter of resignation, illustrated the contrasting perspectives graphically when he stated categorically that 'there is one thing that participation cannot mean, and that is initiation of the proposals'. The factors leading to this attitude are various, not only do personality and bureaucratic variables have a place, but also the expression or organisational and role survival. These defences are required to counter the underlying fears based upon a reluctant awareness of the economic and demographic vulnerability of the whole project.

What were the expectations and grievances of the members of Planwatch, an organisation which describes itself as seeking to promote maximum public participation in the planning of Central Lancashire? The expectations included a far more open approach to information. More specifically a genuine commitment to participation, it argued, should begin by the CLDC releasing unconditionally all survey material and reports produced by the consultants, by publishing full details of all alternatives which had been considered and by consulting with 'all interested parties with a view to exploring how best the Skeffington report on People and Planning may be implemented in the central Lancashire situation?' The road appraisal reports, it also argued, had little or no relevance to the consideration of the strategic road network.

The grievances entered upon the restricted information flow, the participation policy to that date, and the workings of the liaison committees. Although Planwatch was not antagonistic to the concept of the new town and had tried to impress this attitude upon officers of the CLDC, it was convinced that Mr Davies was entirely correct in asserting that the corporation's commitment to public participation was only 'a verbal and paper one'. The most Planwatch could say in favour of the CLDC's participation exercises at that time was that they did not 'represent a complete embargo on information'. In criticising the form and content of the current 'participation' policy, Planwatch asserted that 'the public would clearly understand that they have no active role to play in the plan formulation'.

The liaison committees were singled out for particular disapproval. These committees were seen to demonstrate what they characterised as the 'on our terms only' policy. They had not been well publicised nor their purpose explained and members were appointed by invitation only. Planwatch described how, for several months, the meetings of the committees had consisted largely of lectures from corporation staff, which gave no real opportunity to engage in decision making, that committee had been given only six weeks to consider the consultancy document and that they had been forbidden to reveal it to the organisation which they represented. Referring to the Ahamed/Howard report, Planwatch stated that this statement remained unanswered five months after submission, an action hardly amounting to consultation, let alone participation.

A significant point was Planwatch's pique at being refused membership, together with Transport 2000, of the liaison committees after offering to send delegates. The action was commented upon adversely by the inspector at the outline plan public inquiry, hinted at in connection with the Ramblers' Association in his report (Rollison, 1975, p.20) and a personal interview (Rollison, 1977). A constructive dialogue and early exchange of views was viewed by the inspector and other observers as an action which would have shortened the public inquiry considerably. The fact that the policy of excluding residents' groups from the liaison committees was partially reversed after the public inquiry gives some indication of informal pressures to change the policy in this area and the initial shortsightedness of the original decision.

Reference has been made to the events which were occurring in parallel to the process of public participation. The national implications of the 'oil crisis' and the intra regional conflict aroused by the strategic plan for the north west may be interpreted as 'interfering' with attitudes and perceptions towards the new town. Above all at the local level within the designated area, the initiatives of the CLDC under Section 6(i) of the New Towns Act and in their seeking compulsory purchase orders, were a prime factor in moulding opinion in certain small, generally isolated, pockets in the local political network.

THE PROCESS OF LAND ACQUISITION

The Development Corporation had initiated a comprehensive policy of land banking as an early organisational objective. This action was one of the more innovatory policies of the CLDC and, although not completely untried, it was unusual for a development corporation to buy up all the developable land in advance of its known requirements! (See Glidewell, LEP, 31 March 1973). This policy was initially opposed by many of the farmers who were approached, but by the middle of January 1973, Mr Phelps was in a position to announce that compulsory purchase orders had been served for a total of over 7,000 acres of land on 400 land owners, of whom 182 had voluntarily opened negotiations to sell (LEP, 15 January 1973).

Voluntary agreements to sell could not have helped the position of the remaining landowners' case, and the credibility of their representative organisations, at the public inquiries held during July and August 1973. As a rule, the expectation was that the public's interest in such proceedings would be limited. This presumption, indeed, was used as a justification by counsel for the development, Mr Iain Glidewell, QC that 'the lack of objections is an indication that the new town policy is right'. (LEP, 31 July 1973). This supposition proved to be a serious under estimate of public concern in two particular peripheral areas, Walton Summit and Grimsargh/Haighton.

Walton Summit

Walton Summit, a rural area peppered with occasional high quality suburban type housing, had been chosen as the CLNT's marketing response to Warrington new town's 'crossover' industrial estate. Its location, enclosed by the junction of the M6 and M61 motorways and skirted by the Preston-Colne railway line, was regarded as ideal, and an essential feature of the growth generation strategy of the CLDC. Housing and farmland were to be compulsorily purchased under the Kellet Lane No.8 CPO with the powers of the development corporation vested in Section 7 of the New Towns Act 1965 being employed. In association with CPO, the CLDC was using its powers contained within Section 6(i) of the New Towns Act to propose development prior to the Secretary of State's overall approval of the outline plan. This application was for a comprehensively planned 'employment area', the description 'industrial estate' being seen as perjorative, and strictly inaccurate,since service and clerical employment were to be included in the scheme.

The proposed development was vigorously opposed by a number of residents in the area and a Walton Summit protest committee was formed, led by a school teacher, Mr Jim Pilkington. A publicity campaign, leafleting,local radio and press advertising, culminated in a very well attended pre public inquiry meeting in the St Bede's Hall, Clayton on 16 August 1973. The effect of this gathering was to stimulate local interest and to motivate residents to attend the public inquiry at nearby Walton-le-Dale the following morning. The numbers expected were markedly underestimated. The council chamber of the Walton-le-Dale UDC had been hired for accommodation but as the writer observed, all those wishing to attend could not find seats in the limited space available. After what has been described as 'a near riot' and delays, alternative accommodation was found in a school hall nearby. During the course of the day, the scheme was noisily and emotionally attacked by Mr Pilkington. Interviews and television coverage of the day's events by BBC's 'Look North' team were transmitted that evening.

Grimsargh/Haighton

Similar community interest was stimulated also when the Grimsargh CPO's for 2,686 acres were considered before the inspector, Mr Rollison on 14 August 1973. The objections were led by spokesmen of the National Farmers' Union (NFU) and the Country Landowners' Association (CLA), but were also supported by many of the local residents through the Grimsargh action group. Almost 200 people were reported to be present in Grimsargh at the opening and 'it was standing room only in the main hall of the St John Southworth School'. (Longridge News, 16 August 1973). The land banking was successfully attacked by the CLA (whose chief legal adviser, Mr Francis Holland, described as 'a totalitarian attitude') by the Grimsargh Action Group, and by the head of the NFU's land use and transport department, Mr Neville Wallace. Most significant was the contribution of the action group, which was not directly involved in CPO's whose Chairman and Vice Chairman made statements criticising the policy for its excessive public expenditure and social dislocation and that it was not in the public interest 'for a public body to acquire land without stating what it is to be used for'. In a final statement, Mr George Jepson, Chairman, asserted

> .... no planning permission has been received or applied for. This is a major departure from time-honoured and accepted principles by public bodies when acquiring land; the decline in population since the consultants prepared their report makes it no longer necessary to acquire land in the Grimsargh area; the corporation's land acquisition policy was prepared by layman without the advice of either an agricultural expert or a planning and development surveyor.

The attractiveness of the north east flank of the area was used as an argument by its opponents against development, but also, from the CLDC point of view, this feature was an asset to attract 'the executive class', according to a statement by Mr Phelps. (LEP, 15 August 1972). In more general terms, the arguments in favour of the policy, were stated by Sir Frederick Corfield, QC, the CLDC's leading counsel, to be that to acquire land before it was needed was not only admissible but necessary, being implicit in the formal designation. To create growth in the area and to attract people to live there, he argued, would involve extensive investment in main services to enable the CLDC to respond to market demands. To have land readily available when needed for executive housing, as well as for large housing estates and industry Sir Frederick contended, was both efficient and economical and could also reduce competition for development land by builders and reduce land hoarding. Thus the process of land banking gave a farmer a 'rare advantage' of maximum time to find an alternative farm, while in the meantime by farming under licence from the development corporation, farmers could have longer occupancy than otherwise might be the case.

Two and a half months later, the draft outline plan was published giving the proposals for the Haighton/Grimsargh area. Its release provoked an angry response from the chairman of the Grimsargh Action Committee who accused the CLDC of proceeding in haste with the CPO in order to 'deprive all potential objectors of substantial grounds on which to base their opposition' (LEP, 26 November 1973).

Moss Side, Leyland and other developments

On the western fringe of the designated area, west of Leyland the small settlement of Moss Side is located. The CLDC planned this area to be another comprehensive village development under Section 6(i) and a public exhibition and public meeting was advertised in the local press (Leyland and Chorley Guardians, 29 November 1973). With a target population of 5,000 this scheme was designed as a 212 acre layout including provision for 1,500 new houses, shops, two new schools, a meeting hall and an eight acre village green opposite the existing village church.

The public meeting was held following the exhibition, on Monday, 10 December 1973 and the notice of submission of Section 6(i) proposed followed on 31 January 1974. There was then a period of twenty eight days for inspection of the proposals at the offices of the CLDC, during which time representations could be made in writing to the corporation.

Meanwhile a number of compulsory purchase orders continued to be sought by CLDC, involving land surrounding their headquarters at Cuerden as well as Clayton-le-Woods and Whittle-le-Woods. The public inquiry into the 236 acre housing scheme at Whittle-le-Woods (Walton Summit No 2) was announced in early December 1973 and bitterly attacked by Mr Pilkington as 'taking them by surprise' and, coming just before Christmas, as a demonstration of 'the heartless tactics of the bureaucratic machine under the name of democratic government' (LEP, 11 December 1973).

At this time (December 1973) the government was under pressure to reduce the public expenditure planned for the fiscal year 1974-75 by 20 per cent. The share of the £1,200 million cutback for the Department of the Environment was announced on 18 December 1973 by the Secretary of State, Mr Geoffrey Rippon, to be £360 million. This pruning was seen to affect all local authorities and the road programme in particular. There was some press speculation suggesting that the CLDC land banking policy might be 'a casualty of the massive cutback in public spending' (LEP, 19 December 1973), but since the exchange of ownership and purchase price could be deferred, and the fact that bousing remained a priority, there was some doubt about the direct impact of the expenditure policy.

This uncertainty, however, did not deter the CLDC in its pre outline plan development stragegy. The official notice indicating the date for a public inquiry to hear objections to the CPO's for Walton Summit No. 2 and to the associated residential area planned under Section 6(i) appeared in the local press on 10 January 1974. The public inquiry held by Mr J.B.S. Dahl took place in the town hall, Chorley, from 29 January 1974. Many of the arguments employed for and against the development were those which would be emphasised later during the outline plan inquiry. These were comprehensively argued by one of the objectors, Mr David Marshall. He questioned the need for the 1,7000 houses planned on the site and suspected that they would not be required if the adjoining employment area was not approved. His principle objection, however, was what he regarded as the unnecessary taking of 'prime farm land' to build a housing estate, for which a need had not been demonstrated. This land was a natural buffer between small townships, according to another objector, Mrs Marjorie Decker, and the road structure serving the area was suspect. This point was covered in the submission of the Lancashire county council who gave their approval to the scheme subject to the provision of a new link road between the A6 and the M61.

Stressing the need for the maximum attractiveness of the new town, Mr Colin Beck, chief planner on behalf of the development corporation, made the point that it was important to provide early housing sites in different parts of the designated area for them to meet demand adequately. The pattern of the early housing sites was, therefore, consistent, he argued, both with offering a wide choice to house buyers and within a concept of 'dispersed growth'.

In an attempt to counter arguments about the decline in existing property values, Mr Dennis Cudworth, chief legal and liaison officer, pointed out that all houses, even if originally rented, would be built for eventual sale, if requested by the tenants. He also assured objectors representing the Roman Catholic church, whose land and parish size were affected, that all their needs would be catered for under the proposed development.

Mr Pilkington made much of the fact that the hospital facilities in the locality would'not be able to cope with the rise in population which would hit the area'. The main point of his objection which was to make the local newspaper headlines and to become a national news item, was his accusation that CLDC had asked surrounding planning authorities to reduce their planning application by 50 per cent. This charge was denied by Mr Beck, but it seems likely that this allegation was an over specific reference to the likely effects of the 'fringe area' policy of the CLDC, which sought to inhibit new development within a few miles of the boundary of the designated area.

Evidence of informal influence was given in a letter to the Chorley Guardian of 7 February 1974, which quoted instances of applications to build 450 and 140 houses at nearby Blackrod and Adlington being refused. CLDC had earlier withdrawn attempts to contest development in the Standish area, north of Wigan, but later succeeded in opposing development at Longton (LEP, 29 April 1974) and, following the outline plan inquiry, at Kirkham in the Fylde. This fringe policy was strongly contested and was a main feature of the case against the outline plan by the Greater Manchester Council and both Wigan and Bolton Metropolitan Councils at the public inquiry which will be described in Chapter 12.

About two weeks after the Walton Summit No. 2 Public Inquiry had been completed, the advertisement giving notice of the intention to proceed with the proposals for Moss Side under Section 6(i) was published (LG, 14 February 1974). This announcement gave 28 days for the public to inspect the plans at the CLDC headquarters and to make representations to the Secretary of State for the Environment. Prior to and following the General Election of February 1974, the Moss Side Residents' Association began its activities, elected a committee at a public meeting on 10 January and started to assemble its evidence for the expected public inquiry. Official approval for the 'village' development was given in the last month of its existence before local government reorganisation by the Leyland Urban District Council's Planning Committee on 11 March 1974. The new adjoining Chorley District Council had no objection to the concept of the plan but made a few minor observations (LEP, 9 April 1974). Similarly, the successor council to Leyland, the South Ribble district council, at its development committee meeting had no objection to the Moss Side scheme, apart from minor improvements in layout, and a request for consultation on some points of detail (LEP, 20 April 1974) The eventual public inquiry into the Section 6(i) application commenced at Leyland Civic Hall on 17 September 1974, which was after the main phase of the public participation process into the outline plan.

At this time, the writer observed an event which took place in Moss Side, Leyland, which had a bearing on local residents' attitudes. This was a well attended public meeting held on 2 May 1974 with the development corporation at the St James's School room, Dunkirk Lane. A great deal of feeling against the development was expressed by a number of inhabitants who opposed the change from the semi rural character of the area and the imposition of a larger than previous mix of public rented housing to private owner-occupied. The earliest development for which there had been least opposition, Astley Park, Chorley, had been almost entirely for owner-occupation. Walton Summit was planned to be about 70:30 mix of private to public housing but, to the concern of many Moss Side residents, the housing envisaged for their area was to be about half rented from the development corporation, with overall the highest net density of dwellings per acre of 12.0. The occasion was observed by the writer and, in addition to discussion and argument about physical detail and social provision 'we want nursery not pub residents' (Leyland Guardian, 9 May 1974), it was significant that many of the exchanges focussed upon public participation and questions asked provide evidence of the impact of the press and, specifically, a recent television programme about the Edinburgh airport runway. The importance of the media in the new town developments has been discussed at length in Chapter 8.

NATIONAL INFLUENCES - THE GENERAL ELECTION OF FEBRUARY 1974 AND THE STRATEGIC PLAN FOR THE NORTH WEST

With CLNT having its origins in a Labour administration, the change from the Conservative Government to Labour in February 1974, led to the assumption, underlined by the local press opinion, that there would be no significant change in policy towards CLNT. Official Lancashire County Council support was stiffened by pre publication suggestions of the proposals contained in the Strategic Plan for the North West (SPNW). This account indicated that the government's investment priorities should be weighted towards the Metropolitan Counties of Greater Manchester and Merseyside with other north west new towns - the so called

'Mersey Belt'. This report 'so alarmed chief officers that a secret meeting between Lancashire and the 14 new district councils agreed to make a common stand against its proposals' (LEP, 7 March 1974).

In the report, CLNT was damned with faint praise and welcomed 'as a major long term growth area, with a slower build up than originally expected but making a major contribution in the later 1980s'. (SPNW, 1973, p.15). This attitude had the effect of reinforcing local authority commitment to CLNT with the leaderships of the major political parties, and encouraging a spirit of intra regional rivalry between Lancashire County and the Metropolitan Counties to the South, which would be enflamed by local press comment to which reference has been made in Chapter 8.

LOCAL EVENTS - THE ANNOUNCEMENT OF WHITTLE DISTRICT CENTRE, THE CLDC FILM AND THE ROAD APPRAISAL REPORTS

Towards the end of March 1974, through the press coverage of the Chorley District Council's Policy and Resources Committee's proceedings, the Clayton-le-Woods multi use complex was made public (LEP, 26 March 1974). This proposal was later to be renamed the Whittle district centre/community school and was the subject of a similar Section 6(i) procedure culminating in a public inquiry the following September.

At this time the CLDC film illustrating some of the features of the outline plan was premiered before an invited audience in the Charter Theatre, Preston and then advertised for public showing at centres throughout the designated area (See LEP, 18 March 1974, CG and LG, 21 March 1974). Although this film was described by Mr Richard Phelps as 'only part of the process of communication and participation culminating with a public inquiry in the autumn', for the purposes of this description the film will be placed within the pre outline plan participation procedure since this technique was only a one way process of fairly bland information giving. It was intended that the outline plan would be published at the same time as the film became available, but this document had been the victim of a number of delays, having been promised in turn for the spring of 1973 (LEP, September 1972), by early 1974 (West Lancs. Evening Gazette, 20 October 1973), and by March (LEP, 11 February 1974) only to be also 'delayed at the printers by the three day working week' (LEP, 19 March 1974).

Another initiative by the CLDC which made the outline plan information process more complex was the prior publication, first through the local press (LG, 28 March 1974) and then through booklets available for reference at public libraries (LEP, 23 April 1974), and the various road appraisal reports. These reports indicated the routes considered and the reasons for the preferred line of various key sections of new roads to be constructed as part of the outline plan transport network.

The official reason for the separation of this element of the outline plan

> .... was to ensure that the public are given the opportunity to participate in the route selection procedure in a similar way to that envisaged for new motorway and trunk road projects. (Public notice LEP, 23 April 1974)

The impact upon the public of abstracting an element of the outline plan is difficult to assess. Much of the information contained therein was complex and could have been obscure to many residents of the area, yet it did serve to give prior and separate warning to those opinion leaders who perceived their implications clearly. Certainly this action could be seen positively, as focussing upon the physical and social impact of sections of the road network, or in some respects negatively in that it diverted attention away from broader implications of the outline plan. The decision to hold separate sets of meetings for the public on the road appraisal reports and on the other aspects of the outline plan had similar opportunities and dangers, in that the agenda could be more focussed and ordered on the one hand, but on the other, energies and enthusiasms could be dissipated and diverted between the two sets of meetings.

SOME IMPORTANT INTERIM DECISIONS BY THE SECRETARY OF STATE

Just as the release of these road appraisal reports was making some impact upon residents, the event which served to underline the relentless progress of the new town machine took place. The new Secretary of State for the Environment, Mr Anthony Crosland, approved the recommendations of the inspector, Mr J. Botterill, that the Walton Summit employment area should proceed with only minor amendments. This announcement was given front page headlines and the emphasis was placed upon 'hopes of 1,000 jobs' (LEP, 2 April 1974). The momentus of the project was underlined by the news release by CLDC a week later. This document stated that the builders had been selected for CLNT's first housing scheme at Astley Park, Chorley and that CLDC were shortly to introduce four more new town schemes ahead of the outline plan to add to the five already submitted under Section 6(i) (LEP, 9 April 1974).

Many members of residents' associations expressed their powerlessness and vulnerability against such a relentless scheme-by-scheme advance. This progress was further underlined by the Secretary of State's approval of the Walton Summit No. 2 Scheme under Section 6(i), subject to an increase in the proportion of rented housing, towards the end of May (LEP, 24 May 1974). (The relevant compulsory purchase orders were confirmed by public notice under Section 7 of the New Towns Act 1965 on 6 June 1974).

THE SECTION 6(i) SCHEMES

At this point it will be useful to summarise the pre outline plan 6(i) schemes which were public before the announcement of the availability of the outline plan on 29 May 1974. Tenders had been accepted for the first scheme at Astley Park, Chorley and government approval had also been sanctioned for the developments at Walton summit, both for the employment area and for the adjoining housing scheme. The secretary of state's approval of public inquiry proceedings were awaited on the housing schemes at Cop Lane, Penwortham and Moss Side, Leyland, and planning studies and an intention to proceed with 6(i) applications had been announced by CLDC for a small scheme at Clayton Hall, the district centre for Whittle-le-Woods, Ingol East and a development at Grimsargh.

Reference has already been made to the complexity of the information processes affecting the attitudes of the residents towards CLNT. The 'domino effect' of the strategically placed and timed decisions on early developments tended to induce expressions and feelings of inevitability in many concerned observers, yet paradoxically there existed a rationalisation expressing CLNT's eventual demise based on the incredulousness that a scheme estimated to require £900 million of public and private investment could be afforded in the current economic conditions. The various residents' organisations, primarily those based on Walton Summit, Grimsargh and Moss Side, had already learned something of the way in which CLDC 'had tried to consult the public directly affected'. The public display of the detailed plans had been effected in each community, and by this action, according to the Chairman, Sir Frank Pearson, CLDC 'could be said to have taken the public fully into their confidence in regard to these schemes' (CG, 14 February 1974). A few minor concessions had been made, but experience to date had shown that the Secretary of State was approving the schemes with a few amendments, which had usually been initiated by the local authorities.

By the very nature of the geographical spread of the Section 6(i) applications, those affected had a long concern and a specific experience of the planning process. Apart from a few unyielding characters within the groups, many residents reluctantly interpreted events as indicating that little would be gained by outright opposition. Many were sceptical of the value of the effort of presenting a case believing that their views would be of little influence and that the main issues were 'cut and dried'.

Evidence of this pre outline plan attitude was gained not only through fieldwork observation, but it found its expression in letters to the local press and ultimately in the vibrations transmitted by the Bernard Davies resignation previously described. This reaction is well expressed and summarised in a letter by councillor Neva Orrell, the Liberal parliamentary candidate for Chorley, writing in the Leyland Guardian of 21 February 1974

> .... The fact that certain schemes have been pushed through before the outline plan has been approved, provides the corporation themselves with a 'bonus'. At the public inquiry, the plan can be presented as already in progress and therefore expensive and inconvenient to interfere with.
>
> The corporation may well blind the public with science to such an extent that there is the danger of a 'fait accompli' situation being engineered; so that, although the public are theoretically able to participate, they will tend to take it for granted that the original plan is virtually unchangeable, too complicated to understand and already accepted in its fundamentals by the local councils, so that only 'cosmetic' alterations are possible.
>
> It is for this reason that groups interested in public participation have been unwilling to accept at its face value much of the material emanating from Cuerden Pavilion.

A few weeks later, the newly elected member for Preston South Mr Stan Thorne, tabled a series of questions to the Secretary of State for the Environment. Those relating to CLNT included asking how much land had been acquired by the development corporation, how many houses required acquisition and whether the government would review the question of land requisition and housing development by CLDC. The question asked about the greater encouragement of participation by community representatives in planning decisions may be interpreted as an expression of his constituents' concern about the process of public consultation to that date. (See LEP, 27 March 1974).

SUMMARY

This chapter has related a number of strands which provide the foundation for studing the main processes of public participation during this period. It has described events and administrative action which would influence participants' attitudes towards the CLDC's programme of public participation (See Chapter 10) which culminated in the outline plan public inquiry (See Chapter 12).

NOTES

1. 'We hope, however, that there are none actively interested in planning matters in the area who feel that they have not had at least reasonable opportunity of access . . . despite the extensive measures taken to inform the public about the contents of the plan they did not generate more in the nature of genuine enquiries in the pursuit of possible alternatives rather than indifference or outright opposition to particular proposals.' (General Manager's Proof of Evidence para. 23).
2. 'It is not easy to define what constitutes inadequate programme of public participation but the aim has been to interest, to inform and to involve as many members of the public as possible . . . Nearly £50,000 has been spent on this and it is fair to say that this corporation has done more than most development corporations in this field'. (Inspector's Report paras. 78 and 79).
3. This was not helped by the poor layout and printing design used. Land uses were shown by superimposing a sepia shading upon an Ordnance Survey base and it proved difficult to decipher the underlying roads and place names.
4. This dispute was eventually made public - "Liaison a 'Mockery' New Town Critic". (LEP, 8 May 1974)

10 Public participation in the outline plan

INTRODUCTION

Whether by accident or design, the phasing of the various stages of public participation in the outline plan was distinctly untidy. For the purposes of clarity it is necessary to include the meetings in connection with the transport network element in the plan since they were very much an integral part, if not a dominant component, in the public's perception of the proposals. Although the descriptive film had been released for a short time, and reportedly well attended (LEP, 8 April 1974), the actual date of the commencement of 'participation' will be taken as 23 April 1974. It was the date that the free summary pamphlet of the outline plan was available in public libraries in the designated area, together with the reference copies of road appraisal reports. These reports relate to eight sections in the road network shown in the land use and transport plan within the outline plan.

In addition to describing the form and content of the road appraisal report and outline plan meetings, this chapter will also make reference to events of significance occurring simultaneously, such as land banking under Section 6(i) powers of the New Towns Act, comments by an eminent local architect-planner on the proposals and Preston Borough Council's policy statement.

THE ROAD APPRAISAL REPORT MEETINGS

The prelude to the meetings

The public notice giving details of the first series of five road appraisal report meetings was published on 30 April 1974. (The week intervening between these two dates had been the occasion of the Davies resignation.) A feature of this notice was the penultimate paragraph which stated: 'To avoid overcrowding and disappointment in attending the meeting priority of admission will be given to TICKET HOLDERS.' Tickets were available, free of postage, from the CLDC.

Such an arrangement requires some explanation. One possible interpretation could be that the embarrassing overcrowding experience at the Section 6(i) inquiries at Walton-le-Dale and Grimsargh required controlling. Though since such instances were decidedly uneven, it is doubtful whether, by newspaper advertising alone, such numbers would have been replicated consistently but it might have been thought well worth the effort of the extra clerical work involved. Certainly the tickets served as useful reminders, and possibly could have induced commitment in some to attend the meetings, but there is evidence that the tickets applied for were not fully used. They did serve as an indication of excess demand for a meeting and a second series was subsequently arranged for disappointed applicants in certain centres.

It is significant to note that no mention was made in the advertisement that special meetings might be arranged for certain groups. (Those meetings which eventually were held at the request of organisations such as the Ashton action group or the Fulwood and Broughton residents' association were certainly among the best attended and the most vociferous.) No doubt the CLDC officers preferred a balanced audience, with a sprinkling of supporters and the uncommitted, rather than a group which was basically antagonistic. It is possible to speculate that the ticket arrangements, if required, could certainly have served as an 'early warning system' for the presence of known activists. Whether justified or not, resentment was expressed by the interviewees at this ticket application procedure.

The initial publicity was supplemented by a sketchmap advertisement of the relevant sections of road for each meeting. The response for tickets was such that, before the first series of meetings had started, the CLDC decided to issue a press release describing the successful response. A new town spokesman was quoted as saying that the meetings at Leyland, Ribbleton and Walton-le-Dale 'were all heavily over subscribed' . . . 'This is public participation in a big way'. (LEP, 15 May 1974). It was at this time that the residents' groups described in Chapter 7 were becoming active.

The Preston north action group announced that it had formed a campaign committee 'to halt new town plans for an eastern primary road through Preston' (LEP, 8 May 1974). This policy was actively supported and encouraged by the Member of Parliament for Preston North, councillor Ron Atkins, who attacked the road proposals during a Preston council debate asserting that they cut across local communities and would destroy them (LEP, 10 May 1974). This attack was sustained by the chairman of the group, fellow Labour Council member, Councillor Dick Evans, at a public meeting at Deepdale Labour club. On one of the first and rare occasions when class interests were openly articulated, Councillor Evans challenged his audience to unite to fight the road proposals which he contended, were being planned to carry people out to housing estates in places like Grimsargh, houses which would not be for working class people who were having their homes threatened by the roads. Many observers have pointed out the balance of advantage towards the higher socio economic groups in society as a result of urban motorway development. This view was given local significance when Councillor Evans stated:

> .... The new town corporation is going to provide luxury houses for those who can afford them. It breaks my heart to see the squalor that some people in Preston have to live in. There are 1,000 emergency cases alone of families who desperately need homes. (LEP, 16 May 1974)

This process is not of recent origins, but, as Simmie (citing Somers Town in London) points out, has been going on for nearly a century. (Simmie, 1974, pp.115-6).

Three news items

On the day that the launching of the new series of road appraisal report meetings took place (in addition to the report of the above, under the headline, "'Unite' warcry for new road fighters"); three further news items relevant to CLNT were published. The first was a series of reports of the town and country planning association's conference on the Strategic Plan for the North West and observed by the writer, which had taken place in Manchester the previous day. It had been a lively conference, well attended by staff from CLDC in support of their general manager, who was to address the 300 delegates and stress that the CLDC would go ahead as fast as possible despite the preferred emphasis upon the Mersey belt in the plan. This particular contribution was ignored in the press reports in the Guardian and the Daily Telegraph, who emphasised the tensions which were expressed in some of those in the shire counties of Cheshire and Lancashire and those within the Liverpool-Manchester conurbation. It was left to the Preston based Lancashire Evening Post to emphasise the implications for CLNT with the headlines, 'New town is snubbed by N.W. Planners'. They quoted Mr Phelps, expressing the view that:

> .... We are not deterred that to some we appear as the Cinderella of the plan. Perhaps the time of the ball has been deferred and midnight may have to be put back. But we shall go ahead as fast as we can. (LEP, 16 May 1974)

The second news item was a short article in the Guardian by John Hudson 'On the planners Lancashire hot pot - Going public', which had all the indications of having been prompted by a local activist. It opened with a direct reference to the first of the meetings:

> .... In Leyland tonight a team of planners, engineers, and central Lancashire new town administrators will meet several hundred townspeople for talks on their future road proposals.
>
> On paper, at least, the operation is firmly in line with the Skeffington proposals on public participation with professionals and laymen coming together in lively and constructive debate. But the atmosphere tonight, and at the series of discussions to follow, is unlikely to reflect such enlightened ideals; both sides are preparing themselves for nothing more sophisticated than a good old fashioned protest meeting.
>
> Nearly five years after Skeffington,and three since the establishment of the new town development corporation, public participation is still suffering an unhappy childhood in central Lancashire. There are those who say that the development corporation has taken only the minimum steps to involve the layman, in reply to which officials can point to an extensive list of liaison committee meetings, film shows, lectures, public debates and published documents.
>
> The only real criterion however, is the extent to which these efforts have encouraged the public to feel that their say is a real and meaningful one. The evidence is that a great many people still need a lot of convincing.

After some discussion of the role of the liaison committees, and quotations from interviews with Mr Phelps and Mr Howard, the article continues:

.... It is over the current road appraisal studies though, that the greatest heat is being generated. Mr Phelps protests that the recently published routes, giving alternative lines for various new link roads, are merely proposals for discussion and may never be required. Arguments in their favour would be more fully explained in the forthcoming outline plan.

Oponents, however, see them as committing the region to maximum private transport, a point taken up by Preston's two Labour MPs. Action groups springing up to resist them are following this line by arguing not against specific road lines, but against the need for the roads at all.

The third item, a letter from Councillor Norman Yates, published in the Lancashire Evening Post under the heading 'Democracy becoming just an illusion . . .', underlines the felt suspicions and doubts expressed to the writer by many involved in the action groups. His initial concern was whether democratic processes would be allowed to operate as the final plans were formulated or would the people's wishes 'be trampled underfoot?' Referring to the public meeting held on 2 May 1974 by the Ashton action group, he cited the fact that the speakers, Mr S. Thorne, MP, Councillor Michael Atkins and Councillor Taylor had all supported the Ashton residents in their protest but had admitted to the audience that "they had 'no teeth' with which to act". He went on:

.... It would appear that those in positions of power and authority have no intention of letting the people's wishes interfere with their plans, which may in some instances be better described as pipe dreams with little basis in reality.

Recent experience indicates that a public inquiry about the new town, or any other proposed development, is likely to be little more than an inconvenient formality and a farce.

Showing a wide knowledge of recent planning experience, he continued:

.... The Samlesbury brewery, the proposed new runway for Edinburgh airport, the Canvey Island oil refinery extensions, the Kenilworth M40 inquiry are recent pertinent examples. Democracy appears to be rapidly becoming an illusion rather than a reality.

In conclusion, he foreshadowed many of the basic arguments about CLNT and the eventual 'last ditch' attempt by activists to change the Secretary of State's decision:

.... Since the idea of a Preston new town was first conceived, Britain's economic situation has changed considerably. Rampant inflation, the world energy situation, building materials shortages and other difficulties demand that the whole idea of the new town requires radical reappraisal, but unless

Prestonians can rapidly acquire a set of exceptionally strong teeth it could be too late and the developers will have free reign!

The climate at the commencement of the public meetings was thus characterised by a generally widening gulf between the local political establishment on one side, who had become galvanised into defending their protege by the lukewarm attitude of the Strategic Plan for the North West. On the other, not only the 'anti new town militants', but also the 'Skeffington idealists' were witnessing the largely unchecked advance of 6(i) applications before the outline plan participation process was initiated, and experiencing an increasing disillusionment with the process of participation from the evidence of the Davies resignation, public statements and letters to the press.

The public response to the road appraisal report meetings

Apart from the Chorley meeting, all the other meetings in this series had been very well attended. The demand for tickets led the CLDC to organise a second series of road appraisal report meetings; one at Bamber Bridge covering the road alignments and reports discussed at Walton-le-Dale, another at Leyland Civic Hall and a further one at Ribbleton. The press announcement for these meetings also coincided with the notice of the exhibition of proposals for the Whittle district centre/community school at the Bamber Bridge public library. By the time the first of these meetings was to take place on 29 May 1974, the Walton Summit housing had been approved by the Secretary of State, the outline plan had become available and the date of the Whittle district centre public meeting had been announced.

The Bamber Bridge meeting, attended by about 80 people, was prefaced by the usual formal statements and a brief review of the areas of concern mentioned at the previous meeting. There was a further opportunity to refer to the A6 traffic and the employment area by a member of the protest committee, Mr Hale, and its chairman, Mr Jim Pilkington once again was present to appeal emotionally to the audience: 'You couldn't call this meeting participation. It is indoctrination when it is too late for us to do anything'.

The second Leyland meeting, also attended by less than 100 people, followed the same pattern, Mr Phelps referring back to the main points raised at the first meeting in Leyland. It was followed by an indication that there would be a dialogue on possible changes (a 'reasoned exchange' in his words) and a decision would be available in July.

The attendance at the duplicate Ribbleton meeting was only 56, although it was claimed that 270 tickets had been distributed. The previous evidence for the need for the eastern primary was reiterated by Mr Garside who told the audience that some new roads would 'inevitably be needed' to serve the 20,000 people living in the Grimsargh area by 1985 and the 50,000 expected by the end of the century. The forty five houses to be demolished and the fifty others affected by noise caused by the chosen route was far preferable, in his view, to the twenty times that number of houses which would be demolished or affected by improvements on existing roads to cater for that population. In response to this statement, Councillor Miller accused the corporation of making road proposals for 'mythical populations' and that it was likely that Preston 'would be lumbered with a road it did not want and that might not be used'. If the road had to be built, he argued, it should avoid the populated areas and be kept east of the M6 motorway to avoid Preston altogether. This suggestion was taken up by Mr Garside for possible consideration, but it was pointed out that the road was also intended to serve other expanding areas in the new town to the west of the M6, such as Fulwood, where 7,000 people would be living by 1985.

The special Ashton meeting, requested when the western primary was discussed at Fulwood, was announced to take place on 18 June 1974 at St Andrew's junior school, Blackpool Road, close to one of the most affected areas. This meeting was advertised in the Lancashire Evening Post on 1 and 4 June, by which dates the full outline plan had become available to the general public at public libraries, or by purchase at £6.00 per copy.

For those reacting to the new town proposals this period was to be one of intense activity, with the Ashton action group meeting proving to be one of the high points. The road appraisal report meeting had provided a focus upon the physical and social implications of the transport network, so that the details released through the local and national press on 30 and 31 May 1974, equipped those interested with more comprehensive information. It also served as a second phase reminder to those who had been aware of the more complete national press coverage at the time of the circulation of the restricted draft the previous November. As if to underline the relentless momentum of the project, this publicity was coupled with the announcement of a public meeting to discuss the proposals for the Whittle district centre/ community school and associated development on 6 June. This date coincided with the recording of the only full television programme to be transmitted during this period on the new town issue.

CONVENING THE MAIN PROTAGONISTS - THE ROLE OF GRANADA TELEVISION

This programme, one of the Granada 'On the Spot' series, was the only occasion, apart from the later public inquiry briefing and its opening session, when most of the key actors from the residents' groups, the local authorities and the CLDC were brought together. In the circumstances, it was only an organisation with the status of Granada which would have been able to arrange such an occasion. This gathering could have been regarded as a central Lancashire community forum 'in embryo', but without the willingness of the CLDC to implement any innovative community development policies, nor the existence of a voluntary agency with sufficient prestige to follow this initiative through, the opportunity was lost. This failure indicates the lack of an existing, well established coordinator of the voluntary sector in central Lancashire with experience in community action. Unlike Liverpool, with its Council of Voluntary Service experienced in convening community groups and enabling them to respond to issues, (1) the Community Council of Lancashire had primarily a rural development remit and had not developed this role. Similarly, the Civic Trust movement in the area was moribund and the only well established amenity society with a degree of influence the Council for the Protection of Rural England, felt restricted by its traditional spheres of concern to involve itself in predominantly urban matters. Planwatch itself and later SCRAP would attempt to provide the services of an umbrella organisation, but without great success.

The recording session in Astley Hall, Chorley and the transmission the following Sunday, were given wide coverage in the local press.

They gave both Mr Phelps and Mr Beck an opportunity to state the case for the new town and a number of leading spokesmen of the residents' groups, some councillors and George Rodgers, MP for Chorley, to make short statements. These points centred mainly on the transport network, the arrangements for participation and the basis for the development of CLNT. Although the headlines, "Meetings are 'New Town Propaganda'" (CG, 13 June 1974) and 'New Town Chiefs in TV lashing' (LEP, 7 June 1974) might give the impression that unbalanced confrontation took place this view was not borne out by direct observation of the event. The new town officials were becoming very adept at handling this type of occasion and, as the editor of the Chorley Guardian commented:

> .... somehow I got the impression that Dick Phelps, development corporation general manager and Colin Beck, chief planner, were batting to bowling which they found very easy in spite of the wicket.. (CG, 13 June 1974)

THE OUTLINE PLAN PUBLIC MEETINGS

The first series of twelve public meetings to discuss the outline plan were first advertised on 7 June 1974. It is curious to note that again there were arrangements for ticket applications and that 'to avoid over crowding and disappointment . . . priority of admission will be given to ticket holders'. A period of intense activity by individuals and local organisations preceded these meetings. The Ashton action group (AAG), maintaining its aggressive stance, delivered a statement to CLDC and the department of the environment, copies of which were issued to the press,the local MPs and the chief executives of Lancashire county and Preston councils. This bulletin claimed that the road proposals were 'monstrous and unjust both in scale and location' and criticised the CLDC for failing to give them fuller details of the proposals. In the absence of such details, the officers ofAAG 'lodged formal objections to any current or future proposals affecting Ashton'.

The only material case of inter party disagreement and controversy at this time centred upon the cross town routes in Preston, based upon Aqueduct Street and St George's Road. The June edition of the Preston North Liberal Association's newsletter 'Focus' accused local Labour councillors of 'scaremongering over the effects of the road plans'. It suggested that, for political reasons, a number of Labour councillors in the area had

> .... drawn their own conclusions from the plan and used them to scare those who live in Aqueduct Street and St George's Road into believing that the development corporation intends to destroy their property to enable it to build a wider road.

Taking the opportunity afforded by its possession of 'a detailed statement' from Mr Phelps to the Lancashire County Council's Liberal group leader, councillor Gordon Payne, the local party adopted a conciliatory tone towards the CLDC giving publicity to the 'positive assurance that the corporation has no proposals for the widening of any of the existing routes included in the plan as principal routes'. In effect, according to Mr Phelps, all that the corporation were suggesting was that, if the area was to be redeveloped in the next few years, it would be wise to make room for possible future road widening. The newsletter went on to say that criticism of CLDC for its 'apparent reluctance to communicate with the public' had been justified, but consistent with its more conciliatory tone, it welcomed the public meetings currently being arranged in small local halls to discuss the plans with the residents affected.

On the evening of a Preston North action group (PNAG) public meeting to be held on 14 June 1974, sixteen Labour councillors from the Preston and Lancashire councils published a reply to the accusation contained in the Liberal newsletter. They argued that the route under discussion was shown on the plan as an 'other major road', its direction involving crossing (the inappropriately named) Skeffington Road and through Basil Street estate containing recently modernised council houses. Referring to the road appraisal reports, the statement asserted that these documents showed the route as a 40 mph district distributor dual carriageway. 'To widen it to that extent would inevitably mean demolition of property on both sides'. They had stressed that this road was not an early proposal and that anyone losing their home would be compensated, 'but their electors did not want that'. While theCLDC might have no scheme for widening the road, 'Lancashire county council might well have widening plans to cope with extra traffic from other new town developments'.

SOME PREPARATORY EVENTS

i) Preston North Action Group

This climate of controversy provided a stimulus to local interest, but had the danger of giving the initial impression that the Preston North action group was virtually a Labour Party 'front' organisation. This political image was largely assuaged by the breadth of interests represented on the platform of the public meeting held in Moor Park school on the evening of 14 June 1974. Not only did the MP for Preston North, Mr Ron Atkins, have the support of a number of Labour councillors but also the concurrence of a Conservative, councillor Dennis Keogh, and a 'non political' secretary, Mr Bryan Hughes, a comprehensive school headmaster.

Mr Hughes gave an account of their committee's activities since the April public meeting and said that they had attempted a dialogue with 'the New Town'. He reiterated that they were against the demolition of property, parks and amenities and against roads becoming 'major highways in towns'. They intended to start organising a petition and he believed that there had been 'a massive fraud in participation'. This point was taken up by councillor Keogh who stated that there had been no participation in the original decision. He regarded roads to be 'among many evils'. In a reference to the Lancashire Evening Post he stated that 'the monopoly press had been pro new city until last week when it published a letter from a Prestonian architect'. (See p.126) They were fighting 'Mr Octopus', the new town was 'a complete and utter waste of money' and they must 'kill the octopus rather than the arm'. Referring to the CLDC, he stated, that 'not one of the officers live in Preston'.

The chairman of Preston's development committee, councillor David Yates, continued this theme by articulating the usual local authority resentment that the CLDC was ' a body of selected persons'. He had yet to see any evidence of public participation, a point supported by councillor Josephine Farrington who declared that 'further information was still not participation'.

The final speech of the meeting was given by Mr Ron Atkins who drew upon his Welsh eloquence to criticise, in particular, the transportation aspects of the outline plan. He was concerned about housing densities from the point of view of the waste of land,as well as the fact that too low densities were detrimental to the efficient use of public transport. 'It is bad to plan the town before you know the needs of the population. The new town authority are guessing whether we shall need new roads', he asserted, 'and it is obvious they have guessed because they have said ridiculous things. Estimates for the future are always wrong that is why many of our schools have been messed up.' Referring to the apparently generous provision for golf courses in the plan, Mr Atkins instanced the example of the proposal for Ingol where new estates were being built and the CLDC had 'planned a big golf course but nothing for the children'. . . 'An elite group planning for an elite group'.

This lively public meeting,attended by about 150 people, was given rare front page press coverage. Mr Atkins' reference to the secrecy surrounding the Grimsargh plans 'because it was considered too sophisticated for the public' brought forward his reported response that 'the most sinful thing about the planners is their attitude that they are an elite people'. This phrase was condensed into the front page banner headline "New town planners 'a sinful elite'". (LEP, 15 June 1974)

ii) The 6(i) and the Grenfell-Baines Intervention

Two further events took place at this period. A further public inquiry at which the CLDC was seeking the secretary of state's approval for additional compulsory purchases of 1,206 acres at Ingol, Grimsargh, Fulwood and Broughton, indicates the relentless progress of land banking procedures. There was also a press intervention by one of the most prestigious professional architects calling for an alternative strategy. Professor George Grenfell-Baines, who played a key role in the designation inquiry and was a founding partner of the Preston based architectural firm, the Building Design Partnership, advocated the use of the investment funds in the towns of the wider north Lancashire sub region. Referring to the outline plan he wrote,

> .... I worry because I believe that all the skill, devotion and money about to be expended could be invested in a much better and more modern way - the way of positive conservation of existing assets, the way of preserving a reasonably human scale in all aspects of our urban settlements not least in the road systems needed to serve them.
>
> So once more it may be asked: 'Is it too late to think again?. Now that all the consequences of the original decision are becoming revealed, it is timely to remember that the quality of life for many people is affected. £900 million is a lot of money, it could do much, given the right objectives. (LEP, 13 June 1974)

The substance of the letter was repeated as a short news item the following day with the heading "£900m 'could be better spent'." This extract included a reply from Mr Phelps stating that it was too late to think again and that it was fallacious that the money spent on the new town would divert resources from other towns in the north west. The £900 million 'represented an estimate of the total cost of growth on the scale envisaged by all the public authorities in the area, and by the private sector'. The intervention continued to reverberate when a few days later, Peter Dugdale, the Lancashire Evening Post's chief planning correspondent wrote an article in response with the title 'Too late to rethink New Town', showing unequivocably his paper's position on the issue. (LEP, 18 June 1974)

iii) Ashton Action Group

Like its predecessor, the specially arranged Ashton meeting to discuss the western primary route was an eventful occasion. It was held in St Andrew's school, closely situated to the most controversial effects of the proposed route, the demolition of houses and the encroachment upon Haslem Park and its lime trees. It was thus the centre of the best orchestrated opposition to the road proposals for the area, that of the Ashton action group. The meeting had been well prepared by AAG's committee and an attempt was made to take the initiative away from the CLDC. There was an initial dialogue between an AAG spokesman and Mr Phelps about the invoice submitted for a copy of the taperecording of the previous meeting. This exchange was followed by a number of technical arguments about road levels where the new route would cross the Blackpool road.

There was vociferous opposition to the road proposals and this view was supported by a vigorous speech by the Member of Parliament for the area, Mr Stan Thorne. He attacked the CLDC for not allowing enough time for local objectors 'to muster their arguments'. It seemed to him that a lot of the trouble that they now faced stemmed from the fact that the consultation with the people of Preston had begun now instead of in 1969 when the original (i.e. designation) public inquiry had been held. He announced that he would be speaking in an adjournment debate in the House of Commons specifically to bring to the attention of the Secretary of State for the Environment the fears and objections local people had to the CLDC proposals. The Secretary of State had already expressed concern to him about the information local people had been able to obtain so far about the new town and its effects. He would ask the Secretary of State to postpone the date of the public inquiry at present due to be heard on 17 September 1974.

In many ways this meeting, held before a capacity audience of some 400 residents, marked the climax of the 'public participation' exercise. The road system had proved to be the emotive issue, and by affecting populous inner areas of Preston it carried greater numerical popular support than the earlier campaigns in the less populated areas of Grimsargh and Walton summit. The organising committees of PNAG and AAG had also largely convinced the members of parliament for their respective constituencies of their case, and they had agreed to speak on the action groups' behalf. The MPs, with their oratorical skills and prestige, gave the meetings a sense of occasion and were attractive to the local press as news items. Indeed, Mr Atkins became a committee member of PNAG, while performing the rare dual role of borough councillor and MP representing the area covered by PNAG.

iv) Preston Borough Council's official policy

The series of outline plan meetings which followed were, in general, far less emotionally charged and attracted fewer people. On the eve of these meetings it was made clear that, despite the views of individual councillors, the official policy of Preston council was to support the concept of the new town. This stance was underlined at a meeting of the policy and resources committee 'when the leaders of both major political groups stressed the town stood more to gain by being in than by opting out of the new development' (LEP, 20 June 1974). Revealing the somewhat negative reasons for the endorsement of Preston's incorporation into the designated area, the chief executive, Mr Harry Heap, was reported as stating that the old county borough (of Preston)

> .... had supported the new town originally because if the new town had only covered Leyland and Chorley, Preston would have been in great danger of having all the disadvantages of a new town on the doorstep and none of the benefits. (LEP, 20 June 1974)

Preston would be 'even greater losers' if they tried to withdraw, and as long as their criticisms were informed and constructive they could restate their support for the new town. In a further significant remark, suggesting the existence of inter local authority tensions, Mr Heap was reported as commenting that they had to bear in mind that there were two other partners in the designated area - South Ribble and Chorley - and while he hoped relations with them would be harmonious it would be wrong to conclude that they would never disagree among themselves. Rather sharply, he continued, 'we already have the position of the one in the middle (South Ribble) thinking it should be directing operations'. It is ironical, bearing in mind how Preston lobbied to be added to the Chorley and Leyland area, that he was reported as concluding

> .... we have to make it clear that not only are we in a position where we take a leading line, but a leading role as our present size and position determines in conversations on the new town. (my emphasis) (LEP, 20 June 1974)

Such an attitude is reminiscent of the watchful, even envious Prestonian eye cast upon the rival Mersey belt as a result of the priorities proposed by SPNW.

The contents of the meetings

The first of the outline plan meetings was held in Penwortham, an area south of Preston which, apart from the Cop Lane development and an improved district centre, had little marked change envisaged for it. The meeting, before a small audience of some 45-50, followed a pattern which was to become standard for the following eleven. It commenced by Mr Phelps introducing himself in a short formal statement which referred to the powers contained in the 1965 New Towns Act, the requirements of the secretary of state for consultation and the objection procedures. The outline plan itself was described with reference to a large sketchmap by Mr Colin Beck. He stated that the development corporation had its terms of reference set by government and this mandate was basically to improve prosperity, and accommodate growth. The task was to 'generate prosperity on a sub regional scale using the New Towns Act'. Within the designated boundary containing 35,000 acres the population would grow to 420,000 by 2001. The area had a broad economic base; there would be a plan of dispersed growth with a wide range of choice. The new town was 'not propped up' by special development area status and had to rely on the free market using relatively low densities and the advantage of varied locations. Admitting that one could never be certain about the future, he stressed that flexibility was the key, but that there would be firm proposals up to 1986 with room to manoeuvre afterwards.

77,000 houses would be built over the planned period, doubling the current building rate. This expansion would include developing existing communities. Houses would be constructed at a density of between nine and twelve dwellings per acre. 80,000 new jobs would be created by the end of the plan period - '25,000 in and around existing town centres, 35,000 in new employment and 20,000 dispersed'.

Describing the hierarchy of shopping facilities, Mr Beck outlined the provision of local shops in the village centres and larger shops for convenience goods in the district centres and stressed that policy was to resist major proposals for new shopping centres with hypermarkets. As far as the transport system was concerned, he believed that motorways should not be used by local traffic - 'the time to pop on and off motorways is coming to an end'. The system of roadways would be as attractive for in town traffic. In his view public transport was best served by the bus, which was more flexible than the railways. Proposals for motorway intersections were beyond the development corporation's control.

Mr Beck cited York as an example of the exploitation of a river for recreation and leisure, and he pointed to the potential of the Ribble valley. There were many play areas in the plan and major tree belts would be planted.

Finally, he summarised that provision would be made for the population growth primarily in Grimsargh, which would grow by 20,000 in 1986 and to a final population of 52,000 in 2001, Preston would marginally increase from its present 123,000 population to 130,000, Leyland would increase by 20,000 by 1986 and although Chorley itself would remain steady, the Whittle/Clayton area would grow from about 7,000 to 23,000. Of the five townships - Grimsargh,Preston, Walton, Leyland and Chorley - he would look at the proposals for Walton township. (Penwortham, the location of the meeting, fell within its boundary). The planning policies for Walton were modest in population growth and in facilities. The developments, he insisted, would have been expected in this area anyway without the new town. There would be three new river crossings and highway congestion would be relieved. The expansion of the area was 'nothing terribly remarkable' and the aim was to reinforce the five existing centres within it. (These were Penwortham, King's Fold, Lostock Hall, Bamber Bridge and Walton-le-Dale.)

Prior to opening the meeting to questions the recording of the proceedings was mentioned. Initially this activity had been done at earlier meetings,somewhat surreptitiously, by a local recording agency, and on one occasion at the meeting on 6 June 1974 to discuss the Whittle district centre a proposition 'to wipe the tape clear' was defeated. It appears that the recent clandestine presence of the recording equipment was seen to cause some resentment and at later meetings an announcement about this arrangement was made following the formal statement. This more open approach proved to be more acceptable to those attending the meetings.

The procedure at the meetings

With minor modifications, arrangements at the subsequent meetings followed the pattern just described. The question time provided an opportunity for local and personal matters of concern to be aired and a response made by the CLDC officers present. The team normally consisted of Mr Phelps, Mr Cudworth (chief legal and liaison officer) who dealt with any legal matters such as compensation, Mr Garside, chief engineer, who was concerned with transport and Mr Colin Beck (and later, on occasions, his successor as chief planner, Mr Desmond Procter) who responded to general planning matters. In addition, various junior members of the CLDC staff might be present and, on one occasion only, was the Lancashire county council to make its presence felt, when at Penwortham, Mr Jeffrey Rowbottom, chief planner and a local resident, made a statement to the meeting in support of CLNT.

The questions and resulting discussions were wide ranging in content and often lengthy, many meetings lasting between two and two and a half hours. Despite the earlier and separate series of meetings already described on the transport network, an analysis of fieldwork notes shows that the issue of transport was raised as a substantive issue at some eleven of the twelve meetings. This concern with transport varied from meetings which were more interested in providing the necessary roads before housing development took place, such as Penwortham, to those which were vehemently against their area being 'used' to the benefit of those travelling between new growth points, the motorway network, and the centre of Preston. At the Ribbleton Avenue meetings (27 June 1974), for example, this concern dominated the discussion and it was an important element at Fulwood (24 June 1974), Ingol (8 July 1974), but less so at other meetings.

THE TRANSPORT NETWORK PUBLIC MEETINGS

There was an additional outlet for technical discussion on transport, when as an admitted response to pressure from Planwatch's planning adviser, a report 'The transport network in the outline plan' was produced, and made available to the public. This document was advertised together with an associated public meeting in Leyland, on 1 July 1974, when the justification for this report was the 'great interest shown in the transport policies in the OUTLINE PLAN' at recent public meetings. This special meeting, which was publicised as one which discussion would be 'linked to these policies', was held at Leyland Methodist church hall on 15 July 1974.

Consistent with previous practice, priority was given to those who already applied for tickets. 134 tickets, it is understood, were requested and 53 persons eventually attended the meeting, 19 of whom were officers of either CLDC or the local authorities. In his introductory remarks Mr Phelps stated that the meeting should focus upon three documents, Chapter 17 of the outline plan, the road appraisal reports and the background document into which the public inquiry was not being held, the transport network in the outline plan. Commenting on the invitation to officers of other local authorities, he made the point that they were there as 'observers rather than participants', a comment borne out by an early question which was directed at the Lancashire county planners by John Hagarty, chairman of Planwatch. Were they prepared to do anything? he asked, to which the reply was that they could not give any views. At this point the general manager was observed by the writer to appear distinctly uncomfortable. One woman also claimed that at none of the public meetings were there representatives of the county council whom they could question.

This point highlights the difficulty of attempting to restrict the agenda to items for which the development corporation had direct responsibility. In many instances, questions on the provision of social services and education were parried and reference was made to the county council's functions. This confusion was particularly marked in the sphere of transportation. Lancashire county council, as the transport authority, was from 1974 required to prepare a transport policies and programme (TPP) every year to provide a basis for grant bids and loan sanctions from the department of the environment. It therefore follows that proposals by the development corporation should be congruent with both the transportation authority's policies for public transport and with the north west road construction unit for motorways and major roads. It was stated that the county council representatives were not prepared to talk since it would be 'wrong to anticipate the TPP'.

The imaginative use of busways in the nearby Runcorn new town also tended to raise expectations of innovatory transportation proposals in other new towns. Questions from representatives of the residents' groups were naturally most concerned about the impact of roads, but they also joined forces with those, such as Transport 2000, who were interested in the wider aspects of traffic management, bus priority lanes and light rapid transport systems. Mr Don Fifer, chairman of Transport 2000 N.W., together with representatives of the Ashton action group, questioned Mr Garside relentlessly about the possible use of railways as the 'primary mode'. There was also some disputation as to the relative importance of public to private transport. This 'modal split', it was alleged, was weighted too much in favour of private transport and therefore of road building. Alan Howard, for example, alleged that the new town dared not show a bias towards public transport 'because it would not attract the right type of people'. To which Mr Garside retorted that this premise was false, since even with maximum private transport, they would still have 'a public transport town'. He would not accept that they were biassed. 'The future will be monitored and policy changes will be in operation.'

Citing the parking provision for 600 cars at the Whittle centre, John Hagarty stated that this figure was not central to transportation policy since this estimate was the ultimate provision for the whole centre. This proposal was the new town 'hedging its bets' and was expensive. Colin Beck, in reply, asserted that this policy was 'trying to cater for a whole range of futures into the 1980s and 90s'. There needed to be a great degree of latitude since the future was unknown. The plans would 'suit both extremes, suit the problems here now and make up lost time'. He believed that they were realistic extremes.

These arguments are rooted in alternative views of transportation policy based upon laissez-faire attitudes towards economic development or a comprehensive planning approach; or alternatively a left of centre concern with the non car owner and residents in poorer, ageing housing, contrasting with an individualistic view of serving and matching forecast trends and the underlying requirement to market the new town in the face of intense competition from other developments. Such disagreements were to become a dominant theme in the public inquiry described in Chapter 12.

SUMMARY

This chapter has described in some detail a number of public meetings organised by the development corporation and the resulting interaction between officials and the public. Some reference has been made to events occurring during this period, further land banking at Ingol, Professor Grenfell-Baines' press intervention and a statement of Preston borough council's policy towards the new town, all of which may be viewed as of possible significance. Major national, regional and local factors which were concurrent into the participation process will be described in Chapter 11.

NOTES

1. For example, from 1966 to 1976 Liverpool Council for Voluntary Service provided the secretariat for a neighbourhood organisations committee which, among other things, reacted to inner city partnership project proposals.

11 Exogenous factors to the participation process

SIGNIFICANT EVENTS CONCURRENT WITH THE PUBLIC MEETINGS

INTRODUCTION

During the period of public participation in central Lancashire a number of national, regional and local events and issued occurred which had an influence upon social attitudes and commitment. In this first section of the chapter a series of factors are described, government policy on rented accommodation, developments in the Ingol area of Preston, a meeting of the Ashton action group at Cuerdon and an adjournment debate in the House of Commons on 4 July 1974, prompted by the MP for Preston south, Mr S. Thorne. In later sections of the chapter major developments in amenity group activity within Fulwood/Broughton and Grimsargh and the campaign for the delay in holding the outline plan public inquiry are described together with the publication of a supplement to this outline plan. The October 1974 general election had an impact upon the politics of the new town and is described in some detail. Finally, to place the participation process in context, the overt policy statements of the main local authorities have been summarised.

Government policy on rented accommodation

The political support for the new town, indicated by both interviews and documentary evidence, is very much linked with the anticipated voting behaviour of the new residents. Much Conservative antipathy towards the project was assuaged by the decision to provide for a significant proportion of owner-occupied dwellings within the development. The outline plan was suitably vague on the pattern of tenure on the basis of the uncertain

> .... forecasts of the purchasing power of our new population and the corresponding extent to which they will need houses to rent or will be able to afford to buy. (CLDC, 1974,p.96)

The working assumption by early 1974 was that the ratio of privately owned to publicly rented would be 50;50. The Chorley Guardian, however, had received information about a likely change in government policy. On 20 June 1974 under the headline 'Renting shock' they disclosed that:

> .... Environment Secretary, Mr Anthony Crosland intends to instruct new town development corporations to build 75

per cent of their new houses for renting.

.... This is expected to anger planners at the Central Lancashire new town development corporation who have been reckoning on a 50:50 split.

This revelation activated the prospective Conservative candidate for the marginal constituency of Chorley, Mr Barry Porter, to write to the Chorley Guardian to express his concern at the reported change.

.... If this instruction is actually given the whole concept of the central Lancashire new town will be changed. In all my talks to the people and representatives of those areas which are to be affected by the new town, I have always had a reaction that they were reasonably satisfied with the proposed fifty fifty split between private ownership and rented accommodation. Almost everybody has said what they did not want was a development which bore resemblance to a new town like Skelmersdale. If this instruction is given it would mean, in my view, that the danger would be very real. (CG, 27 June 1974)

This concern was strongly supported by one of the idiosyncratic leading articles written by the managing editor of the Chorley Guardian in the same edition. Somewhat sensationally he contended:

.... The ill fated central Lancashire new town is on the brink of disaster. That is the inevitable conclusion to be drawn from reports that environment secretary, Arthur Crosland (sic), is minded to reverse the existing housing policy so that 75 per cent of the houses will be let and only 25 per cent for sale.

It is of course easy for Labour to adopt such a course. Almost everything they do is for votes and the political tendency is for council tenants to vote Labour, it is said.

The social class, and therefore the electoral implications, of either a predominantly rented or owner-occupied series of housing schemes was observed to be a central component of the attitude towards the new town by many politically aware residents. The three constituencies which encompass the major part of the designated area were all regarded at that time as marginal constituencies with a tendency to change their political allegiaances in line with the party forming the government. Any significant shift in the socio economic composition of the constituencies could be electorally damaging or beneficial to one of the major parties. The awareness of this situation and the possible effects on existing property values of new extensive rented estates prompted an interest and questions at the public meetings which otherwise might have been less marked.

The Ingol exhibition and the 6(i) application

On 21 June 1974, the day on which the second of the outline plan public meetings was to take place, a public notice advertising an exhibition and an associated meeting in Ingol, north west of Preston, was published in the Lancashire Evening Post. Another instance of the complexity of events and the relentless implementation strategy of CLDC, the Ingol east 6(i) application was proposed as an initial stage towards developing a post war Preston suburb into a small town of about 20,000 population. The 432 acre scheme which involved about a third of the envisaged complete township consisted of a comprehensive housing development of 2,000 units arranged around 18-hole golf course set around the wooded valley of the Sharoe Brook.

The public meeting was advertised further in the press on 24 June 1974, but publicity for this occasion was unofficially assisted by the distribution of leaflets locally by two Planwatch activists. The procedure for admission by tickets was omitted and the meeting in St Margaret's church hall was well attended by about 70 people. The meeting, chaired by the general manager, dealt in a broader way with the area plan for Ingol, within which the Ingol east 6(i) formed an initial phase. The area layout was described by Mr Procter, who by now had replaced Mr Colin Beck as the chief planner. The importance of a range of house styles was stressed and the provision of two 2-form entry schools and two village centres was outlined. Above all, the central feature was the integration of the golf course, open space and housing. The development, it was explained, would be implemented as quickly as possible, initially in the south east of the area and moving in a clockwise direction, taking a five or six year period of growth to complete.

The early questions focussed upon the dominant feature of the golf course within the development and in the new town generally. It was pointed out that although golf was a minority sport, it was a growing one and the provision proposed reflected the advice received from the sports council and consultants. The reason why other sports and amenities were omitted was that these facilities would be incorporated in the local plans, whereas it was important at the outline plan stage to show golf courses as they were significant users of land. This reply did not satisfy the chairman of Preston Borough Council's leisure and amenities committee, Councillor Harold Parker, who complained that the corporation (CLDC) had put too much emphasis on golf courses in the outline plan and asserted that he was sure that the sports council would have recommended more than four football pitches in Ingol. In reply the legal and liaison officer, Mr Cudworth, explained that there was provision for seven more football pitches in the scheme if Preston council were to buy the land involved.

This concern with golf courses and football facilities may be interpreted as a thinly disguised articulation of the cultural priorities associated with different class interests. The development corporation requiring to rely upon the natural attractiveness of the area rather than the direction of population through overspill agreements, was intent upon creating the lure of a 'golf course habitat' for its more prestigious initial developments intended for purchase by management and professional clients. Those attending the Ingol public meeting understandably were intent on expressing likely disadvantages to those already resident in the area by such developments rather than the undoubted attractions to be created for the 'incomers'.

Disadvantages expressed included the impact upon the existing footpath network and the implications for pedestrian safety from golf balls. This feat was discounted by the development corporation whose spokesman assured the meeting that, although the golf course was in the residential development, it would not be too close to it. In any case they were being advised by experts who were conversant with new courses which had been designed in this way in the United States and Australia which had proved highly satisfactory. The final probe into the golf issue was

CENTRAL LANCASHIRE NEW TOWN

PUBLIC MEETING AND EXHIBITION

INGOL - proposed residential and associated development

There will be a Public Meeting in St Margaret's Church Hall, Tag Lane, Ingol, at 7.30 p.m. on

FRIDAY, JUNE 28th, 1974

for an explanation and discussion of proposals for residential and associated development at Ingol.

The proposals will be on display in St Margaret's Church Hall from Friday, June 21st to Friday, June 28th at the following times:-

Friday, June 21st	10 am to 7 pm
Saturday, June 22nd	10 am to 7 pm
Monday, Tuesday and Wednesday, June 24th, 25th, 26th	10 am to 1 pm
Thursday, June 27th	10 am to 6 pm
Friday, June 28th	10 am to 1 pm

R.W. PHELPS

General Manager

Central Lancashire Development Corporation,
Cuerden Pavilion,
Bamber Bridge,
PRESTON PR5 6AZ.

Lancashire Evening Post 24 June, 1974

made by Councillor Bunker who sought to discover who would benefit from such a proposal. He was concerned that 'the new golf course, club house and squash courts would be a gold mine for some private owner, charging exclusive entrance fees and keeping local residents out'.

It was predictable, however, that such a meeting, although focussed upon a specific part of the designated area, should return to a number of issues which dominated the generals eries of public meetings. The need for the roads to service this area, their width and intrusiveness upon the older Preston communities, the density and renting/private mix of the housing, the provision of services such as shops, schools, and transport were all topics to be aired in a lively exchange of views, described by Roger Beam as ' a barrage of questions from angry Ingol residents and Preston councillors' (LEP, 1 July 1974). Although, initially, the Ingol operation might be viewed entirely as an indication of the determination of CLDC to implement as many of its schemes as far as possible prior to the full approval of the outline plan, it did serve as an extra public meeting on the outline plan since wider issues were discussed. It also served to alert the opposition to CLDC to the north of Preston and to stimulate the eventual formation of the Fulwood and Broughton residents' association (FABRA).

The Ashton Action Group at Cuerden

The vociferous opposition to the road proposals through the Ashton-on-Ribble area of Preston was articulated by the Ashton action group. The public meetings promoted by the development corporation and held within this district had been well attended and prepared for by the officers and their 'core activists', the so called 'forty thieves'. In response to this activity and prompting, the chairman of CLDC, Sir Frank Pearson, suggested that a private meeting be held between members of the group and senior officers of the corporation (LEP, 22 June 1974). This took place at CLDC headquarters, Cuerden Pavilion on 2 July 1974.

It became common practice on such occasions that many of the groups made it plain that they were not opposed to the concept of the new town as such, but details of its proposals. Ashton action group, through its chairman, Arthur Jones, professed such an attitude. This stance was based on the view by some that much new town planning would be superior to the standards exhibited by the existing local authorities, but above all, as an acknowledgement of reality of the new town designation and as means of gaining some credibility with the CLDC staff in a disparate negotiating situation.

This unevenness of power relationship is shown by the records of such meetings, where information sought is either diverted to other authorities, or subject to prevarication of many of the exchanges.

The adjournment debate initiated by Mr Stan Thorne, MP

Much of the activity of the Ashton action group was relayed to the Member of Parliament for the area, Mr Stan Thorne, and he had publicly stated his trenchant views on aspects of the CLDC's policies. He took the opportunity to initiate an adjournment debate on 4 July 1974 to voice his concern about the lack of opportunities for public consultation and siscussion. He contended that when people looked at what had been produced by the central Lancashire development corporation, they were very much in the position of being told the planners knew best.

Introducing his theme, Mr Thorne said that the north west was an area that had a denser population than any other part of the country, because of this factor, land was of vital importance and its use should be planned. In June 1972, the then Under Secretary for the Environment had said that ample opportunity would be given to the public for discussion of the eventual plan for the new town.

Drawing the House's attention to his allegation of lack of consultation, Mr Thorne said:

> .... In order to obtain a consensus within a large area about what is of value, a whole range of organisations and institutions must be consulted. I am certain that the central Lancashire development corporation has sought consultation with the Chamber of Commerce in Preston, Chorley and so on. Other organisations will have been embraced, but the list of organisations that have certainly not been consulted is immense. The trade unions within the whole of this area have not been consulted, nor have the trades councils, voluntary organisations, residents' associations, the women's voluntary service or the family service unit. All these are organisations that are vitally concerned with the social and economic structure that exists in the area.
>
> What I am concerned with is consultation with people about the nature of the housing developments that will take place. The whole question of roads has presented already immense problems to the community because whilst the concept of the new town goes back to 1969, and the board was set up in 1972, the actual consultation taking place is minimal in the extreme.

He went on to point out that

> .... People were asking if roads were the only means of transport the corporation considered viable.

He was aware that the Skeffington report had recommended that people ought to get information throughout the preparation of a plan and that representations were to be considered continuously while the plans were being prepared. 'Unhappily, these recommendations have not been implemented in the central Lancashire new town area.'

Foreshadowing the later campaign for the postponement of the public inquiry from the date of 17 September 1974, Mr Thorne pointed out that there was considerable pressure for a delay in the timing of the inquiry since 'it gives an inadequate time for the people of Preston to make their objection to a plan that they have not had the opportunity of participating in the preparation of'. (<u>LEP</u>, 5 July 1974 - later editions). In the debate, Mr Thorne was supported by Mr Ron Atkins, Labour MP for Preston North, who criticised the road proposals, and Mr George Rodgers, Labour MP for Chorley, who disapproved of the membership of the board of the development corporation.

In reply, Mr John Silkin, Minister for Planning and Local Government, did not hold any strong promise of a chance of a change of date for the inquiry but promised an investigation ...

> .... At the moment, I am not thinking in terms of deferring the date, but in view of the representations, I will look at the matter during the course of next week. If I come to the

conclusion there really is a case for deferring the inquiry, I will do so.

In the event, the delay was granted, following a campaign described later in this chapter, and the outline plan inquiry did not commence until 5 November 1974. With the existing approvals under Section 6(i), their spokesman conceded that such a minimal delay did not inconvenience CLDC greatly (personal interview) but the few extra weeks were to provide valuable extra time for the preparation of evidence by the action groups.

Developments in Fulwood/Broughton and Grimsargh

Reference has already been made to the formation of the main Preston residents' groups, which took place prior to the outline plan public meetings. Consequent upon the meetings, however, was the rather later development of the Fulwood and Broughton residents' association and the resuscitation of the Grimsargh and Haighton action committee. Evidence of this galvanising to action of certain key individuals at this time is a long, well displayed letter to the Lancashire Evening Post on 5 July 1974 by Mrs Sylvia Pickering. The interpretation of the information gained through the outline plan meetings and associated publicity was employed by her to draw attention to the likely impact of the road proposals in areas of Preston, not covered by the PNAG or AAG. These were mainly in Fulwood and Broughton to the north of the town.

The main focus of concern was the extension of the western primary road from the new township of Ingol to link with the proposed employment area at Midgery Lane, and the difficulties likely to occur at the junction with the A6 road. The letter states:

> .... This issue is a local one like the Haslam Park road, but it relates to the traffic concept of the New Town as a whole, and those of us who do not like it may well be moved to look further into the Outline Plan, and be disturbed by what is happening to other areas.
>
> The opportunity to find out more about the plan as a whole is still here, as Outline Plan meetings are taking place at Roper Hall, Friargate, on July 11th and 16th at 7.30 p.m.
>
> Even if we are not interested in the fate of the threatened communities of Ingol and Grimsargh which are being devoured by the developers, we ought surely to concern ourselves about Preston as a whole and to find out as much as we can before it is too late to present one's objections - the closing date for this is July 30th 1974! ...

She continued:

> Any action has got to be taken in the next two weeks because the Public Inquiry, starting on September 17th will consider only objections to the Outline Plan, which has been in circulation for some time, and most areas have not had their detailed plans explained to them yet because, we are told, they are not yet ready.
>
> No further public inquiries are at present being visualised, and the quality of communication between the Development Corporation and the public as so far manifested leads one

> to be pessimistic about the value of the future consultations promised to us.

Corroboration of Sylvia Pickering's emerging role with the action groups is given in her penultimate paragraph:

> .... Anyone wishing to find out more about how the New Town will affect life in the Fulwood and Broughton areas is welcome to write to me personally. I have contacts with the Ashton Action Group, the Preston North Action Group and Planwatch, and am hoping to have some material to show to the public tomorrow at Broughton C.E. School's fete, in the old school.

Following this letter and the response to it, it was possible to organise the information of the Fulwood and Broughton residents' association. The first major task of the informal grouping had been to ask the development corporation to hold an additional public meeting in a venue more centrally placed within north Fulwood. This event was advertised in the Lancashire Evening Post on 13 July 1974, without the ticket requirement and took place on 22 July with an attendance of nearly 200. Following a lively meeting, during which 'New Town Chiefs fail in bid to reassure public' (LEP, 23 July 1974), the steering committee was in a position to hold its own inaugural public meeting the following Thursday, 25 July 1974, elect its committee and commence its activities formally.

Simultaneous with the announcement of the additional Fulwood meeting was the advertisement stating that there was a 'notice board displaying' the proposals for residential and associated development for Grimsargh village. This display was to be followed by a public meeting to be held on Friday, 19 July at 7.00 p.m. This meeting took place in a very full Our Lady and St Michael's church hall in Grimsargh. Although primarily attended by local residents, as with the Ingol meeting, it did attract a number of Preston councillors and members of nearby action groups. It proved to be one of the most hostile and aggressive of the series. Early in the proceedings Councillor Tony Parker, the local ward member on Preston council at that time, articulated the reason why Grimsargh was to be the only area to be unequivocably anti new town. They had been listening to the proposals for fifteen years and at the time of designation they had fought desparately to stay out of the new town and "even with 80 per cent of the village against the new town we lost. We were 'steamrolled'". Now he insisted, 'we want some say in the future of the village in which we live'. He was concerned with how the village developed and the council should not be fed 'a morsel at a time'. Amid applause, he asserted that proposals for four storey dwellings had been 'thrown in to knock off again'. If they remained, he warned that the 80 per cent opposition to the 'high density estates' was the fear of admitting 'undesirables' to the village as a 'ghetto for Preston'. When pressed about the possible vetting of tenants by the corporation, Mr Phelps states that 'the development corporation cannot exclude members of the community'.

Consistent with other areas and residents' groups, the reasoned arguments for the new town had been accepted by some. Such an attitude was represented by Dr Douglas Watt, who, during the meeting admitted that he had been one of the supporters of the new town, since he regarded planned development to be better than haphazard development. The corporation, he alleged, had 'squandered goodwill' by its 'cynical disregard' of their views. as an example he cited that the parish council had only been told about plans after they had been sent to the secretary of state, and there had been a great deal of delay and prevarication over the site for a new village hall. Such statements from respected members of the village community could only assist the recreation of a consensus against, not only the new town itself, but the officers representing its policies and attitudes to local opinion. This orientation was reinforced at the climax of the two hour forty minute meeting when a local doctor accused the general manager, amid uproar, as being 'as slippery as a wet orange pip!'.

Such an occasion provided the stimulation and encouragementfor the revitalised Grimsargh and Haighton action committee under the chairmanship of Mr Ray Johnson and for the eventual formation of the anti new town alliance under the title SCRAP. (The Society for the Confirmation and Reaffirmation of Anti New Town Policies).

THE CAMPAIGN FOR THE DELAY IN THE COMMENCEMENT OF THE PUBLIC INQUIRY

Planwatch, at this time the only active group with an overall interest in the new town, decided to bring together all known groups in order to coordinate their various approaches and to avoid contradictions in their cases to the public inquiry. This meeting held at the Bridge Inn, Penwortham on 17 July 1974, succeeded in convening a total of eleven groups of very diverse objectives and prejudices. While on many topics and attitudes tension was observed , particularly over the acceptance by many of the new town principle, there was one problem which emerged as common to all groups. This difficulty was a concern about the lack of time in which to prepare detailed evidence for the public inquiry due to commence on 17 September 1974.

In a press statement issued following the meeting, John Hagarty, chairman of Planwatch, summed up their views as follows:

> .... There was a very strong feeling that the development corporation and their consultants had had three years in which to prepare their case, yet we're only left with three months. When you realise that members of the various groups all have separate livings to earn, there is much less than three months available to us. The representatives felt a clear need for a delayed start to the inquiry, and urged everyone to write to the minister, Mr John Silkin, asking for a postponement of the date. Some groups have already done this. Others would now do so. (LEP, 19 July 1974, Leyland edition only)

This initiative was given further impetus by the action of the members of parliament for Preston North and South, and Chorley. They formed a deputation to visit the Parliamentary Under Secretary of the Environment Mr Gordon Oakes on 24 July 1974. At this meeting they were disclosed to have sought 'a major postponement in the inquiry so that local objectors to the development plan could have more time to develop their case'.

Mr. Oakes was reported to have pointed out that 'if the date date was changed, there could be difficulties in finding a top official who was available to take the inquiry'. (LEP, 25 July 1974). He apparently stated that he was anxious to avoid delay but after what the press report described as a 'forceful exchange of views' and described by Mr Rodgers himself as 'a long and at times ferocious discussion', (LG, 1 August 1974). It was understood that Mr Oakes had promised to investigate but had insisted that the inquiry should be held before the end of December 1974.

Two days after the deputation, Mr Oakes announced in the commons that the public inquiry into the outline plan would now commence on 5 November 1974, a postponement of some seven weeks. It was made plain, however, in the correspondence to the three MPs that the deferment had only been made with 'some reluctance' and that this had involved 'some considerable rearrangement' of the department of the environment's inspector's programmes. Under no circumstances would he consider any further postponement of this inquiry. The decision was met with approval by both the MPs and the chairman of Planwatch, who pointed out that three months - with a holiday in the middle - had not been sufficient for people to prepare their evidence. 'Now it gives them time to do a proper job. I think the three MPs have done very well for us.' (LEP, 26 July 1974).

A SUPPLEMENT TO THE OUTLINE PLAN

On 31 July 1974, CLDC puplished a supplement to the outline plan which listed the major points raised by the public at meetings and in correspondence and gave replies to some of them. (This document could be regarded as a brief form of reactions report which may be found in structure plan procedures.)

The corporation stressed that, in publishing this commentary, it had in no way amended the outline plan as published, and submitted to the Secretary of State on 3 June 1974. The public inquiry would be concerned with the plan and the road appraisal reports as submitted and it would be for the Secretary of State to consider any changes when he considered his inspector's report on the evidence submitted at the inquiry.

Ten points of general public concern and four local ones were listed; some of which were answered and others noted. For purposes of information the main contents have been summarised in an extended footnote. (1)

FURTHER PROPOSALS UNDER SECTION 6(i) NEW TOWNS ACT

On the date originally intended for the outline plan public inquiry, 17 September 1974, notice was given that two proposals for development under Section 6(i) New Towns Act 1965 would be subjected to a public local inquiry at the Leyland civic hall. The postponement of the outline plan public inquiry, it seemed, was not going to prevent further progress of key advance schemes. The two to be scrutinised were the Leyland Moss Side residential development, which consisted of about 57 hectares (142 acres) and the district centre and community school at Whittle-le-Woods of about 24 hectares (60 acres).

These schemes were to be criticised by the Moss Side residents association and commented upon by the Clayton-le-Woods parish council respectively. Moss Side residents had a small effective committee and submitted a well produced case setting out their requirements which would make the development 'more acceptable'. This submission included a stipulation that there should be no housing more than two storeys high, similar densities for rented and private housing with only 50 per cent of the total housing for renting, and the provision of more green space and play areas together with a larger community centre.

Councillor John Livesey of the Clayton-le-Woods parish council presented their case before the inspector, Mr J.B.S. Dahl. He asked that the 6(i) application should only be confirmed when the outline plan transportation network had been resolved and sought essential safeguards, such matters as the height and general design of buildings, and the preservation of trees, ponds and hedgerows.

Other Section 6(i) proposals and decisions were also being made during September 1974. The secretary of state confirmed without modification a compulsory purchase order for land at Cop Lane, Penwortham and a further 6(i) application was made for development of land for a tree nursery at Charnock Richard.

These decisions were made public on 26 September 1974, the day on which the main local authority protagonist, the Greater Manchester Council, announced its intention to object to the speed with which plans were going ahead for the CLNT. This disagreement was justified since it believed that the programme would have a detrimental effect on the towns within its county. (Daily Telegraph, 26 September 1974). The following day the Secretary of State gave his permission for the first housing scheme in Penwortham - on the Cop Lane site - but stipulated that this should be in phase with road construction requirements for the area. This decision was essentially a compromise verdict, for both the Lancashire County Council and the South Ribble Borough Council had pointed out that an early start without the road building required would create traffic problems. This action was one of the last major decisions on the new town before the general election campaign in October 1974, but by this time the development corporation had already committed expenditure on capital projects of more than £17 million (See LEP, 17 October 1974).

THE GENERAL ELECTION, OCTOBER 1974

The new town had not been a significant local issue in the February 1974 election, but this position was to change by October. By this time the new Labour Members of Parliament for Preston North and South and Chorley had become involved in representations on the new town. The Preston MPs, in particular, had become closely identified with action groups in their constituencies. By far the most significant factors in bringing the new town to a central position in the campaign were the intervention of SCRAP, the uncompromising anti new town position taken by the Conservative for Chorley, Mr Barry Porter, and the views expressed on the Strategic Plan for the North West.

There had been evidence of tension between the leading members of the residents' and planning groups. The 'Skeffington - idealists', from such groups as Planwatch, tended to be in favour of the new town concept, and many of the members of action groups based on an area 'under threat' ('the local protestors') were either indifferent to the concept or wished to keep the topic covert in order to maintain unity of purpose. The greatest concentration of anti new town feeling was evidenced in the Grimsargh area and in the leaders of the Walton Summit protest committee. By the second meeting on 8 August 1974, the attempt to coordinate all shades of opinion by Planwatch was faltering. Following public meetings in Grimsargh and Whittle-le-Woods on 16 and 19 August 1974, the ground was ready for the formation of an organisation committed to the demise of the new town completely.

At the Whittle-le-Woods meeting, Ray Johnson attended from the Grimsargh action group. He advocated the need to fight the total concept of the new town, to oppose the 'early development programme' (that is schemes promoted under the new town act Section 6(i)) and called for an organisation to promote the anti new town point of view. Local councillors and MPs were alleged to be misrepresenting the people if not reflecting public opposition to the new town. The press report of the meeting, under the sub heading 'Votes' quoted Mr Johnson as saying, 'They have got to realise that they cannot rely on our votes in the future. I feel now is the time we have got to stand and fight'. The threat was made more explicit by Mr Jim Pilkington who was reported as saying:

> .... If we fielded independent anti new town candidates then our voice would be heard. That would put the cat among the pigeons and even if we lost it's the number of votes that we would get which would be the important thing. (LEP, 20 August 1974).

The threat of 'nuisance candidates' in the three highly marginal constituencies was not repeated in the press statement formally announcing the intention of launching SCRAP and the holding of a public meeting in Preston 'to extend the idea to other groups and individuals'. (LEP, 26 August 1974). By the time the public meeting was held the proposal to the meeting was to have one candidate to get publicity particularly through the use of the free mail to each voter, but press reports added that 'if enough money can be raised to fight three seats, then Preston south, Preston north and Chorley will probably be chosen'. (LEP, 5 September 1974).

SCRAP met with a cautious response from the other action groups, many of whom had a greater affinity with the 'Skeffington idealists' of Planwatch and, in the event, only six people of the sixty or so present voted in favour of the idea of a candidate.

SCRAP met with a further rebuff when Mr Ron Atkins, MP, speaking at a FABRA public meeting on 12 September 1974, urged the meeting not to oppose the concept of the new town when they lodged their objections at the public inquiry. The chairman of PNAG, councillor Dick Evans, confirmed that the group would focus its attacks upon the roads and it was left to the chairman of FABRA to state that the association would be working with 'Mr Johnson's Organisation', SCRAP - a statement he was later to retract.

In the event, the proposal was not pursued and in a letter to the Lancashire Evening Post, the SCRAP treasurer stated that the idea had been rejected 'because it would cost too much'. The exercise had, however, contributed to the public's awareness of the issue during the period prior to the October election.

This was particularly focussed upon the Chorley constituency, an area including Leyland, which, ironically was to suffer least from the road proposals. Mr Barry Porter, the prospective Conservative candidate, in a letter to the Chorley Guardian, stated his attitude firmly when he stated:

.... Nobody has yet convinced me that the new town development corporation has done anything save to spend an enormous amount of public money and loose planning blight throughout the area. (CG, 8 August 1974).

His contention was that the existing county and district council planning departments had 'sufficient power to regulate growth'. He followed this with a statement that he would 'campaign for the abolishment (sic) of the central Lancashire new town development corporation in his manifesto for the next election unless someone convinced him that the corporation is necessary'. (Guardian, 19 August 1974).

The prospective Liberal candidate for Chorley, Neva Orrell, called for 'drastic modifications' in the proposals and greater accountability of the CLDC to the local community through its elected representatives. Greater stress, she urged, should be placed on urban renewal, the use of derelict land and the conservation of agricultural land. Keeping very much to the Planwatch view, she pointed out that since on the basis of the economic situation it might be necessary to 'suspend, curtail or even abandon the exercise, it seems reasonable to hold back unspoilt country until we are absolutely sure we need it'. (CG, 5 September 1974).

The Labour candidate, George Rodgers, was seen as giving the new town plan his qualified approval - not surprising according to the Daily Telegraph political reporter Trevor Bates - since 'New Town growth should put the two Preston seats and Chorley firmly in the Labour camp'. (Daily Telegraph, 30 September 1974).

Mr Porter was strongly rebuked for his stance by an editorial in the Lancashire Evening Post, showing that journal to be more pro new town than pro Conservative. Under the heading 'New Town politics', it stated

.... Mr Barry Porter, the Conservative candidate at Chorley has made his position on the central Lancashire new town 'absolutely clear'. It is absolutely clear that he does not understand the subject as well as one might expect.

After pointing out some errors of detail in Mr Porter's adoption speech it goes on:

.... It may also be of interest to Mr Porter to know that at the time of the February election, Mr Heath told us 'There is to be development of a major new town in the Preston-Leyland-Chorley area. Eventually it will accommodate some 430,000 people, an injection of about 120,000, and it represents the investment of around £500 million in the region'.

This figure is itself on the low side, and a figure of £900 million is often quoted. Is Mr Porter saying that such investment is not wanted in central Lancashire or not wanted in Chorley? If he is planning to spend the next five years going around Whitehall and Westminster saying that this money is neither needed nor wanted, then we must very much doubt if he is the right man for Chorley to send to Parliament. For he is in effect inviting the direction of investment - in better housing, better jobs and a better quality of life - to other parts of the region and the country which will welcome it with open arms.

> Mr Porter is courting short term political advantage. But the view he represents is damaging to the long term interests of the area, as the leaders of his party clearly appreciate. (my emphasis) (LEP, 27 September 1974).

This editorial provided the cue for the most unequivocal declaration of the anti new town platform adopted by Mr Porter. Not only did he reply to the 'Post' by letter, but he also took the opportunity of referring to the editorial in one of his campaign meetings.

In his letter, he conceded that there were many local Conservatives who were in favour of the concept of the new town and that he was aware of the policy expressed by Mr Peter Walker and Mr Heath in 1970 that a Conservative government would not interfere with any new towns already designated. Rebutting the jibe that he was trying to 'pick up cheap votes', Mr Porter stated that he would have 'nailed his flag to the mast' of SCRAP, but he had made it clear to the chairman of SCRAP that 'his views were not coloured by electoral considerations'. He went on:

> .... The plain fact is that on the doorstep I have found, and this has been confirmed by survey canvassing, that a substantial number of people are very concerned about the new town. Their views range from outright opposition to the whole thing to bewilderment as to how it will affect them as individuals . . . I ask for a reappraisal from the new minister so that quickly the arguments from both sides and especially from the bewildered middle can be heard finally. It seems to me an entirely appropriate time for a change of government and the impending public inquiry for this to be done.

It was pointed out at the election meeting by Mr Jim Pilkington, chairman of Walton Summit action committee, that the other conservative candidates did not share his views on the new town. In reply to this suggestion of a party split on the issue, Mr Porter maintained that the new town must not be viewed from any political standpoint, it was too serious a matter.

Referring to the leader article in the previous Friday's 'Post', Mr Porter defended himself and accused the 'Post' of 'applying double standards' (LEP, 2 October 1974) (my emphasis).

> .... 'The Evening Post' should apply the same standards to the new town as it does when accusing the north west Regional Health Authority of being undemocratic . . . The development corporation is no more democratic than the health authority.

Towards the end of the campaign the new town appeared to subside as an issue. Little difference was shown between the parties in Preston north and south, apart from the fact that the labour candidates issued a joint statement on the 'lack of consultation with the public' by the new town planners (LEP, 1 October 1974).

The attempt to make the new town an election issue throughout the area by SCRAP and others manifestly failed. The local success in Chorley with the conservative candidate proved to be short lived and must have lacked impetus when the leader of the party, Edward Heath reaffirmed their commitment to the new town at a Manchester press conference and stated that Mr Porter was 'perfectly entitled to hold his views'. (LEP, 4 October 1974).

It was left to another planning controversy to stimulate inter party differences, the Strategic Plan for the North West. As described earlier in Chapter 9, the contents of this document had been widely leaked in the spring of 1974. During September 1974, a critique of the methods employed by the plan was published by the Centre for North West Regional Studies, University of Lancaster. The team was led by Professor Alan Mercer (also a board member of CLDC), and it called for a totally new strategy based on developing a number of centres throughout the region. The publication of the Lancaster report was followed by its endorsement by Lancaster council.

Often undeclared by the opponents of the strategic plan was the fear of domination by the metropolitan masses of the Mersey Belt. It was left to the Lancashire Evening Post to articulate this anxiety. Exhibiting some of the double standards to which Mr Porter was to refer, a leading article on it on the one hand was to state:

> .... It is a source of great delight to us, therefore, that Councillor Jim Mason, leader of the minority Labour group on Lancashire county council, should have spoken out so firmly in Manchester last week, in favour of 'a strong element of democracy being injected into regional decision taking'.

This sentiment is very much congruent with the newspaper's stand on bureaucracy and secrecy within the health authority. It goes on to explain that

> .... the North West Labour Party is calling on the Department of the Environment to study its proposals. These would not only bring regional planning but also other government regional policies under full democratic control.

When it follows this call for regional accountability to its logical conclusion the 'Post' loses its nerve:

> .... The publication of the strategic plan, however, which isolates preferentially the Mersey Belt from the remainder of the region, causes one to see potential difficulties in making regional planning and administration democratic. It would be no democracy if the Mersey Belt were to outvote the rest of the region in its own interest every time. (my emphasis).

Underlining the connection between the new town and SPNW the Post concludes:

> .... We note that already Greater Manchester has its eye on the investment scheduled for central Lancashire under the new town plan, Lancashire's labour men should raise this with their Manchester colleagues. (LEP, 30 September 1974).

Such near xenophobic anti metropolitan sentiments stirred up by SPNW were given expression in the rivalry between the Labour and Liberal candidates in Preston South. Mr Ron Marshall, the Liberal candidate declared that the Labour candidate, as a member of the Merseyside lobby and a resident there, could not be relied upon to press the claims of Central Lancashire. He questioned whether he would more naturally support the implementation of SPNW which,

.... Could deprive central Lancashire of the much needed resources to accelerate the pace of industrial development, extend democrary in industry and encourage vitally needed investment to make Preston prosperous.

He asked whether Mr Thorne was 'prepared to forget his Merseyside lobby commitment' (LEP, 7 October 1974). This attack was viewed by the labour candidate, Mr Stan Thorne, as an act of 'sheer desperation' and declared that 'he would strongly oppose any attempts to solve unemployment and economic problems on Merseyside at the expense of the central Lancashire area'. (LEP, 8 October 1974).

Thus with the background of all party disapproval of SPNW in the Lancashire county council, it tended to become an issue of who could disapprove of SPNW the most vehemently. This tactic also gave the spokesmen the opportunity to leave their options flexible for the resources retained rather than state a rigid view on new town activities.

This failure to make the new town a party issue in the election serves as a pointer to the more complex interests and loyalties linked with shire county/metropolitan county stresses which overarch party lines. An examination of the attitudes towards CLNT, as a central feature of regional strategy, in terms of local authority policies within the north west will provide a convenient summary and it is with this review that we conclude this chapter.

LOCAL AUTHORITY ATTITUDES

The attitudes towards the CLNT can be analysed on a spatial rather than on a party political basis. With all party support and historical commitment to the project in the county council, opposition tended to be strongest in the beneficiary counties of SPNW - Merseyside and Greater Manchester - and acquiescence weakest in the Lancashire districts nearer the periphery of the county.

Preston

Preston is the seat of county administration and 'self styled' senior district within CLNT. The town had lobbied successfully to be included in the Leyland/Chorley proposals and had undertaken extensive investment such as the Guild Hall complex, on the expectation of a rapid growth of population. As such, the commitment generated by officials and senior members of council was high. But it was necessary for them to reiterate this view on a number of occasions during the months preceding the public inquiry. The council made a declaration of support in June 1974 and the issue was debated again the following month. On this occasion 'critics from both sides of the chamber were routed and the two political parties united in support of the £900 million development'. (LEP, 18 July 1974).

Once again the SPNW influenced attitudes. One councillor, Arthur Taylor, admitted that his support was coloured by a negative factor, since 'if they did not join it, they would find all the benefits going south of the Ribble, and Preston would suffer'. He warned that they now had to 'beware of the greater danger of the claims of the Mersey Belt, where there were already three other new towns, and had powerful friends in high places'.

The pressure placed upon some of the ward members from road protestors during the summer months proved effective. The policy and resources committee submitted its draft recommendations and, while criticising some aspects of the outline plan, it proposed support for the building of most of the eastern and western primary routes and their feeder roads. The debate was lengthy and there was a back bench revolt by both labour and conservative members. Party lines in local government although less rigid than nationally, are broken only occasionally (See Jones, 1969, p.284). The weight of the deputy Conservative leader - representing Ashton - Councillor Arthur Taylor, and Councillor Ronald Atkins, MP, representing the PNAG area, was sufficient to defeat the western primary route through Ashton and the Aqueduct Street/St George's Road cross town route, but not enough to delete the council's approval of the eastern primary. This debate, conducted over three sessions, was one of the most remarkable observed by the writer. It illustrated the tension between the interest of a district area and that of the felt benefits for the wider community - a microcosm of the sub regional rivalries and stresses.

The resulting policy from this twelve hours of debate was an insistence on a greater emphasis on public transport in the outline plan inquiry and the recommendation that no further 6(i) proposals should be allowed to proceed until the outline plan itself had been finally approved.

Chorley

The Chorley borough council approved a written summary supporting the new town at a special meeting on 17 September 1974. A number of pointed observations were made. There was a need for local public inquiries when detailed plans were published so that objectors would have an opportunity to give their views on developments. There were also detailed comments on aspects of housing, the environment and industrial sites, but by far the most significant was the defence of Chorley against the superior weight of Preston. The agreed report stressed that Chorley should be strengthened as one of the three centres in the new town. It was aware of the danger of the existing communities being neglected in favour of the new districts.

Although there was evidence from interviews and press reports that Chorley residents and some councillors were anti new town in their statements, it would appear that there was a greater degree of consensus within Chorley Borough itself than in Preston. Chorley was to benefit first from a joint urban renewal scheme with CLNT and it was to suffer lease disturbance from road schemes. The greatest degree of change was projected for the periphery of the borough in Clayton/Whittle, in Euxton and in Runshaw. This part of the borough is where more criticism and opposition was demonstrated. The views of the Walton Summit group and the Clayton Parish Council have already been described. In Euxton the opposition to plans for their village was more vigorous than in Clayton. This resistance was expressed at a special meeting of Euxton parish council in August 1974 where a number of specific objections to the outline plan were agreed. One member of the council, and also a Chorley Borough councillor, Jim Moorcroft, also called for a complete reappraisal of the new town. (LEP, 2 August 1974).

Fylde and Lancaster

The official policy of Fylde borough council was to support the outline plan, provided it was part of a comprehensive plan for the whole of

Lancashire designed to distribute investment through the county 'in accordance with priorities determined by the county council'. (LEP, 2 August 1974). This sentiment was the view expressed by a longstanding campaigner against CLNT, Councillor John Gouldbourn of Lytham St Annes. Councillor Goldbourne accused his colleagues of relying too much on official advice and forming their opinions as a result of seeing 'official documents and prissy films'. In reply, the establishment view was expressed by Councillor Travis Carter, chairman of the planning and industrial development committee. His committee fully supported the concept of the new town.

> .... I am sure that relations with the new town development corporation are proceeding along amenable and satisfactory lines. It is going to take time to get down to brass tacks. But I cannot see at this stage that the Lancashire county council should do anything other than support the new town.

Further north, the Lancaster borough council formed a special committee to comment upon the SPNW in July 1974 and at that time indicated that CLNT was receiving too much attention. This view was confirmed by the all party committee's report which stated that the proposed development did not reflect the needs of the area north of Preston.

> .... The group suggests that existing centres of population in the region should be examined for potential development to give the correct balance of population. They consider the area north of Preston well suited to meet the current trend towards the 'green field' industrial development.
>
> The area was capable of attracting the small type of labour intensive engineering and scientific based industries, says the study group, emphasising the need to establish job potential for school leavers.

Giving some hint of rivalry between the city and the administrative centre it concluded that:

> .... The group recommends that the government should be asked to consider providing financial help for the development of facilities for an estimated population of 150,000 for the Lancaster area. (LEP, 16 September 1974)

Most of these views would be represented later at the public inquiry, but it is noteworthy that the increasing disquiet with the proposals can be correlated with distance from the project.

SUMMARY

This chapter outlined the context in which the initial stages of the participation process in central Lancashire occurred. It describes a series of local, regional and national events which impinged on social attitudes towards CLNT. These have ranged from housing policy, parliamentary debates and a general election at the national level to local group formation and activity in the immediate vicinity of the new town itself.

NOTES

Roads

The supplement rejected objections to the need for an eastern primary road through the Ribbleton area of Preston and the suggested alternatives, but there were possibilities of minor amendments to the route. Similarly, radical changes to the western primary at Moss Side, Leyland and Strand Road to Ingol were rejected, though the corporation was willing to assess the route of the road through Ashton by taking in some surplus railway tracks alongside Haslam Park. Amendments to the plan which CLDC was willing to accept; if proposed at the public inquiry, included the provision of a bridge to keep Slater Lane, Moss Side open, an improvement of a proposed footbridge to an occupation bridge at Bannister Lane, Farington and a revised road line near Longsands Lane, Preston to avoid the demolition of two houses on Fulwood Row.

Housebuilding

It was noted that concern had been expressed that rigid ratios for rent and for sale might be imposed.

Public transport

The point had been made that relatively low densities of residential development would impede the prospects of a viable and efficient public transport service.

Land

Many had expressed the view that derelict land in urban areas should be used up before taking agricultural land.

Offices

It had been emphasised that the continued growth of office employment on the scale envisaged by the outline plan would cause increased and unacceptable pressure on local roads.

Schools

It had been alleged that the Lancashire county council would not promote an adequate school building programme to deal with the extra population or that an adequate programme, if prepared, would be approved by the Department of Education and Science. This shortfall would increase overcrowding in existing schools.

Population

The lower population forecasts contained in the strategic plan for the north west indicated a need to question the assumptions of population growth contained in the outline plan.

Transport policies

It had been suggested that the development corporation was either not sufficiently concerned with, or had inadequate powers to promote, an adequate. it had been proposed that the corporation should seek a much wider role in either the operation or subsidisation of public transport. To some extent this involvement would be as an alternative to the road construction programme.

Traffic

Many had proposed that the early completion of the proposed motorway box around Preston was essential. The closing of any existing motorway junction should be avoided so that external traffic did not use the town roads. (A possible reference to the fact that the eastern primary was being seen as 'a duplicate M6' along one of its more overburdened lengths).

Sport

There had been considerable comment on the fact that golf as a minority sport was being given 'exceptionally favourable treatment' in comparison with other sports.

Matters of more local concern which had been noted were that in Fulwood it had been pointed out that Lightfoot Lane would become overloaded; in Euxton industrial development should not be promoted south of Euxton Lane, and an additional rail halt should be considered; and in Bamber Bridge an additional rail halt should be provided south of Brownedge Road.

12 The outline plan public inquiry

INTRODUCTION

The climax of this period of local political involvement and activity is the public inquiry into the outline plan. This chapter describes the proceedings, the principal protagonists and outlines the role of the inspector in a public inquiry which commenced on 5 November 1974 and continued, with a break for public holidays for almost three months until 24 January 1975. This public inquiry, which placed within the context of organisational analysis suggested in Chapter 5 may be viewed as an occasion for a 'set piece' in inter organisational relations providing insights into bargaining and power relationships. It would be impossible within the limits of these pages to include detailed reports of the proceedings which, with few exceptions, were observed from the press tables by the writer. The first section of the chapter will therefore include some remarks on the conduct of the inquiry and a broad summary of the arguments offered by the main participants.

THE MECHANICS OF THE PROCEEDINGS

The general form which the outline plan inquiry proceedings should take was discussed at a procedural meeting at Leyland on 11 October 1974, under the chairmanship of a senior inspector of the Department of the Environment, Mr S.W. Midwinter. The meeting was intended primarily for the 'official' objectors, the local authorities and the major amenity societies and action groups, although a few individual objectors were present and a commercial objector, notably Whitbread's Brewery, who were to be represented by a former Secretary of State for the Environment, Mr Geoffrey Rippon, QC.

Each objector present was asked to state whether or not they would be legally represented, the length of their case and whether it would take the form of a statement not open to 'cross examination' by the corporation or of evidence by witness which it would be permissible to probe any questions from the corporation's counsel. The inspector pointed out that due note would be taken of whether or not an objector would permit questioning, 'more weight' being given to the latter. On behalf of the CLDC, their counsel, Mr Iain Glidewell, QC, gave details of the accommodation, programming and facilities for objectors. In a major initiative, the corporation suggested that the inquiry programme be split into various categories of objections, transport, specific lengths of road, general objections (1), etc., but this proposition was strongly resisted, particularly by Greater Manchester council, who pointed out that they would be required to return on a number of occasions and that this arrangement would be inconvenient. The opposition to this proposal was clearly noted by the development corporation and as the official minute of the meeting states 'it was agreed however, that objectors should only need to present one case even if this covered several categories' but that 'General objections were best heard in the early part of the programme'. It was agreed also that it would be preferable for onjectors where possible to present grouped cases. This proposal was particularly significant in the instance of the district councils of north east Lancashire who indicated that they would be appearing under the 'umbrella' of the North East Lancashire Development Association.

The official minute also notes 'The corporation gave notice that they intend to submit to the inspector that objections about the concept of the new town or about designation etc., were not relevant to the inquiry'. The minute failed to note that an 'etc.' was the subject of participation, a warning whcih was later to ensure that Planwatch was aware of basing its evidence on participation clearly upon the outline plan.

The form taken by the inquiry's proceedings, subject to the inspector's ruling, was also explained to the objectors present. The inquiry would commence with an opening statement on behalf of the corporation and would be followed by 'the evidence in chief' from the corporation's three witnesses. There would be no cross examination of these witnesses by the objectors at this stage and an opportunity to do this questioning would be given later, provided reasonable advance warning was given. The objectors' cases would then commence.

On the opening day of the inquiry, 5 November 1974, after the inspector had 'had sight of' the various objectors present at the Guild Hall, Preston, a procedural wrangle occurred over the right to reexamine witnesses where a matter might require clarification. It was eventually agreed that this practice was permissible for both sides and as a result the inquiry proceedings became quite complex and difficult for laymen to follow, particularly those who were not able to 'sit in' for some considerable period. As a result of this additional stage the order became in its most lengthy form as follows:

(1) Cross examination of corporation's witnesses, if required, by objectors' counsel.

(2) Opening statement by objectors' counsel.

(3) Witness called by objectors' counsel - case read and copy distributed.

(4) Witness cross questioned by corporation's counsel.

(5) Reexamination of witness, if necessary, by objectors' counsel.

(6) Additional proof of evidence produced, where appropriate, by development corporation witness and 'guided through' and reexamined by counsel.

(7) Objectors' counsel cross questions on additional evidence.

(8) Corporation's counsel sums up.

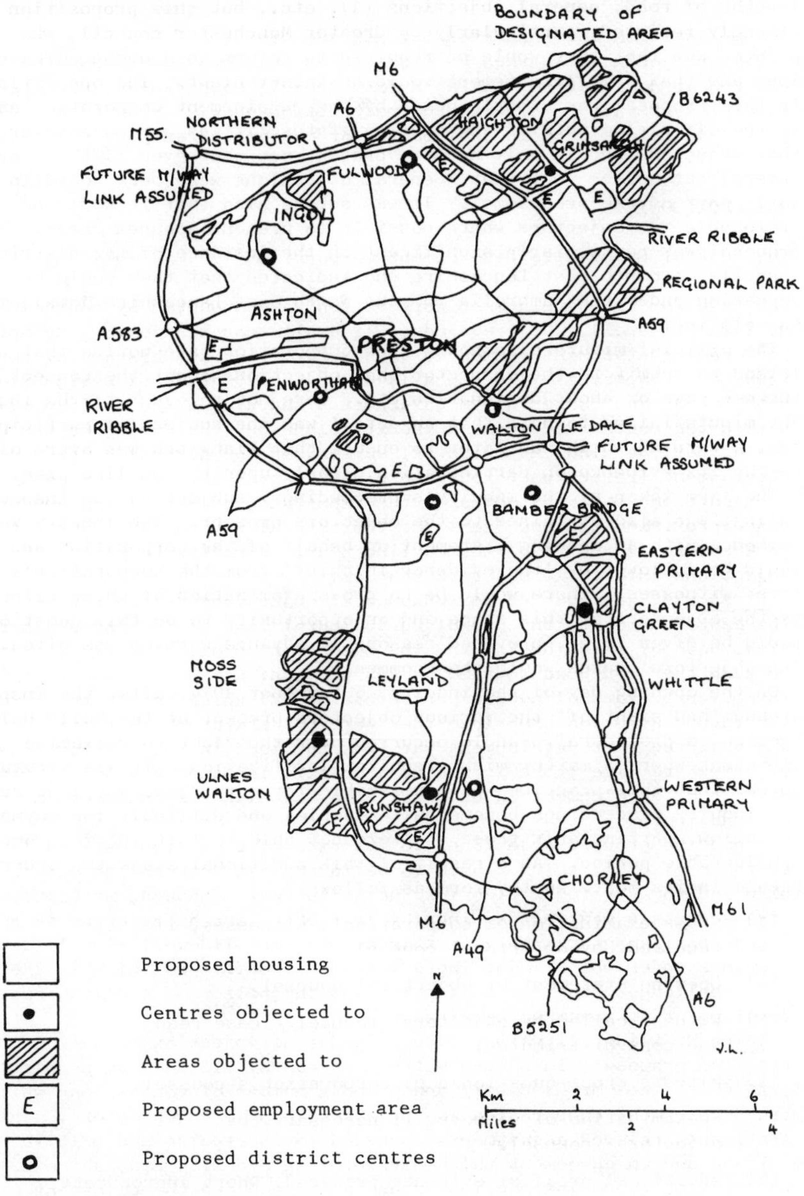

CENTRAL LANCASHIRE NEW TOWN

Diagram of principal areas of objections voiced at public inquiries September 1974 and November 1974 to January 1975.

(9) Objectors' counsel sums up.

and at any time the inspector may ask questions.

The proceedings can thus be regarded as an improvement upon those adopted at designation, taking a form broadly comparable with motorway inquiries at that time, with the restriction upon probing into earlier policy decisions such as designation or national transport policy.

THE PROTAGONISTS

The Central Lancashire Development Corporation

The case for the development corporation was conducted by counsel, Mr Iain Glidewell, QC, (now Judge Glidewell) and his junior, Mr McLeod. His opening statement commenced with a review of the history of the new town (See Chapter 2). He emphasised the confirmation of designation by both Labour and Conservative governments and placed the outline plan within the context of local authority planning. Referring to the published outline plan, Mr Glidewell summarised the general pattern of development (referring to outline plan, Chapter 12, p.25), aspects of transport and the road network, the importance of recreation and open space provision and the 'care for the natural environment' demonstrated in Chapters 11 and 21 of the outline plan. Finally, he placed the objections into three major categories:

First what he regarded as fundamental objections to the concept of the new town, or to the use of agricultural land inside the designated area, both of which he invited the inspector to exclude from the inquiry because they had been settled by designation; complaints about administration or lack of public participation (2) which he claimed were not the inspector's concern since they were not statutory matters; those who objected that development was 'taking place in the new town instead of somewhere else'; the fringe area policy, leading to a 'close restriction of development in boundary areas', which was inherent in the designation.

Second he grouped objections to its rate of expansion between 'such as those of GMC', which tended to be 'a contest between the outline plan and the strategic plan for the north west', though, Mr Glidewell stressed, this was 'not an inquiry into SPNW' and he referred to a recent parliamentary reply on this point. Mr Glidewell then listed ten headings under which major ingredients or specific policies in the plan were challenged, the first of which was the policy of simultaneous development at a number of sites.

Third Mr Glidewell referred to a number of objections relating to detailed proposals into such matters as roads, villages or property.

At this stage Mr Glidewell announced a number of concessions which the development corporation was prepared to make to objectors. This statement included adjustments conceded to Courtaulds and British Leyland and an agreement which had been reached with Lancashire county council for rephasing housing areas in Fulwood and the deferment of development in Haighton (on the east side of the M6) to an unspecified date, possibly post 1986.

Finally, Mr Glidewell observed to the inspector that the object of the inquiry was first to approve the outline plan generally 'with modifications you recommend' and to approve and endorse pages 180 to 182 of the plan - a summary of the principal policies and proposals. In closing, he stressed that the new town was of 'the greatest importance for the future of the whole region'. (An emphasis which was later to be referred to on Radio Blackburn in reporting Mr Glidewell's speech that the new town was the 'best thing to happen to the north west this century'.)

The general manager was then called to present his proof of evidence. This report with appendices amounted to 48 closely argued pages. In his accompanying verbal submission, Mr Phelps attempted to negate the major objections to the outline plan. He insisted that designation was a fait accompli and it had already established the use of agricultural land for the new town, so objections on these points he argued, were inadmissable at the inquiry. Requests for alternatives, he asserted, were out of place, since these arguments had already been weighed by the consultants in 'Study for a City', and the preferred option decided upon. Dealing with public participation, Mr Phelps cited the development corporation's publications, exhibitions, public meetings and a film, expenditure upon which had totalled over £40,000. Referring to his proof of evidence he pointed out that the development corporation's public participation had 'set a new standard in the area' (3) (CLDC, 1974b, p.6).

The general manager showed how the outline plan would relate to the central north Lancashire structure plan, (which was still awaiting completion five years later) and to local plans to be made by other planning authorities. He referred to the limitations of functions of the development corporation; they were not responsible for the provision of schools, hospitals and social services; the local authorities had to provide these services, so requests should go to them. He went on to contest the arguments of Greater Manchester council, based upon the SPNW questioning the need for the new town and the rival claims upon government resources of towns in the Mersey Belt. Turning to the objections to major ingredients of the plan, Mr Phelps discarded responsibility for changes in government policy about the modal split between rented and private housing. The development corporation had to provide what the government asked for (4), but they would not be building high rise flats as some objectors had inferred, unless requested to do so.

Turning to transportation, Mr Phelps contended that it was not the business of the development corporation to produce a transport policy; this function was the responsibility of the highway authorities, the County Council and the Department of the Environment. He refuted the accusations of some action groups that the new town roads could lead to a large number of property demolitions. The high figure of demolitions carried out recently by the local authorities had been part of their slum clearance programmes and not connected with road construction, so he argued the comparison was biased. Finally, he defended the outline plan's much criticised acceptance of continued maximum use of the private car; public transport alternatives had been considered and the network was suitable for them, but, he suggested, people liked to use their cars.

The former chief officer for public planning, Mr Colin Beck, presented his brief proof of evidence outlining the proposed pattern of physical development. This statement was principally a reiteration of his presentations at the series of public meetings held before the inquiry (See Chapter 10). Mr David Garside, the chief engineer, in presenting his proof of evidence repeated the arguments he had used for the road network and answered some points raised at the public meetings. Objectors had the opportunity to put questions to the development corporation's witnesses about their evidence either at this stage, or immediately before presenting their own cases and a number of questions of clarification were asked by representatives of the action groups and local authorities.

The official objectors - the local authorities

The Greater Manchester Council presented a major objection to the outline plan (which had the blessing of Merseyside County Council) and were supported in separate proofs of evidence by two of their constituent district councils, the Metropolitan Borough of Wigan and Bolton Metropolitan Borough Council. This powerful group of local authorities whose territorial responsibilities lie to the south of the designated area, related much of their evidence to the findings of the SPNW in proposing a slower rate of growth for the CLNT. Representatives of Greater Manchester Council, with the support of Merseyside County Council, suggested that the 'uncertain investment' in central Lancashire would be a waste of limited resources, and that it was preferable to concentrate these resources upon the existing programme of new towns in the region, Runcorn, Skelmersdale and Warrington, and making any additional funds available for environmental improvements.

> .... in the disadvantaged areas of the north west which are mostly in the Mersey Belt and north east Lancashire.

It was stressed that, since the decline in population projections and the change in emphasis from redevelopment to rehabilitation in older housing areas, it was advisable to defer the construction of additional dwellings in the region, particularly bearing in mind that the existing new towns in the North West had an intake capacity of about 130,000 remaining.

The policy of simultaneous development over much of the designated area was criticised since there was a distinct possibility that many of the resources expended on advance site works, large road schemes and multiple sewerage schemes would be underutilised because of the greater attraction of the nearby special development area. This policy was condemned by the director of administration of Wigan Metropolitan Council as 'a maximum risk strategy'.

Planning to maintain the current situation of a new inflow of workers to the area and to control development on the 'fringe' areas adjoining the designated area boundaries also formed a strong element of the objections by the Bolton and Wigan Metropolitan Councils. An objection to 'unreasonably restrictive' fringe area policies was also made by a representative of West Lancashire District Council, in whose boundaries Skelmersdale New Town is located.

In cross questioning, CLDC's counsel treated this coordinated objection as a criticism of government policy in the allocation of resources, and attempted to discredit SPNW and its recommendations. Designation had been established by the previous inquiry he argued, and funds saved by doing away with the new town would not go to the Mersey Belt but to other new towns. He attempted to meet criticism based upon SPNW by referring to the extension of the new town's time scale from twenty years to thirty. Criticism of the fringe area policy indicated that its critics expected the new town to succeed, it was already in operation and had been upheld at a recent planning inquiry by the Secretary of

State. These arguments were central to the intra regional rivalry between CLNT and the Mersey Belt strategy of SPNW and were given some coverage in the national press (See Chapter 8).

There was also some continuing disquiet remaining from fears of relative disadvantage. These were expressed in their evidence by number of local authorities from within the 'sponsoring' county of Lancashire. For example, concern about the effect of the concentration of growth on the new town and the impact on the rest of the county focussing much county capital and revenue expenditure on the area was voiced by the Blackpool, Fylde and Wyre Borough Councils. This disquiet was also one of the main points expressed by the North East Lancashire Development Association, a body representing the unanimous views of seven district councils in Lancashire. One of the constituents of the association, Rossendale Borough Council, includes an area whose pressure was instrumental in seeking compensatory measures to offset the influence of the new town in north east Lancashire. From the submission it is clear that there was growing uneasiness about the likely effectiveness of these schemes. The statement of case of the association put this strongly when it was stated:

> .... That various undertakings, given with a view to maintaining competitiveness in north east Lancashire with the impact of a new town in Central Lancashire have since been eroded or rendered totally ineffective.

In effect, the objections of the councils of the north east Lancashire towns were similar to those that they had expressed at designation, and were an articulation of the fear of the rival attractions of the new town over its neighbours with less natural advantages.

The Fylde Council's objection mirrored those of Wigan and West Lancashire to the south. They were opposed to the new town's fringe area policy. This they believed would be likely to inhibit their own freedom to develop. In this context, special reference was made to a large housing estate being planned (and shortly to be submitted to public inquiry) for the former RAF station at Kirkham, to which the CLDC was known to object.

Although the new town was the 'brainchild' of the Lancashire County Council, the proceedings revealed that a majority of its constituent district councils had severe misgivings about the project, if not overtly about the principle of designation, certainly about its form and rate of development.

This strain in organisational relationships between county and district councils has been marked in some examinations-in-public and of a number of structure plans. This difference may be quite marginal in, for example, the amount of land required to be zoned for industrial use - as in the North East Lancashire structure plan. It is possible, however, through a failure to consult, that wide divergences of policy emphasis can occur, as during the examinations-in-public of the structure plan of the Greater Manchester Council. Such inter organisational differences or disputes between local authority levels may thus purely reflect incompatibilities between perceived strategic (county) or local (district) interests. Perhaps purely from lack of experience within a limited period of implementation, this factor has not been discussed in some post-local government reorganisation texts in public administration (Hill, 1976; Smith and Stanyer, 1976) and only briefly touched upon in terms of disputes (Stanyer, 1976, p.209). Buxton, however, in his legal text, does point out that the ethos of the non metropolitan district, with housing as a central part of its functions, 'will tend to concentrate more on particular local cases than upon policy making in the proper sense' (Buxton, 1973, p.263).

More significant from an organisational behaviour standpoint, is the failure of diplomatic 'boundary spanning' roles in communications aspects of inter organisational behaviour. The key relationship between districts and their county are in themselves worthy of research, and the examinations-in-public provide a rare opportunity for observation of overt differences by future researchers.

The local authorities as 'supporters'

In a brief five page typewritten statement Lancashire County Council, by virtue of its pre inquiry negotiations, was able to present a case broadly sustaining the submissions by CLDC. The council had argued that initial development within the designated area should be adjacent to existing settlements. This policy was to ensure that the available physical and social investment could be utilised more economically than the preferred CLDC 'dispersed and simultaneous' development pattern. The concession previously announced in Mr Glidewell's opening statement that some developments were to be rephased, were spelt out, together with understanding that in the event of a failure to agree that the parties (that is the county, Preston Borough and CLDC), through the Section 6(i) procedure 'will represent their respective views to the Secretary of State, in the knowledge that a final decision will be taken by him having regard to all these views'.

This tripartite agreement, the contents of which were recommended to the Secretary of State, is direct evidence of the precarious balance of inter organisational power between these local authorities and the CLDC at this sensitive pre inquiry period. Temporarily at least, leverage was finally tilted towards the county council, for it would have been damaging indeed if CLDC had been deprived of this major local authority support at the public inquiry. This uneasy alliance found common cause in its attitude towards the SPNW where the CLDC general manager's arguments and data were given full support, in an approach which was entirely the same as (the county's) own. The two organisations were thus to close ranks in the face of the possible threat of the diversion of government priorities from new town to the Mersey Belt.

The county in its statement attempted to construct a collective view on behalf of its fourteen constituent districts. The statement sought to reconcile some of the divergent positions or emphases of its districts, notably those who are members of NELDA, and made the point that it 'is being very conscious of its responsibilities in securing a proper and adequate allocation of resources in all the fourteen districts'. In a thinly disguised admission of some district's diffuse and often competing interests, it stressed that the 'potential and needs of the Fylde, Blackpool and Wyre and the Lancaster and Morecambe areas must also be recognised and catered for and all this means that the new town should not have a monopoly of investment from government, the county council and the private sector'. (my emphasis).

The county council had 'no objection in principle to the primary road network contained in the outline plan' but, as the highway authority, they raised 'strong objection to the proposals for the possible closure of the motorway interchange on the M6 at Leyland and of the north facing slip roads on the M6 at Samlesbury'. With this notable specific exception, to be resolved under highways acts procedures, the county reiterated its support for the new town and its commitment 'to assisting in its successful realisation'. Yet its statement implies how uneasily it reconciled its role as the strategic planning authority, and the representative organisation of fourteen districts, with an unequivocal support of the outline plan.

Similarly, the district councils within the designated area, Preston, South Ribble and Chorley boroughs, had all continued the historical commitment of their major predecessors prior to local government reorganisation. Yet, although they all professed support for the concept of the new town, they also had severe misgivings about the outline plan and about their relationships with its originator, CLDC. Some of these differences and strains were openly, if cautiously, expressed in the statements which they presented at the public enquiry. Not articulated, yet no less real, was the disquiet they felt at the lack of consultation between themselves and CLDC, much of which was contained during the period of the public inquiry,(4) but which was to be unleased in the following months.(5)

Elected members of councils were appointed to the board of CLDC by the Secretary of State as individuals and not as representatives, and their consequent inability to be used as channels of communication was resented by the local authorities. Preston district councillors in particular, had been lobbied by their ward electors about aspects of the outline plan, notably the major road proposals. There was also pressure concerning the proposed early development of Haighton and Grimsargh, and the employment areas (such as Midgery Lane north of Preston). Fears were also expressed about the new district centres envisaged, notably that planned for south of the existing Leyland town centre at Runshaw which, it was argued, could develop as counter-magnets to the other shopping centres.

The statements presented by the three district councils were in the main couched in the most diplomatic language. Each proclaimed its undoubted support in the concept of the new town, yet in turn they all presented differing points of emphasis and areas of disagreement with the outline plan. Preston Borough Council in its statement expressed concern that it wanted to see the new town implemented in the most advantageous way, and any comments it made were 'intended to be constructive rather than destructive', (para.1.2). Touching upon a sensitive point about the pre-empting of the wider scheme by advance section 6(i) applications, the statement continued:

> .... the Council consider that any Section 6 applications submitted before approval of the outline plan, concerning our area, should not themselves be approved or implemented in advance of a decision on the outline plan, (para.1.4).

Chorley Borough Council, while stating that it fully supported the concept of CLNT, reiterated the arguments of the Lancashire County Council when it:

> .... contended most strongly that during the earlier part of the plan period priority should be given to developing and strengthening existing urban communities and neighbouring areas in order to take maximum advantages of the services, facilities and social infrastructure which already exist and which in many instances will form

a basis of support for the present and incoming population, (para.1.2)

Calling for a 'close coordination and collaboration' between the outline plan, the county structure plan and subordinate plans, Chorley Borough Council anticipated some submissions later made by action groups when it sought inquiries for 'area plans prepared by a development corporation', 'held on similar lines to a public local inquiry into a local plan', (para. 1.5).

The Borough Council of South Ribble, in turn, in its 'Statement of Views', expressed support for 'the development of the new town as a general principle' and made the point that its statement was 'therefore not by way of objection to the outline plan but an expression of wide based and enthusiastic support'. The matters it raised were put forward as 'suggested improvements' . . . 'Not as fundamental attacks' . . . but somewhat acidly, it added:

.... Nevertheless the suggested amendments are firmly advocated and are not merely presented as insignificant trifles thought up to give South Ribble something to say at this inquiry, (para.1.1)

The transportation schemes and policies contained in both the outline plan and the supporting documents 'The Transport Network in the Outline Plan' had proved to be the most contentious of CLDC's proposals. This tension is reflected in the fact that, under the heading of transportation, the widest divergencies of response by districts occur. While Chorley had 'no objection in principle to the road network as indicated in the outline plan' and only made observations on detail it its brief seven page 'representation', and South Ribble put forward amendments to two of the road proposals, it was left to Preston to state that this policy was an area where their views 'were fundamentally different from those of the development corporation', (para.5.1).

Using arguments also presented by some of the action groups, Preston, in eleven closely argued pages pointed to the need to amend the outline plan which should:

.... stress that the early completion of the 'Motorway box' around Preston is a vital prerequisite to the provision of a satisfactory transportation system for the designated area as a whole, (para. 5.1)

In common with Lancashire County Council and some action groups, it also opposed the proposals for changes on the M6 motorway junctions, but it was most significantly in this third point, on travel options, where they differed from CLDC 'about a basis philosophy'. The statement continued:

.... For our part, we say that in the last quarter of a century the only realistic policy which can be advocated is one which not only relies heavily on public transport but which also discourages the use of private transport for journeys to work and as you will be aware we are not unique in holding this view . . . We say that the plan could come out boldly and say that the Development Corporation intends to use all its power and influence in the furtherance of the earliest possible promotion of the maximum use of public transport and adopt a strategy which will control and deter private computer traffic throughout the designated area ... (my emphasis).

It was in strong opposition to a specific proposal of a major road route through the town that Preston's submission was reflecting the electorates pressure, strongly represented through Preston North Action Group and the Member of Parliament for Preston North, Mr Ron Atkins, who was also a councillor at this time. The route would involve new road construction in the section between Blackpool Road and Skeffington Road and 'presumably a major improvement from Skeffington Road through St George's Road and Aqueduct Street' and, as Preston Borough Council pointed out, 'implementation would substantially restrict any general improvement work in the St George's Road area'. It estimated that not only would 145 houses have to be demolished, but some 494 houses would be affected by 'environmental damage'. In any case, the statement argued, 'the reasons advanced by the development corporation for the proposal are, in our view, untenable'. In the face of this uncompromising position CLDC was eventually pressured into making a verbal concession on this route, quite unexpectedly, during a public inquiry session.

Falling some way short of this last minute concession was a protracted negotiation about shopping policy with South Ribble. While Preston concurred in general terms with the outline plan's policy to resist proposals for any new major regional shopping centre within the designated area, Chorley specifically requested that CLDC should investigate the likely impact of the shopping facilities at the proposed Runshaw district centre on existing centres 'to ensure that the new shopping development is not excessive in scale and will be phased to minimise such impact' (para.6.1). South Ribble Council, however, through the statements presented, provide strong evidence of serious inter organisational differences between it and CLDC. The original statement included statements, later superseded, to the effect that the Runshaw district centre would be opposed ... 'The council . . . feel that a district centre would have very serious repercussions on the Leyland proposals and in all the circumstances would not be justifiable', (para.6.8 deleted). The degree of lateness of such negotiations is shown by the submission of a supplement to the original statement which presented new replacement paragraphs on shopping and open space. The new paragraph 6.9 reflects the compromise so recently reached on shopping policies when it states:

> .... In their discussion with the officers of the corporation the council's officers believe they have secured general agreement that the intentions of the council were not inconsistent with the general approach of the corporation and it is understood that the corporation would not expect to introduce any significant shopping development in Runshaw until the early 1980s, by which time it should be possible to assess the developing potential of Leyland and determine if there is a need for a district centre.

Although the response to these observations by R.W. Phelps 'Welcomes the constructive and positive way in which the South Ribble Borough Council's views are expressed in their statement', it is evident that the last minute agreement had been hard fought. The fact that such differences had been made public was clearly resented by CLDC. In support of this view the response continues:

.... With respect to (the Borough Council) it seems to the Corporation that in the main (their views about shopping) are matters which will more satisfactorily be resolved at Area Plan stage than at present. In part also they can be more suitably pursued through direct consultation and discussion with the Development Corporation. ('Rather than bringing such matters into a public area' was left unsaid). (my emphasis)

In the light of this strong rearguard action by CLDC, it is evident that some considerable tension existed in the relations between South Ribble and the CLDC, and this truculence is reflected in the unconventional opening remarks about their amendments not being 'insignificant trifles'. As far as the 'supporting' local authorities as a whole are concerned, though nominally in support of the new town, it is evident that their misgivings were primarily focussed upon the consequences of their organisational relations with the CLDC rather than upon the new town itself. Many of the differences, such as on the phasing of development, transportation and shopping might have been avoided through better organisation diplomacy and by a greater awareness by CLDC of the importance of boundary spanning roles. This flaw was a point which the inspector himself would note in relation to many of the objections presented by local organisations and individuals.

The voluntary sector

The local action groups and other voluntary organisations presenting objections may be grouped into two broad categories. First those which presented a case dealing primarily with the designated area as a whole and second, those who were mainly concerned about the outline plan's proposals for a community or district, or even about an individual street or property.

Among those taking the broader strategic view were Planwatch, who presented their evidence in association with Transport 2000 Northwest and the Lancashire branch of the Council for the Protection of Rural England, the Ramblers' Association (Lake District and Manchester areas) and an organisation with a title 'Society for the Coordination and Reaffirmation of Anti-New Town Policies' (SCRAP).

Planwatch, in parallel with a number of the local authorities represented, noted the uncertainty of future growth and suggested that the secretary of state should review and determine the rate of growth needed and that these forecasts should be expressed in ranges rather than in single figures. Anticipating Levin's advocacy of a 'salami' or 'slice by slice' approach to new town development (Levin, 1976, pp.303-4), Planwatch stressed that the targets and the performance of the development corporation in relation to them, should be 'the subject of independent reviews into full public involvement'. There should be included in the plan

.... a detailed and precise exposition of all current policies and those proposals that are expected to be implemented in, say, the first five years. In the event of policy changes being necessary these could be dealt with as the need arose, possibly involving a review of the plan, and later proposals could also be dealt with on subsequent submission.

The policy of dispersed and simultaneous development was strongly opposed. Separate evidences were presented dealing with conservation, recreation, rural environment, housing policy and design and a 33 page alternative commentary offering generally constructive alterations and emendments of the outline plan was also submitted to the inspector, Mr S. Rollison. Transportation, above all, became the most detailed, technical and complex issue. This subject was considered in turn, by a member and planning adviser. One assessed the environmental impact of the overall road proposals and gave a criticism of the footpath networks. The other presented a technical appraisal of the Transport Network in the Outline Plan (a document accompanying the Outline Plan), which took the view that the two extreme environments used to formulate and evaluate the transport policy options were

> .... not radically different extremes, but that they both contain in-built bias towards the use of the car such that the net results will in every case be to over emphasise the importance of car trips and under estimate the role and contribution of public transport. (Turner, 1974, p.10)

Such was the complexity of some of the transportation arguments that the inspector suggested that the parties should adjourn to discuss them and the alleged existence of an economic evaluation (6) of the transport network. (The writer, as an independent observer, was refused admittance by CLDC.)

Objections to what was regarded to be an inadequate appreciation of the contributions of public transport, and the need for an integrated transport system which incorporated some railway development, were made by the chairman of Transport 2000 Northwest in an associated submission.

In his summing up of his three evidences as an adviser to Planwatch, Mr C.S. Turner expressed 'very real and deep seated doubts about the social implications of the outline plan and the development corporation's actions'. In a similar vein the corporation's approach and attitude to the contentious issue of public participation were criticised by a member of Planwatch. Planwatch, as a group led by what have been classified as 'Skeffington idealists' (See Chapter 6), had a particular interest in public participation. The group, represented on this occasion by a college lecturer, Mr M. Middleton, criticised the construction of the master sample social survey, which had been under taken allegedly to assist the development corporation to assess the effects of the new town on existing residents. He pointed out that results had not been available in time to be incorporated into the outline plan. In his associated evidence, Bernard Davies, a founder member whose resignation from a new town working party had been reported nationally, (See Chapter 9), suggested methods by which the public might in future be able to participate more fully in planning. In reply, the development corporation questioned the feasibility of involving the public to the satisfaction of all parties, and quoted evidence of their attempts to 'inform and involve' the public in the designated area, but had been discouraged by some of the poorly attended public meetings which had resulted.

Lack of opportunity to participate was also an important element of the submissions by SCRAP who, unlike Planwatch, made no secret of their continued opposition to the fact of designation. Although warned by the inspector of the 'irrelevance' to the public inquiry, since this

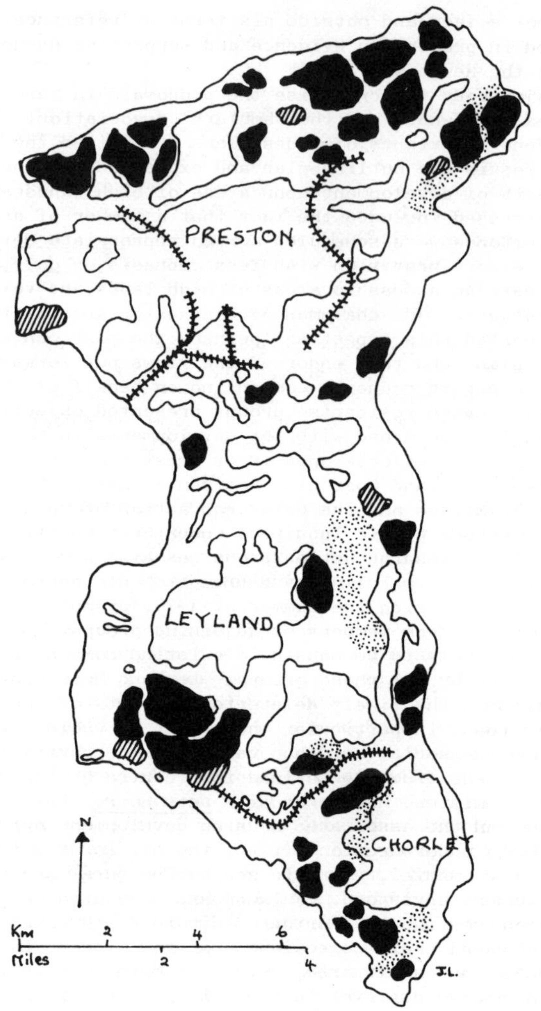

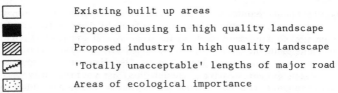

Existing built up areas

Proposed housing in high quality landscape

Proposed industry in high quality landscape

'Totally unacceptable' lengths of major road

Areas of ecological importance

Summary of Environmental Objections, submitted by the Ramblers' Association at the outline plan public inquiry decision was not a fact and outside his terms of reference, members of SCRAP persisted in presenting evidence and supporting documents opposing, the concept of the new town.

The third major body to scrutinise the proposals in terms of the designated area as a whole was the Ramblers' Association. This group, anxious to defend the rights of pedestrians, criticised the lack of footpath policies in the outline plan and expressed 'a genuine concern' about the effects of development upon areas of high landscape value. Major points stressed included the fact that a number of areas of major ecological importance were scheduled for an appropriate development, a more balanced leisure provision with less emphasis on golf, a concern for easier pedestrian access to areas of high landscape value, but above all the road network. The chairman of Manchester area of the Ramblers' Association regarded this aspect as 'perhaps the most contentious part of the outline plan' and they endorsed the views put forward by Planwatch.

In addition to parish councils commenting on behalf of their areas, a number of locally based residents' groups presented objections. Of these, four were primarily concerned with the developments in the peripheral areas and two with the effects upon inner Preston of proposed urban roads and routes. Leyland Moss Side Residents' Association, Walton Summit protest committee and the Grimsargh action group had already made objections at previous public inquiries under Section 6(i) of the New Towns Act, and the Grimsargh action group was also active at the time of the designation inquiry. Fulwood and Broughton Residents' Association was the last to form during the summer of 1974, prompted by the initiatives and spin off from members of adjoining groups.

The disruption likely to be caused to existing communities was the dominant point made by all these groups. Leyland Moss Side Residents' Association stressed the likely deleterious effects of the proposed western primary road, in particular the effect it would have upon existing property and the social hardshop caused by the physical division of the Moss Side village from the Leyland town centre by the route. Walton Summit protest committee, having had its <u>bete noire</u>, the Walton Summit employment area and the associated housing development approved by the Secretary of State under Section 6(i) of the New Towns Act, continued to object on environmental, economic and agricultural grounds to the scale of development envisaged. Fulwood and Broughton Residents' Association, representing the northern surburban and rural fringes of Preston, concentrated their objections upon the Midgery Lane employment area (like the Walton Summit area, to be sited in an existing agricultural belt), a proposed district centre, the phasing of the residential areas at Haighton and Ingol and the roads required to service these schemes.

Although all these groups were principally concerned with the effects upon their own areas, it must also be pointed out that most of them in their evidence also included many wider issues and strategic points similar to those made not only by objectors such as Planwatch, SCRAP and the Ramblers' Association, but also by the dissenting local authorities. Grimsargh action group, although dealing vociferously and at length with proposals for the Haighton/Grimsargh area, included evidence in their 103 page submission on such terms as land acquisition as part of the growth policy, publication, presentation and public participation, population, housing, transport, community health, growth (cost and phasing) and employment and regional considerations.

Two major residents' groups had been formed, both with the support of their appropriate Member of Parliament, to represent the urban areas of Preston; one covering the northern and north eastern areas of the town and the other western districts based upon the Ashton area of Preston. Preston North action group was formed specifically to oppose the 'cross town highways' indicated in the outline plan. In the public inquiry, the group made a very strong case against the eastern primary road (which was designated to serve the new developments proposed for Haighton/Grimsargh) and also the associated district distributor based upon the widening of St George's Road/Aqueduct Street (which the development corporation eventually withdrew - see the objection by Preston Borough). In addition to the evidence of the likely social impact of the roads, members of the group also made some well argued points about transportation in general.

Ashton action group however, were the most focussed of all the groups. They based their submissions upon their implacable opposition to a specific section of the western primary road. Members of the group, without external technical assistance presented social, environmental, statistical and technical evidence to challenge all four routes considered in a supporting document to the outline plan, road appraisal report No.2. This presentation, of all the submissions, was perhaps the most emotive since it involved such issues as the likely encroachment upon a public park by the preferred route (including the felling of mature trees) and the unavoidable demolition of a number of properties in Ashton-on-Ribble.

Fulwood and Broughton residents' association was fortunate to find that a solicitor, whose house would be affected by a road proposal, was prepared to present their case. He expressed the association's opposition to early development at Haighton to the east and Ingol to the west of Fulwood, since they would justify the construction of a road to which they objected. They also objected to the development of land in the triangle between the M6 and M55 for housing , on the grounds that it would be unsuitable because of traffic noise.

A number of common themes emerged from the objections of the various groups. The over optimism and impracticability of the population targets was raised by local authorities, groups and individuals alike, such arguments tended to be supported by official projections made since the publication of the outline plan and these figures were often quoted. These forecasts were countered by arguments on the net household formation and the area's magnetism as a 'natural growth point'. CLDC's policy of dispersed growth and its phasing of development was consistently attacked both on regional and local grounds. Not only were doubts expressed over the viability of the parallel development of a number of sites, but conservation, agricultural and general amenity arguments were employed against the development of green field sites prior to the infilling and use of existing opportunities in the three major urban centres. These arguments were summarised by Leyland Moss Side residents association when they stated:

> .... Urgent considerations should now be given to the reprogramming and development in areas such as Moss Side and Grimsargh which should be put back and finished by the year 2001 and in their place bringing forward those areas more centrally located which, although currently scheduled for 2001, we feel would if completed by 1986 help to consolidate the new Town. Areas such as Ulnes Walton and Runshaw are by and

> large 'greenfield' sites which ought not to be developed at all but left to farming/smallholding, etc. . . . To take quality agricultural land such as is found in Ulnes Walton and Runshaw and begin development with the possibility of curtailment because of policy or cash problems would in our opinion be a blunder of gigantic proportions.

The economic and financial implications of the new town in terms of the national economy, regional priorities and the likely costs of servicing amenities were pointed out by a wide cross section of objections. The significance of the transportational proposals, a major financial item was a constant theme. Not only were car ownership projections often challenged, but also the alignment and necessity of many of the major and minor road schemes which formed an integral part of the plan. Among the constructive suggestions made by a number of objections was the early completion of roads on the line of the land reserved for the motorway box around Preston, a scheme for which Preston North Action Group coined the maxim 'round rather than through'.

While local authorities hinted at disquiet about the CLDC's lack of consultation, the voluntary associations tended to criticise the CLDC's lack of sensitivity and the inappropriateness of such a body for the further development of a well-populated area. Indeed, there was the view expressed by many objectors that new towns legislation provided inappropriate machinery and inadequate levels of participation. This viewpoint was not articulated at this time by the relevant local authorities but was later to be forcefully stated by Sir Kenneth Thompson, chairman of the Merseyside County Council, in reaction to the Secretary of State's proposals in 1979 for an urban development corporation for Liverpool's dockland. The strength of feeling on this issue is typified by the reply made by Mr Alan Howard of Planwatch to the general manager's comment that Planwatch 'fail to understand the purpose of the outline plan'.

> .... We understand the purpose of the outline plan very well indeed. It is to secure for the development corporation, a non elected body, very wide and far reaching powers to initiate changes in the physical environment of 235,000 people now occupying 55 square miles of central Lancashire, uninhibited by public debate, unfettered by electoral responsibility, or unrestrained by further public inquiries. Such powers might be justified in the hands of a body which was superhuman in wisdom and in concern for the welfare and well being of the people. Despite its many excellent aspects which we have duly noted in our evidence, the outline plan demonstrates that the development corporation is limited in both wisdom and concern, and we suggest that its powers should be limited accordingly.

Industry, commerce and individual objectors

Britain's 'biggest industry' agriculture, was represented by the Country Landowners' Association and the National Farmers' Union. Unlike most manufacturing industry, the NFU supported the arguments contained in SPNW as the best use of available resources with CLNT having a longer term role 'if the growth materialised'. But in the meantime they argued, it was necessary to guarantee food supplies. It supported the Greater Manchester arguments which 'tackles the urban problem at the root'. The expert witness for the NFU, Mr Merridew, expressed concern at the potential disruption of development to the remaining farmers in the area. In continuing the argument that the bulk of the land was classed as Grade 3 under the Ministry of Agriculture's national land classification, he pointed out that this grading should not be seen 'as an indication of the productive capacity, but rather as a broad physical assessment on a national scale'. This argument was then applied to the 'greenfield' development proposed for the Grimsargh/Haighton district which were described as 'highly productive areas, profitable and efficient and likely to remain so if left in their present state'.

Several large companies submitted observations expressing concern about the land use boundaries shown on the outline plan which, they argued, might restrict possible expansion. Pre-eminent among these was a major employer, British Leyland UK Limited, which had a major plant of the truck and bus division located in Leyland itself. The administration of this division was based in Leyland and on the Leyland site the factories, at the time of the inquiry, employed 'a total payroll of over 10,000 people' making British Leyland 'the largest employer of people within the influence of the Central Lancashire Development Corporation'. The 'representation' placed before the inspector by Mr A.D. Fogg, staff director, made it clear that inter organisation discussions had taken place. British Leyland declared that it was 'grateful for having had the opportunity to meet and discuss the proposals . . . over the last few months'. They affirmed that 'the objectives of the Central Lancashire Development Corporation are in the interests of the Leyland area as a whole and in the interests of the Company'. They therefore expressed their 'full support for (the outline plan) proposals', but on certain points made specific representations. They first underlined the results of prior negotiations, for zoning land for expansion rather than being left unallocated, which had been referred to in the general manager's proof of evidence; others referred to road alignments and land in ownership becoming green belt. A major unresolved objection was the proposal to close junction 28 of the M6 motorway.

Changes proposed for a motorway junction also gave rise to an objection by another major company, Whitbreads. The siting of their new brewery at Samlesbury had been a controversial planning decision in which the then Secretary of State, Mr Peter Walker, had overruled the recommendation of his inspector. The choice of site had been based partly upon its ease of access to the motorway and the proposal to close a slip road at junction 31 was vigorously rejected. Counsel appearing for Whitbreads was, quite remarkably, a former Secretary of State for the Environment, Mr Geoffrey Rippon, QC. The two expert witnesses from Whitbreads were closely cross questioned by the CLDC counsel, Mr Iain Glidewell, on the company's distribution process and argued that the Samlesbury interchange was 'unlikely to be affected before the M65 was opened', (i.e. the proposed Calder Valley motorway). Mr Rippon did not choose to cross question CLDC witnesses but in his submission he 'specifically requested the Secretary of State to delete all reference with regard to the slip road. It was not the proper time or forum to consider such matters'. He noted that it was 'not only objected to by us, but by Lancashire County Council, North East Lancashire Development Association and by Preston Borough Council'.

Many individual objectors were also associated with residents' groups and submitted additional, personal points. There was the emotional submission by the chairman of the Ashton Action Group, Arthur Jones (See Chapter 9) and the deeply felt observations by postman and keen rambler, Cyril Spiby. Arthur Tyldesley spoke eloquently and without rancour of the flowers and wild life in the quiet country lane in Ingol, where he lived, which he believed would be endangered by the development there. The Runshaw development was attacked by George Birtill, editor of the Chorley and Leyland Guardian, who despite Mr Glidewell's accusations of inconsistency (by quoting his newspaper pronouncements), firmly held his new position. He was supported in his view by a Leyland elder statesman and former UDC councillor, Mr Stanley Kelley.

One of the most unusual objections arose from the agreed amendment to land use submitted by CLDC to the inspector. The result of the concession to British Leyland was that properties previously unaffected by foreseeable development were to be sited in land scheduled for industrial us. Mr & Mrs McKeown submitted a late personal objection to the inquiry supported by a petition on behalf of other residents in that area, which received prominent press coverage, (LEP, 14 January 1975). CLDC in its list of amendments stated that 'the industrial area has been further amended to leave a strip of land unallocated on the easterly side'.

THE ROLE OF THE INSPECTOR

The central figure presiding over the inquiry and serving as the official channel and filter of information is the inspector. He is normally a member of the permanent staff of the Department of the Environment's inspectorate. This complement is currently a cadre of about 130 who have been recruited almost entirely from the appropriate professions, such as town planning, surveying or civil engineering, from outside government service. As recruitment advertisements demonstrate, there is the requirement of sufficient experience in a professional career to gain entrance to the panel. After a thorough selection procedure and subsequent training, they are gradually introduced to the control of inquiries by superintending inspectors.

An explanation of the attraction of the role is offered by Wraith and Lamb; it lies in temperament:

> .... An inspector's work offers responsibility, varied interest, movement and a freedom from routine, attributes of employment which some value highly. (Wraith and Lamb, 1971, p.182)

This generalisation applied to the motivation of the CLNT outline plan inspector, Mr S.H.A. Rollison. He regarded the work as fulfilling and interesting and appeared to make much of the independent nature of the inspectorate with its apparent remoteness from the rest of the civil service and its tenuous links with bureaucracy. (Personal interview 10 May 1977). The inspectors attend seminars on planning issues, such as 'out of town' shopping centres. They also receive planning policy statements, having apparently been aware of changes in policy about six months ahead of their formal announcement.

The role demands the creation of an aura of distance and impartiality. The inspector is required to hold himself aloof from anything other than formal contact with persons who may be a party to the inquiry. Much of his time is spent in hotels weighing the evidence and writing reports.

Indeed, in parallel with the judiciary, it is maintained that inspectors have no informal links other than within the inspectorate and tend to be unaware of the processes following submission of their report which is a 'personal document'. (Interview 10 May 1977). Current personal links may be restricted, but common backgrounds, experience and perception shared with other prominent figures are evident. Mr Rollison, for example, like many senior new town officers, had spent a period in the colonial service.

The remoteness required through professional ethos ran counter however, to Mr Rollison's relationship with the local press. The LEP, consistent with its house style, proceeded to mount a photograph of the inspector adjacent to many reports. It appears that a 'special status' was accorded to Mr Rollison by the press. In turn, the inspector regarded the reporting of the inquiry by that paper most favourably. Towards the end of the outline plan inquiry, special photographic coverage of the helicopter flight surveying the designated area ('Inquiry takes to the air!', LEP, 11 January 1975, 'On top of the problems', LEP, 15 January 1975) and a special interview by Peter Dugdale provided "a fascinating insight into the thoughts and life style of one of Whitehall's 'Men in a suitcase'". (See attached reproduction of the article 'Our future will be decided in the heart of Kent', LEP, 29 January 1975).

Most remarkable of all was the news item stating that:

> .... one of the country's top planning inspectors is to use 'Lancashire Evening Post' reports to help him write his own report on the Central Lancashire new town outline plan inquiry.

It continued:

> .... Department of the Environment inspector Mr Stanley Rollison said he was so impressed with the accuracy of the 'Post' reports on the inquiry by our chief planning correspondent, Peter Dugdale, that he was keeping cuttings from the paper for his own inquiry assessment, along with his own notes, written evidence and other documents. (Inspector praises 'Post' reports, LEP, 28 January 1975)

An inspector through his conduct of proceedings, by his interventions and relative flexibility or rigidity, sets an individual stamp on each inquiry. Mr Rollison, though not tested to react to extreme cases of public disorder showed a calm, patient authority. In the particularly lengthy and detailed evening sessions which were specially arranged for SCRAP he permitted evidence to be presented on designation, despite the fact that this submission was out of order and outside the terms of reference for the inquiry. Twice, during an evening session of some three hours duration, he interrupted evidence to make formal warnings about the lack of relevance of the submission, but on one occasion adding 'I shall hear it, but it is costing a lot of public funds'. Despite its inadmissibility, he undertook to bring the minister's attention to the documents containing ant designation views, 'even though they were not part of this inquiry'. ('Objections out of order - but still heard', LEP, 8 January 1975.)

While admitting that professional advocacy was useful for linking evidence and a 'good exercise in public relations', Mr Rollison expressed a preference for 'amateur appearances'. (Personal interview). This view was given support by Mr Rollison's occasional, yet obvious

Our future will be decided in the heart of Kent

Inspector Stanley Rollison leaves the nine-week inquiry and steps into the complex task of reporting on New Town to the Government.

PETER DUGDALE meets the man with the big job of mapping out the future of Central Lancashire. Picture by ROY PAYNE.

OFFICIAL papers, maps and documents are piled high on the study desk of a Kentish farmhouse. A white-haired, slightly-built man pores over them.

That is the scene this week as one of Whitehall's top planning inspectors begins his task of draughting the report on which the future of Central Lancashire —— and to some extent, the whole North West —— depends.

On those slim shoulders hangs the weight of evaluating the New Town development corporation's £900 million outline plan — a plan which will change the face of 56 square miles of the county's heartland over the next 30 years — and the validity of more than 500 objections to it.

To Stanley Rollison, the Department of the Environment inspector who has just come to the end of a marathon nine-week public inquiry into the plan," the hardest part has yet to come."

Draught

It is to the quiet of his country home that he has gone to re-read all those papers, maps and documents again, to look up his own "shorthand" notes, and then write his report and recommendations for his boss, Evironment Secretary, Mr Anthony Crosland.

And so big and complicated is his task that he estimates it will be the end of March — two months — before the completed report is handed in.

Mr Rollison has, in fact, three reports to prepare — one on the main plan, and one each for smaller, detailed plans for early development at Ingol and Grimsargh.

"I shall probably draught the smaller ones first, because it is possible they could be submitted independently of the outline plan" he told me.

After re-reading all the mass of statements, evidence and documents, the inspector will categorise them into subject groups —— objections from other areas like Greater Manchester and North East Lancashire, those against the eastern primary route, those against the western primary route, and so on until he gets to those like Planwatch and the Ramblers' Association whose objections covered a variety of subjects.

"By doing it this way, I think I can shorten the report without omitting anything of importance, and so make it easier for the Secretary of State to assimilate all the objections and the type of objections" he said.

"I hand-write my report, several times, draughting and re-draughting it. The only facility we inspectors are provided with by the Department is a tape recorder, which I use at short inquiries, but would be unlikely to use in a complex and complicated one like this."

"The report is then sent to the typing pool at Portsmouth, and then back for checking before submission."

How long he takes to write his report is up to the inspector himself — providing he does not take too long! And if he finds he is running out of time with his next inquiry looming up, he can put in a request for some other inspector to take the next one for him.

This has already happened to him with the Central Lancashire inquiry. He came in November, expecting an inquiry lasting three weeks. It took nine — spread over three months. So other inquiries he had booked for January, February and March have had to be allocated to others in the 120-strong inspectorate.

In his 15-years experience in the Department, Central Lancashire now goes down as the second-longest on record. It was only outlasted by an inquiry into the Hertfordshire county development plan review, which lasted six months — and took two inspectors working alternate weeks.

"That was for the whole of the county, and there were lots of objections" said Mr Rollison "but we didn't work at quite the same pressure as we have done here. We didn't have evening sessions, and we normally finished at four, each day.

Notice

At Preston, however, he had no fewer than 10 evening sessions, and several of the 36 day-time sessions ran on into the evening. A finishing time of 6 pm was nothing unusual.

During that time, millions of words must have been spoken for and against the plan, but the man in the middle maintained a remarkable command of the entire situation, listening patiently, questioning pointedly, and ruling authoritatively as the occasion demanded.

No-one could leave the inquiry with a genuine complaint that he had not been given a full and fair hearing. And if completing a person's evidence that day meant switching to another venue, Mr Rollison was willing if necessary to do that, too.

All told, the inquiry was heard in no less than seven different rooms because of other bookings, the Guild Hall's Grand Hall, Charter Theatre and Avenham Suite the Town Hall's council chamber and Number 1 committee room, a committee room at County Hall and the Roper Hall — a local social club.

"I take off my hat to the development corporation in having to move all those papers, equipment and plans," said Mr Rollison.

And, after nine weeks' study at close hand, he is also complimentary about the people and places he has met and seen in Central Lancashire.

"I congratulate the people in this area for the very high standard of representations they have made at the inquiry. I admire their courage in persisting to say they still don't want the New Town, although I repeatedly said this was not a matter for this inquiry," he said.

What was all the more remarkable, he felt, was that most of the objectors prepared and presented their own cases, without professional help. "They have done it off their own bat and the standard has been remarkably high, although I suspect that some of it was misplaced because they were bucking the original designation, and they failed to realise that a New Town means urbanisation of the designated area," he explained.

On the other hand, he hoped that the development corporation would take more notice in future of views expressed by some of the "amateurs."

Those nine weeks in Preston — living out of a suitcase in a town centre hotel — also gave Mr Rollison a better than average opportunity of getting to know the area well.

Assets

"I think Preston is a most attractive town. It has wonderful assets in its river and parks and streams and woodland. I would imagine that with good design, the New Town will be a wonderful place to live in."

Whatever the findings in his report, Mr Rollison believes that there is still a big future for New Towns, and he knows of no plans for cutting back on development in them.

As he puts it "housing is still one of the most important issues in this country, and New Towns are one of the most important means of providing them, providing they can produce jobs as well."

"But those" he said "are my opinions, not official ones."

The official opinion on Central Lancashire New Town is not likely to be known until mid-summer, at least, to give the Department's top brass a full chance of assessing his report.

It might even be longer, if the economic climate is the deciding factor.

On the other hand, there could be some indication that the Government is intending to give this plan a priority rating in the fact that Mr Rollison is now being asked "almost weekly" when the Secretary of State can expect his report.

Before he can answer that question with any degree of accuracy, Stanley Rollison will have to wade through that sea of paper on his study desk, and come up with some tricky answers.

But none of us who have seen the hours of concentration he has put into the nine weeks of this inquiry will begrudge him if he takes at least one extra day off work to celebrate his birthday. He is 62 this week!

Thanks for help

Reader's letter

MAY I, and I am sure all the people who have been connected with the issue over the New Town inquiry, say a big "thank you" to Mr Stanley Rollison for the painstaking concern and interest he took in the private persons' objections, the help of the leading men and all those who have worked to get the issues on an even keel.

We all know you cannot stop progress, but you could not stand by and see part of your heritage taken away without fighting for a just outcome.

I think that after it has been sifted through, we will have been helped by putting our objections to the inspector. Homes are just as important, and at the present time more so, than roads.

The Press I thank also, and for anyone to knock them is bad business. They have limited space and other people have to be included. — "Worried Prestoner," Ashton.

An article in the Lancashire Evening Post on 29 January 1975

Reproduced by kind permission of the Lancashire Evening Post sympathies. During the emotional submission from Mr Arthur Jones, chairman of the Ashton action group, he was observed to be visibly moved. Yet the role requires an inherent detachment. This non involvement in turn, as in the judiciary, can lead to a remoteness from everyday affairs and even obvious lapses in current technical terminology. Evidence of this aloofness may be cited when Mr Rollison was heard to ask a Planwatch witness 'What is this term - gentrification?'

In many public inquiries the demeanour of the inspector is a crucial feature in determining its acceptability to the public. He may become the embodiment of authority and a focus for resentment, or alternatively he may inculcate an impression of detachment and integrity. Interviews with objectors at the outline plan public inquiry tended to show that mosttook the view that Mr Rollison, with his calm authoritative manner was regarded as a reasonably fair and balanced official. His ability to suffer SCRAP's 'irrelevancies' could certainly be regarded as an astute means of allowing objectors to air grievances and to avoid the development of too much resentment and frustration. In this way, Mr Rollison, no doubt assisted by the local press coverage, became one of the preeminent participants in the inquiry. He, in turn, was later to agree that this inquiry was one which 'stood out in his memory'. (7)

THE BALANCE OF INFLUENCES : THE PUBLIC INQUIRY IN THE URBAN RELATIONS SYSTEM

The public inquiry, as a British institution, provides an overt episode in the whole process of political decision making. The procedures, the inspector's report and recommendations, and the eventual ministerial decision, may all be regarded as part of a central/local system of information and decision making making flow with a direct feedback to the local-urban relations system.

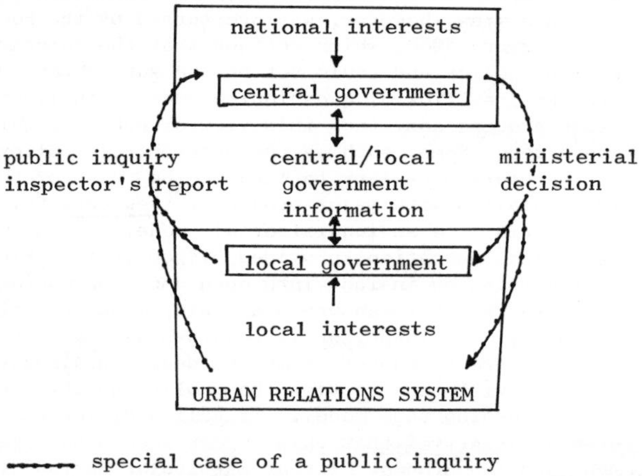

The interpretation of the public inquiry procedures will depend upon the organisational or individual role and relative position of influence. Local authorities will tend to view the inquiry process as a means of balancing and reconciling interests. On occasions, they themselves are required to justify the 'public' interest against private property rights in local public inquiries. It follows that when the local authority is a subordinate, interested party - as the district councils were - or an objector in a clash of elites - as Greater Manchester Council - then consistency requires an acceptance of the ground rules and the legitimacy of the procedures. A 'reconciliation' model would thus appear to provide a common framework for bargaining from the standpoint of the regular participants in public inquiries such as local authorities.

A model of 'information exchange' presupposed a free flow of relevant data from each side and comparisons may be made with 'disclosure of information' provisions in collective bargaining. Arising from this assumed reciprocation, a great understanding of the various parties' position should emerge and participants will experience 'political education'. (Again, one might draw parallels here with the 'all that is required is better communications' school of industrial relations.) As with other negotiation settings, information tends to be disproportionately accessible, regarded as 'irrelevant' or restricted by 'the rules'. The dispute about the M40-M42 public inquiry illustrates this point. Bushell's recent case against the Department of the Environment was based, among other things, upon the refusal of the inspector to permit cross questioning of the department's witnesses about traffic forecasts, on the grounds that these were government policy. In the court of appeal, Lord Denning disagreed with the inspector's view,

> .... They are just as much matters of fact as the evidence of a medical man as to the prognosis of a disease.

and for almost six months this decision placed the Department of Transport's motorway and trunk road programme 'in disarray' (Guardian, 13 July 1979). Lord Denning was concerned to reestablish confidence in highway inquiries and used the court's authority 'to see that the inquiries are conducted fairly in accordance with the requirements of natural justice'. This view, however, was overturned by the House of Lords judgement in February 1980, which decided that the forecasts were a matter of government policy and could not be the subject of cross examination. With the free flow of questioning once again limited, the information exchange process and, thus this view of public inquiries, tends to become devalued. Some, such as the outer circle policy unit, insist that it is therefore necessary to 'change the rules of the game' for public inquiries dealing with major projects, (New Society, 14 June 1979) from the adversarial 'to an inquisitorial' mode. Given current practices, the 'political education' provided by public inquiries, rather than their providing an insight into open decision making and the balancing of interests, they can breed a cynicism and belief that, in Lord Denning's words, 'the inspector is regarded as the stooge of the department . . . just there to rubber stamp the decision already made..'

The inspector himself will tend to view the public inquiry according to to the information processing task model. Mr Rollison, for example, stressed in a personal interview that this report should be regarded as a personal document and the product of that particular period of time. The outline plan inquiry proceedings, the supporting evidence and documents, together with tours of inspection, all require digesting, filtering and ordering so that a report might be produced. Mr Rollison took the view that 'this long inquiry has to a large extent been an exercise in public participation from which I suspect everyone has learned.'(Report para. 680.)

The static nature of the document, a stage in the process of ministerial decision making, gives rise to two issues. First, whether the minister should consider new evidence and second, the extent to which the continued activities of pressure groups should be regarded as legitimate during the period of covert activity during which the ministerial decision is decided.

On the first issue, the Franks committee took the view that:

> .... so far as new 'factual evidence' was concerned, the parties ought to be told, and that the Minister should not reach a decision until he had had their observations. (Wraith and Lamb, 1971, pp.169-70)

closely linked with this argument is the second question, the activity of groups and persons seeking 'post inquiry pressure', (See Chapter 13). Well organised organisations are aware of the need to continue lobbying, but others having been 'educated' by the public inquiry process seek 'a second bite at the cherry', when they are able to employ less formalised procedures than hitherto. Many objectors as individuals, or as members of organisations, are experiencing a procedure for the first and maybe the only time. They find that they are at a distinct advantage. As Wraith and Lamb concede:

> .... They then have to learn in a hurry about things of which they have never heard, the knowledge they acquire is probably incomplete, and they may become apathetic and think the whole thing is beyond them. (Wraith and Lamb, 1971, p.309.

Post inquiry lobbying may thus be viewed as an extra inquiry attempt to redress an imbalance of both information, experience and expertise. The extent of the imbalance of the parties and the public inquiries themselves varies considerably.

A significant feature is the lack of experience of public inquiries by many objectors. Indeed for many organisations as well as individuals their appearance before the inspector could be their only experience of the procedures. This unfamiliarity may vary from locality to locality depending on the rate of local development and the quality of the leadership of the voluntary and civic organisations, but in most instances it will be impossible for objectors to achieve role efficiency on a 'one off' basis. Though the inspector will profess to make allowances for inexperience and nervousness, it is apparent that in comparison with say, a lay shop steward in an industrial setting, the non professional public inquiry objector is at a distinct disadvantage. Just as in industrial collective bargaining, there has to be the expectation of a reasonable chance of some gain by the objector for the institution of the public inquiry to remain valid. Thus the planning inquiry, as an equivalent of a 'formal conference in procedure' in industrial relations has within the urban relations system to be viewed similarly as legitimate and fair. Ministerial decisions, particularly since the Samlesbury Brewery case and Torness, as Robert Waterhouse points out, have led to the realisation that 'It is plain enough to most objectors that the public inquiry is not the best place to win battles',(*Guardian*, 24 September 1975).

More recent examples, not only in planning issues but in the nuclear policy field, have provoked even more savage criticism. As Cowan puts it:

.... What is objectionable is the use that is increasingly being made of public inquiries on major and controversial planning issues to fool the public into thinking that they have a real opportunity to influence the decision. By pretending that the purpose of public inquiries is to let the public participate in making policy, government ministers are trying to defuse politics by concealing where the real decisions are being made. (Cowan, 1980)

It was this emerging wider understanding of the process of influencing decision making and the realisation that the public inquiry was not the only mode of exerting pressure, that prompted the many amenity societies in Central Lancashire to cooperate and mount a belated national campaign for a reappraisal of the need for CLNT.

SUMMARY

This chapter has described the pivotal period of the research fieldwork, the outline plan public inquiry. The ritual formalities of the proceedings have been outlined, together with the principal individual and organisational participants.

The important role of the inspector has been analysed.

NOTES

1. This practice is usual in the examinations in public, now replacing the public inquiries into structure plans.

2. 'the extent and depth of public participation was a model of its own'.

3. (This statement had some validity since the development corporation was the first new town to be affected in its early stages by the recommendations for public participation sent to General Managers in September 1972.) See DOE letter, NT circular No. 276, dated 15 September 1972.

4. 'If the government of the day were to decide that in future we would all live in wooden huts - I suppose the Development Corporation would start building wooden huts'. (CLDC, 1974b p.8.)

5. Even during the period of the public inquiry, Lancashire County Council were reported to have made 'strong representation to the Development Corporation regarding the failure to consult with it before proposing an alteration to the outline plan' ('County protest at plan changes', Chorley Guardian, 27 February 1975).

6. By March 1976, all three District Councils within the designated area were reported to have 'soured relations' with CLDC, and alleging that statements and promises by CLNT were being broken and that one local authority was being 'played off against another' ('Angry councils want new town showdown', LEP, 31 March 1976). Previous to this, even Lancashire County Council had accused CLDC 'of steam rollering plans through without permission', ('New town footpath

steamroller halted', LEP, 9 February 1976).

7. The existence of this report was not admitted initially by CLDC but it was produced after pressure by Mr Turner with the claim that its findings, which were not entirely favourable, should be disregarded, (Turner, 1975).

8. He referred by name to the outstanding contributors, Mr Jim Pilkington, Mrs Sylvia Pickering, Mr Arthur Jones and of course, Mr Glidewell and Mr Phelps. (Personal interview 10 May 1977).

PART V
ASSESSMENT, EVALUATION AND REVIEW

13 Influencing decision making after the public inquiry

INTRODUCTION

This chapter describes the central and most important occurrence in the concluding part of the study, the emergence of the hitherto disparate local groups as a coherent interest group seeking to influence national decision making. The hypothetical basis for the functioning of interest groups, the concepts of networks and urban social movements was outlined in Chapter 4. These notions are drawn upon in this chapter to analyse the post public inquiry activities of the local groups, politicians and MPs, as well as the networks of the various organisations.

THE ACTIVITY OF LOCAL GROUPS

After the public inquiry into the outline plan, new town development continued as before under the existing Section 6(i) approvals. Despite the apparent information vacuum from the centre, the DOE, such activities served to keep the groups viable, though the incipient rivalry between Planwatch, its allied local groups, and SCRAP denied the possibility of a coordinated grouping.

At the prompting of some members of Planwatch, who felt it was desirable to continue to mount pressure on the secretary of state, but were unsure of the best methods, plans for an inter-group conference were suggested in November 1975. This event took place in March 1976, and delegates from local action groups were given talks by three speakers on aspects of influencing decision making. From the central office of CPRE, Robin Grove-White described the lobby process from his experience as a member of a pressure group.

Dr Noel Boaden, a member of the linked research project into public participation in structure planning, gave some observations on the relationships between groups and local authorities and Robert Waterhouse whose 'Guardian' articles on planning issues had excited attention at this time (1), gave some of his reflections on planning in general and new towns in particular.

The most significant aspect of the conference was the emerging understanding and awareness of the possible importance of national lobbying, which was given credence to the writer by noting the questions from delegates (2). Finally there was a proposal that the various groups should coordinate their efforts with a view to presenting a report seeking reappraisal of the project in the light of changing circumstances since designation. With a far greater degree of cooperation

SOMEWHERE NEAR the top of Mr Anthony Crosland's in-tray lies the inspector's report on the Central Lancashire New Town Outline Plan inquiry. The Environment Secretary can be forgiven for not rushing to endorse the inevitable qualified approval read by the inspector, Mr Stanley Rollison, on the development corporation's proposals. At this time of crisis and cutback is it correct to embark on major spending programmes for a supercity that every day looks less relevant to national and regional objectives? That question, whether he likes it or not, haunts Mr Crosland's decision.

Not that the outline plan inquiry—which lasted all of three months last winter—was supposed to question the rational basis for this new town. That, according to Mr Rollison and the development corporation, was all sorted out at the designation inquiry back in May 1969. But accounts of that inquiry show that the then Minister of Housing and Local Government, Mr Anthony (later Lord) Greenwood, offered the 670 objectors little hope of any radical reassessment; he submitted a written statement at the inquiry's opening affirming his belief that the Preston-Leyland-Chorley area was the best place for Lancashire's rejuvenation, population growth and overspill requirements.

Meadowland at Runshaw (above) that will give way to homes contrasts with neglected housing in Hindley, Wigan, which won't benefit from the New Town. pictures by DENIS THORPE

Lancashire hotchpotch

Plans for a super city around Preston await the Government's approval.

But is it needed?

Can the planning juggernaut be stopped?

ROBERT WATERHOUSE sifts the evidence

consultants' report, an "impact study" which ran to twice the length of the CLNT study. Amid a welter of facts and figures, the conclusions were unsurprising. Yes, Blackburn and Burnley would lose population to the new town, but only Blackburn was close enough to be directly affected and it was capable of looking after itself. There might even be positive "spin-off" developments, and job opportunities within the new town for lower paid Blackburn workers.

Reproduced by kind permission of the Guardian

than hitherto, key individuals formed a drafting committee following a conference of delegates at Samlesbury Hall on 8 May 1976. This situation was significant since for the first time links with CPRE nationally would be employed to influence.

The Local Groups Working Party, as it became known, prepared a report on 25 May 1976. It was sent with the support of 21 local groups to the Secretary of State and to many key individuals nationally. The Conservative MP, Edward Gardner supported the report and in July, Christopher Hall (then director of CPRE) attempted to arrange for the representatives of the local groups to meet the Secretary of State. This initiative was not successful. In May, Peter Levin's book 'Government and the Planning Process' had been published (Levin, 1976). Though this book had been reviewed critically locally by Peter Dugdale (LEP, 12 May 1976) this opinion did not deter the working party and it was now employed as further evidence by Chris Hall.

It can be argued that the most important planning policy statement of the period between the public inquiry and the Minister's decision letter of April 1977, was the Secretary of State's Manchester speech on the inner cities in September 1976. This address stimulated renewed lobbying and press comment, notably in the Guardian, 20 September 1976, and The Times, 22 November 1976. The CPRE taking up the anti CLNT cause nationally, sent out a briefing note to all MPs from the north west. This information was in preparation for a Standing Committee on Regional Affairs debate on the north west held on 17 September 1976. There was a press report of the committee in which north west MPs were quoted as sounding a warning that there "must be 'no drawing back' from commitments to develop Central Lancashire New Town", (LEP, 18 November 1976).

Further correspondence included a dialogue between the director of the Town and Country Planning Association, Mr David Hall (following the pro CLNT line and echoing some of the arguments employed by Mr Phelps) (See The Times, 3 December 1976) and Mr Christopher Hall, director of CPRE.

The arguments were brought together in an adjournment debate on the CLNT on 23 December 1976. 37 MPs from the north west were sent a full briefing on behalf of the anti CLNT lobby by Christopher Hall pointing out what he regarded to be 'fundamental flaws' embodied in the arguments employed by 'apologists for the new town'. CPRE, 1976).

Through this phase of national lobbying, a wider experience of political process was introduced to many action group members. It is to some implications and lessons drawn from this period that we now turn.

PRESSURE GROUPS - A REASSESSMENT

How might the observation of late entry of the local groups working party into national pressure group politics provide us with any further insight into the analysis of pressure group activity? Initially, some assessment of the reasons for this delay through the close observation of their activities should be possible.

First, most residents' and action groups were locally based, parochial, and with limited horizons. The identity of interests which might have been forged between them was further weakened by the process of Section 6(i) inquiries and CPOs.

Second, there were no established experienced organisations willing to lead and coordinate a united opposition or dialogue. The Preston

Civic Society was moribund, the possible coordinator of voluntary activity in the area, the Community Council of Lancashire, had primarily a rural remit. Planwatch, a new organisation, attempted this role but had to build up a network and had not the initial expertise nor proven leadership as credentials for such a position.

Third, there was an initial failure to link up with national organisations. CPRE's Lancashire branch liaised with Planwatch mainly on rural aspects and significantly there was no national CPRE consultation until the local groups' initiative. Planwatch was affiliated to the Town and Country Planning Association, who used their planning aid service. TCPA although sympathetic with participation, as such, found it difficult to oppose a new town, since as the former Garden Cities' Association it has a vested interest in the success of the concept. As Aldridge comments: 'The association is, after all, one of the mose effective pressure groups operating openly in the country' (Aldridge, 1979, p.189 ; See also Wootton, 1978, p.21; Ross, 1973, p.332 and Bryant, 1974, p.244).

Fourth, links with people in the other new towns or planning action groups had not been forged. From noting committee proceedings it appeared that there was a general lack of awareness of the campaigns on the third London airport or the London motorway box. The only national issue which appeared to be in the public consciousness was that of the 'Edinburgh runway' and more locally that of the Samlesbury brewery. Both of which had seemed more likely to have induced resignation than defiance. As a consequence, lobbying and organisational skills which might have been imported were not pursued. Methods employed in the Aire Valley, Archway or Winchester public inquiries by the Friends of the Earth and John Tyme were therefore not countenanced.

Fifth, having been involved in the administrative process of consultation and a public inquiry, many organisations might feel reluctant to use other channels of influence. As Ryan puts it:

> .... It is now taken for granted that if a pressure group wants something it goes to the administration first; and even if it returns empty handed, there are constraints on an approach to Parliament or the press since there is an unwritten law which declares it 'bad form' for either pressure groups or the administration to embarrass the other. (Ryan, 1978, p.18)

This hesitancy has meant that little attention has been given to parliament by pressure groups, and contacts with Whitehall have taken priority. This balance appears to have been redressed in recent years not only by backbench revolts, but by the increasing influence of parliamentary committees (See New Society leader, Power in Parliament, 14 August 1980), and the use of question time, an example of which will be described later in this chapter.

The traditional view of the predominant pressure groups having a closed secretive relationship with Whitehall let to many having an ambbivalence about the activities of such groups. Indeed, most studies of such organisations have shown a traditional bias, as Ryan puts it:

> .... that is, an almost exclusive concern with the powerful, those groups whose legitimacy is unquestioned and where access to those who determine public policy is regular and easy. (Ryan, 1978, p.1)

Yet the received truth in a pluralistic society is one in which all groups can organise and compete without restraint in the policy making process. This situation may be attacked from both the Left and Right. From a Conservative viewpoint, Norman Lamont, (Daily Telegraph, 3 May 1978) sees the negative aspects of a society dominated by major interest groups, who in turn become an arm of government and thus part of an emerging corporate state. Its antidote, an open economy with an emphasis on the individual, can also be equated with the danger inherent in the 'mass society'. Kornhauser, in a seminal work on this study, viewed the function of groups to protect the isolated citizen from the manipulations of totalitarian tyrants (Kornhauser, 1960). From a contrasting standpoint, the image of a society of competing groups is attacked by Marxists, who believe that a capitalist state, with its vision of a plural world of competing values is false. Rather it is a consensus imposed by the interests of the dominant ruling class.

In both cases, the over generalisation of this criticism may be demonstrated by the refinement of pressure groups into categories. Wootton, for example, by his four fold classification (3) illuminates the reasons underlying the reactions by some commentators in attributing to pressure groups the stagnation in the political system. By employing the additional dimensions of degree of political specialisation and degree of openness of membership (Wootton, 1978, pp.19-21) and from the diagram on p.186, it is clear that the charge of pluralistic stagnation' if it can hold at all, is most likely to reside with representative (type 2) groups; all other three types giving evidence of initiatives in public policy providing flexibility in the political system (Wootton, 1978, pp.173-82).

Bearing this classification in mind, it is possible to construct a continuum of pressure group accessibility and influence.

Naked political pressure ⟷ *'whitemail'* ⟷ *Acceptability* ⟷|⟷ *unacceptability*

(e.g. WARA) (institutionalised blackmail - Hayward, 1976)

PLACING THE JOINT GROUPS WORKING PARTY INTO CONTEXT

The chosen course of action of the coordinated groups was firmly based upon working within the established machinery of influence. There was no evidence of the need to emulate the anti Cublington campaigns (4) of the third London airport protestors (WARA) nor the civil disobedience of the Aire Valley motorway protestors. Apart from the will and need for leaders of such persuasion, the groups did not possess the expertise within their ranks, the public relations resources, nor the political clout of the airport campaign (McKie, 1973; Perman, 1973). This limitation meant that influence had to be based on acceptability. The action groups, by the adoption of their cause at national level by CPRE, had effectively transformed their classification from representative (type 2) groups into the category of expressive (Sector 3) groups who, since they 'give their minds to things other than political pressure, they seem likely to save most of their ammunition for the times when they are outraged or otherwise stimulated by government'. (Wootton, 1978, p.174). This mutation also meant that it was possible to bridge the divide between acceptability and unacceptability, or in Benewick's

POLITICAL SPECIALIZATION

MEMBERSHIP	LOW	HIGH
CLOSED	1 T & G, NUR British Aircraft, Burmah Oil, London Rubber Industries, House of Fraser, Hill Samuel Law Society Townswomen's Guilds, Women's Institutes National Federation of Pakistani Associations Urdd Gobaith Cymru (Welsh League of Youth) Saffron Walden Countryside Association (Operational)	2 TUC CBI, ABCC, NFU, British Road Federation British Legal Association National Joint Action Campaign for Women's Equal Rights League of Overseas Pakistanis (Tower Hamlets) Welsh Language Society Saffron Walden Anti-Airport Committee, Stansted Working Party (etc.), WARA (Representative)
OPEN	3 National Trust, Georgian Society, Ulster Architectural Heritage Society, Association for the Protection of Rural Scotland Friend Society of Individualists National Allotments and Garden Society Workers' Educational Association (Expressive)	4 Conservation Society, FoE, Population Stabilization Campaign for Homosexual Equality Justice, Amnesty, NCCL Child Poverty Action Group, Shelter CASE, FEVER, PRISE (Propagational)

A Typology of Pressure Groups Wootton, 1978:20

terms between the various worlds of the pressure group universe - from those who challenge the existing rules, priorities or decisions (the third world) to an accessibility which is either continuous (first world) or accepted or intermittent (second world) (Benewick, 1973). They were thus able to have a second chance to exert influence by regrouping under a national organisation. Prior to this action, many activities and group members had been willing to accept Catanese's Axiom II that 'special interest groups can be more effective through overt political actions than through involvement in the planning process' (Catanese, 1974, p.25). It is this weakness, and lack of coherence, of locally based urban social movements to which reference was made in Chapter 4. Yet the need for some form of network to form, in response to a policy proposal or administrative decision, however transitory or disjointed, is an important ingredient of an urban relations system. It is to a short description of these local networks which formed at the time of the most active period of CLNT activity 1974-77 that we now turn.

NETWORKS WITHIN AN URBAN RELATIONS SYSTEM

For the purposes of this study it is desirable to anchor a network on an individual or group. In our case the extent of multiple group membership within action groups makes it imperative to employ a group as an anchor - in this case Planwatch; just as it is to use the CLDC as the nodal point in its network. It is suggested, however, that it is unnecessary to be too stringent about the exclusivity of the individual or group alternatives and it is a more realistic representation to permit both in network diagram representing relationships at the time of the outline plan public inquiry in 1974.

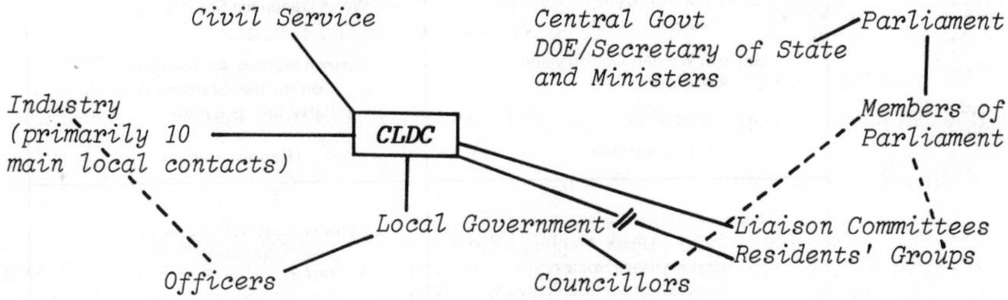

The Network of the CLDC

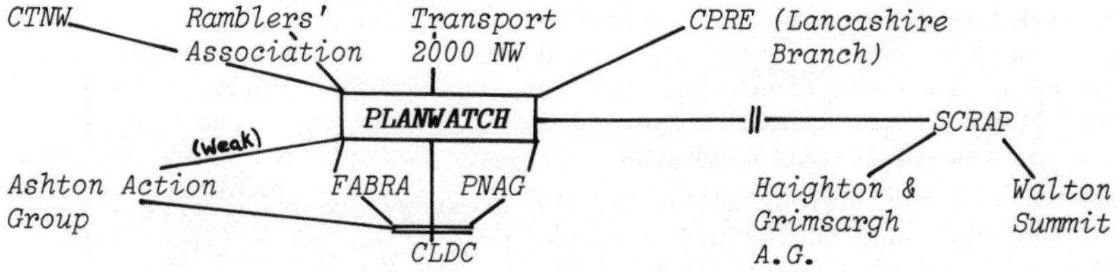

The Network of the local Action Groups

In both diagrams it will be noted that a distinct cleavage is depicted within the local urban relations system; that between the networks of the CLDC and that of what, ultimately, will become the nucleus of the local groups' joint working party. This distinct dichotomy tends not to be based upon crude class or status criteria, but in terms of values, what has been termed after Parsons the pattern maintenance axis,

(Laumann and Pappi, 1976, p.4). Even within an essentially systems perspective it has therefore been necessary to delineate a separate elite subsystem (Laumann and Pappi, 1976, p.13), or what Sarason and his colleagues term 'a public decision making network', (Sarason, et al, 1977).

It has thus not been necessary in this section to adopt a perspective which incorporates conflict, rivalry or a dialectical approach to the urban relations system to show the evident discontinuities which existed in the network at this time. Much of the evidence has shown that linkages between the local groups and that of the development corporation have been tenuous and intermittent. Nevertheless, CLNT, as a significant organisation, would tend to dominate any network and it is suggested that a distinctly organisational perspective, incorporating a political economy approach to networks rather than that of general network theory might prove more relevant to this study.

THE ORGANISATIONAL PERSPECTIVE WITH CLNT AS A NODAL POINT

Organisational decision making

Unless a researcher is in the fortunate position as a participant observer within a management team (Dalton, 1959), he is limited either to data from a partial interview/observation programme with selected staff, or he has to rely upon the limited access to organisational gate keepers and the observation of key personnel in extra organisational situations such as public meetings. The methodological limitations imposed on the researcher in this context have been compensated by the official documents of the CLDC, by the considered writing of the general manager on his organisation's structure and management objectives, and above all from the formal and informal contacts made directly or indirectly with the general manager, his staff and former staff.

Each new town development corporation produces an annual report, and summaries of each new town's progress may be reviewed annually in a special February edition of 'Town and Country Planning', the offical journal of the TCPA. Although the management structure of CLDC was made available to the liaison committees, the more detailed central government directives on the management of development corporations, to be found in the New Towns handbook, are confidential, and according to evidence given to the expenditure committee, are not available even to local authorities (Expenditure Committee, 1974, p.167). In addition to the Financial Times article, to which reference was made in Chapter 7, it is most providential that Richard Phelps should seek to explain and justify his organisational design in a contribution to a book (Apgar, (Ed.), 1976) and in a published report to the Tehran Congress of the international new towns association, (Phelps, 1977).

In common with local government after the adoption of the Bains report, (HMSO, 1972), corporate management principles provide the main obvious criteria for decision making. The main feature of this is that there should be a team of departmental chief officers headed by a chief executive, who has no major departmental responsibilities of his own. All officers of development corporations are responsible through their chief executive to a board of independent persons appointed by the secretary of state; and those from local authorities sit as private individuals, not as representatives of elected bodies. There is, however, no standard organisational structure, but Phelps had identified three main types within the various corporations in Britain. A departmental structure with chief officers heading separate functions such as architecture, planning, engineering, estates management, housing, finance and administration is the most common, with a second type with a slightly more restricted range by combining certain specialities such as architecture and planning.

Management structure for a New Town
Alternative A

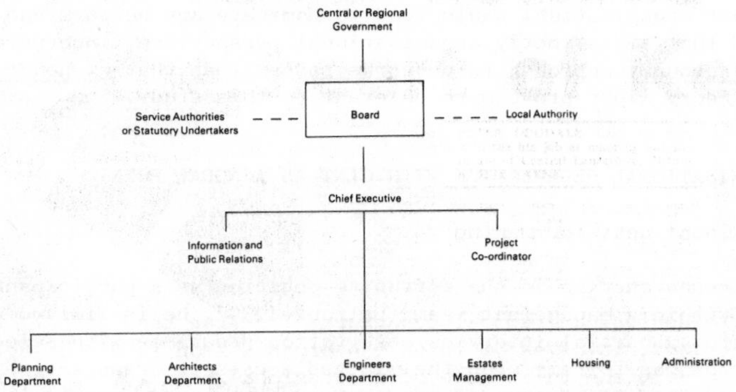

Management structure of a New Town
Alternative B

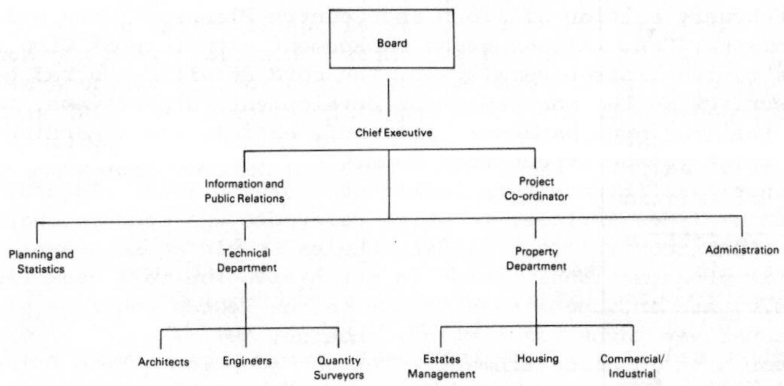

A third and more complex structure incorporated area delegation with separate departmental specialisms developed. (This arrangement compares with area teams in some local authorities.)

Management structure of a New Town
Alternative C

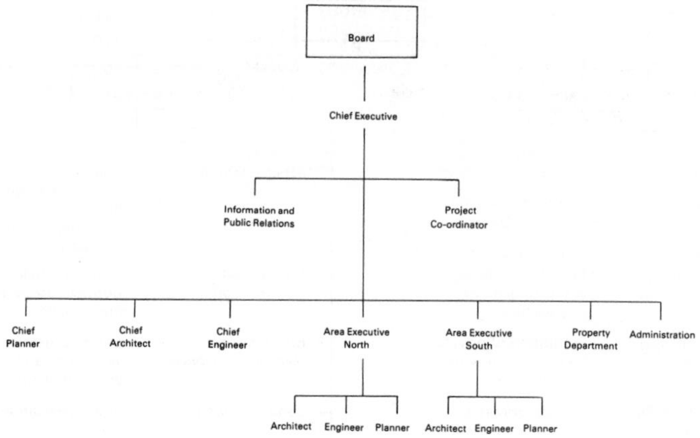

A fourth design, a 'radical departure' from the traditional structures described, involves dividing the organisation into two sections, 'each embodying the full range of professional activities required'.

> .... The policy and planning group deals with all aspects of general policy, including negotiations with other authorities, and general physical and social planning. The executive servises group takes over from the planning side the fairly detailed briefs for each project and executes them, where the works concerned are to be carried out by the corporation. (Phelps, 1976, p.211) (See figure overleaf.)

It is crucial to examine the official justification and intended effects of this structure and to compare this claim with the actual effects on the informal, even covert, intentions of the general manager. The two stranded self contained group structure of the CLDC organisation was justified by Richard Phelps in his contribution to Mahlon Apgar's book as stemming from 'the size of the area designated and the very substantial existing population' . . .

> .... We felt it essential from the outset to set up an organisation that would be able to cope with the effective control of dispersed construction operations over a large area, and with the political (in the broadest sense) problems inevitably arising in an area with such a large existing population and so many established institutions. (Phelps, 1976, p.211) (my emphasis)

The effective control of dispersed operations was thus not formalised within the organisation structure as in model C but here 'best carried out by multi disciplinary working parties or executive groups under independent chairmanship of a programming administrator' (Phelps, 1977, p.6). The political problems would appear to be regarded as more in

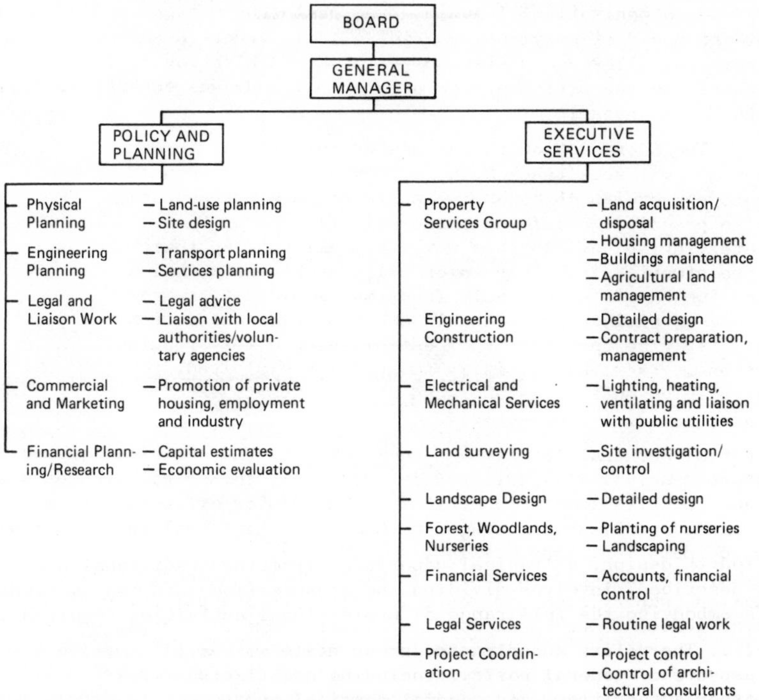

Central Lancashire Development Corporation

Phelps, 1976:212

the province of liaison with the statutory and local government bodies rather than the mass of the population; the subsuming of 'social facilities' under legal and liaison is evidence of this view.

The justification for dividing the organisation into two sections 'each embodying the full range of professional activities required' in the later paper is internal organisational effectiveness rather than as a response to task environments or inter organisational relations.

> .... The advantage of this structure is that there is an inbuilt safeguard against those who should be dealing with policy matters becoming bogged down with all the detailed problems that must inevitably arise in the development process. (Phelps, 1977, p.6)

A negative outcome of this approach was the effect on the morale of technical staff, in their ability to follow a project through from planning to execution, and the lack of delegation. The structure counters the findings from organisational studies that increased diversity of tasks is usually accompanied by increased influence and delegation to middle levels of management, (See Lawrence and Lorsch, 1967) and that innovation requires organismic, flexible organisational structures (Burns and Stalker, 1961).

A third, more personal, justification is hinted at in Richard Phelps's summary of the contribution to the book where he emphasised 'the crucial importance of thinking hard about organisation and structural problems, if possible even before the top level appointments are made' (Phelps, 1976, p.217). This occasion was a unique opportunity to construct a tailor made organisation, learning from past frustrations and breaking out of the mould of previous experiences. In order th ensure this new structure was allowed a gestation period, the selection of loyal staff sympathetic to the notion of the separate strands was essential. As Richard Phelps puts it:

> .... The introduction of the new organisational form met general acceptance because, having decided upon it before recruitment began, we could discuss our proposals with potential chief and principal officers at the interview stage. In this way, they all took up their appointments with clear information about their duties and the way in which their functions would differ from those of similar positions in other development corporations. The opportunity of establishing a new organisation is rare; <u>but if it is to be fully exploited, the principles must be established at the outset</u>. (Phelps, 1976, p.212) (my emphasis)

The initial personal loyalty and commitment to the organisation was therefore crucial. As indicated in Chapter 7, common backgrounds and previous organisational connections of the senior officers were more that coincidental,and encouraged mechanisms of informal solidarity within the corporation, (See Collins, 1975,p.304).

The key to the decision making in CLDC was the effectiveness of coordination, supervision and control of the two groups, which gives 'greater independence of action to a wider range of professionals in report to coordinating and directing managers' . An alternative viewpoint sees professional expertise and various disciplines being dispersed and thus each becoming a potential source of influence. Speed of decision making requires 'the bringing together of a variety of professions and disciplines so that each is working to a common good'.

> .... Team work is essential, and individuals of each profession or discipline must be able to understand and see theproblem of others and so <u>adjust their ideas to the common good</u>. Individuals or separate departments, working on their own, <u>without regard to others</u>, have no place in the management structure of a new town. (Phelps, 1977, p.7) (my emphases)

The above statement suggests that a development corporation could be a battleground for competing professional and individual interests, and the organisational structure 'as a network for applying controls so that certain tasks can be carried out' (Collins, 1975, p.709), and style of decision making as a means of gaining compliance. The centrality of decision making is the key feature of CLDC and this focalisation assures the pivotal position of the general manager.

The person, in this case, has not only designed the structure but also performs within the power, deriving from the position in the organisation. As Handy points out, this so called 'position power' gives the occupant potential control over some invisible assets such as information flow, access to a variety of networks and to exercise the right to organise work methods (Handy, 1976, p.117). The actual use of the position and the quality of decision may therefore be crucial. In his case studies of GEC and British Leyland, Turner takes an anti Galbraithian view stressing the importance of the individual decision making of Lord Stokes and Arnold Weinstock, (Turner, 1975). In studies of the development of local government, the influence of officers in Lancashire County Council, and the dynamism of individuals in Wolverhampton have been highlighted (See Marshall, 1977 and Jones, 1969, p.348).

The importance of decision making style to the commitment and job satisfaction of those lower in the organisational hierarchy has a tendency to be underestimated. The desire for central control by senior management stresses uniformity, while those in the project groups will seek diversity and control to be devolved. This tension may be rationalised as a 'failure of recruitment selection' and it may be resolved by attrition and resignation, but as Handy so aptly states:

> .... No structure, however well related to the diversity of the environment, will work effectively without a culture appropriate to the standard and people appropriate to the culture, and links between the cultures. The designer of the organisation forgets this at his peril. (Handy, 1976, p.305)

The style of decision making must therefore take cognisance of the aspirations of organisational members as a whole. The expression of dissatisfaction with this style and the method of its publication was to be a significant event in the evolution of CLNT.

INTER ORGANISATIONAL RELATIONS

In Chapter 5 reference was made to the possibility of viewing inter organisational relations as a political economy. In this approach the network itself is analysed, not a focal organisation and its environment. Power, upon which inter organisational negotiations are largely resolved it is argued, lies with those who control resources, which are principally money and authority (Benson, 1974). By virtue of its dominant position in terms of designated area and resources within the planning environment in Lancashire, and indeed within the north west, during the mid 1970s, it is inevitable that in examining inter organisational relations the CLDC is focal in this sphere. In any analysis of the urban system in central Lancashire, even if CLDC had not been chosen as a focus for research observation, it is contended that in terms of political capacity alone, attention would have been drawn to its preeminence as a regulating organisation (See Turk, 1977, p.137). (5) Further, by applying Benson's dimensions of relationships, it can be demonstrated that an uncritical acceptance of a network without a power dimension of inter organisational relationships would be unrealistic. In central Lancashire many resources are concentrated, rather than dispersed, and the domination of participants is an obvious feature of the network. By the nature of the legal/administrative terms of reference of a development corporation, it is intended by the government that such an organisation should be dominant in its planning environment. This ascendancy brings the development corporation into the normal sphere of activity of the local authorities. It is not surprising that the relationship with the local authorities has been identified by the field work as predominant.

The public inquiry provided some overt evidence of the tensions which may exist between local authorities and development corporations. This relationship is typical of the partial competition or partial accord in inter organisational relations which derive from the pursuit of different interests at different times. Local authority inter district or county district disputes and those with the CLDC may be subsumed by the higher level interest of a common rivalry with the Mersey belt metropolitan authorities. As Turk puts it:

> .... That organisational actors tend to be in partial conflict with one another does not belie the possibility of partial but enduring accord with respect to certain higher level interests or standards. (Turk, 1977, p.87)

Thus the long standing commitment derived from initiating the idea of CLNT is bolstered by a perceived common threat of resource diversion to another part of the north west. Attempts to diminish inter organisational discord are also a by product of the appointment of local authority members on development corporation boards. Although they are attending in a personal capacity, it is one means of dampening divisiveness, since it constrains members of one organisation attacking another organisation to which one of the members belong. In addition to this form of cross cutting organisational affiliations, other devices for diminishing conflict include extensive interaction between personnel of the various organisations. This fraternisation is a difficult activity since there is not only one set of actors with which the development corporation has to relate. A balance has to be sought between the relationships with elected members and those of the officers. CLDC's awareness of this complexity could only have been improved by the legal and liaison officer's previous experience as a town clerk. Technical discussions with local authority staff might be complicated by the complexities of the local authority structure,particularly in the separation of planning matters between the county and districts, but direct evidence of this difficultv is not easily substantiated. More tangible is the directive given to CLDC staff that they should not converse with elected members at one period.

Relations with local authority staff can illustrate a special case of inter organisational relations: that of inter organisational decision making (See Tuite, et al (Eds.), 1972). This area of specialisation may be viewed as a natural development of interest in inter organisational behaviour, from the emphasis upon the single organisation, to that of its environment, and finally to complex systems of interacting organisations. Since 1974, the main strategic planning functions together with responsibility for education and social services have been the responsibility of the county councils in non metropolitan areas. The motivational factors bolstering an inter organisational consensus between the Lancashire County Council and CLDC flow from the longstanding commitment to the proposal of the new town and an acknowledged interdependence on such matters as educational planning and social services provision. Variations in the quality of inter organisational relations with the district councils within CLNT's designated area may also be evidenced by different approaches to inter organisational decision making, particularly in the field of housing rehabilitation. Initial conflicts of interest, based on power or local prestige, may be resolved by having a joint unit, as in a Chorley rehabilation scheme. This form of joint decision making 'intervention' permits changes in organisation structure to facilitate the solving of the joint problem and encourages the possibility of problem solving, rather than of bargaining, between the personnel involved. This strategy is seen by

Tuite as an objective of a theory of optimal inter organisational decision making: moving from 'conditions of mixed conflict cooperation to conditions of pure cooperation', (Tuite, 1972, p.3). One should not assume in reality that power differences based on the availability of funds, or qualified staff, are not providing impediments to optimal decision making, and to the possibility of bargaining remaining as a method of decision making, and the distributional behaviour for subsequent rewards.

The relations between CLDC and the voluntary sector, particularly the residents' groups, have been observed to be less intense, a possible consequence of the relative lack of staff and organisational development. The under emphasis of this aspect of inter organisational relations has been acknowledged in the United States by the precondition in Model Cities programmes which required 'explicit inter organisational coordination before funds were allowed', (Turk, 1977,p.77). Thus this control of funds by the central authority 'provides a powerful intervention by which cooperative decision behaviour can be encouraged' (Tuite, 1972, p.16).

Inter organisational relations with the voluntary sector is also an aspect of participation, which in addition to legal, administrative and moral pressures to conform, has also in certain circumstances a financial resource sanction. Within this approach it is possible to evolve a paradox. On the one hand, in a community where there are few organisations, it is more likely that power may be exerted over an unorganised mass, yet on the other hand 'respectable' urban social movements, and in particular local political parties, can themselves limit dialectical conflict, since they can stress the need for conflict resolution among mambers and constituent groups. By bringing together varied, yet familiar, interests it is possible - as Turk points out - to:

> .... encapsulate various social cleavages under a few broad ones, simplify issues through compromise and exchange support, and otherwise mould issues to a form in which they can be dealt with, (Turk, 1977, p.114).

In this way also, conflict is more likely to be minimised and the elite are permitted to dominate, through superior negotiating skills and bargaining power.

The CLDC's interest in activating inter organisational relations with residents' groups was required by the expectations of government and the standards set by other public bodies, yet it did not wish this function to be uncontrolled, nor too demanding on staff time. Professed complaints about lack of community involvement were not countered positively by the provision of resources for community development but by the severely criticised and limited liaison committees (See Chapter 9). These meetings may be viewed as a restricted form of inter organisational forum, and one in which power and information differentials often proved to be a barrier to effective relations.

In reviewing the theory of inter organisational relations and relating this perspective to the evidence derived from observing aspects of a particular network it is important to see the validity of various approaches. Two main schools have been identified (Kolarska, 1980): one based on systems and consensus and another based on power and 'the ability to acquire and maintain resources' (Kolarska, 1980, p.14). Perhaps the most well developed of the first school is that of the organisation-set model (Evan, 1972). This model follows Gross, Mason and McEachern's use of the term 'focal position' in their analysis of roles, (Gross, et al, 1958, pp.48-74), and the 'focal organisation' is seen to interact with a complement of organisations in its environment, that is, its 'organisation-set'. Its approach can have the disadvantage of undervaluing individual personal elements in inter organisational relations - what Evan acknowledges as the 'danger of hypostatising organisations, i.e. treating them as disembodied entities', (Evan, 1972, p.188).

In this respect boundary roles are seen as a crucial element in what is termed 'the network of role-set relations of boundary personnel of the local organisations, with their role parties in organisations comprising the input - and output - organisation sets'. The key dimensions in organisations of boundary personnel have been delineated and have a bearing on our interpretation of CLDC's relationship with its public-in-contact. Their numbers, expertise, relative autonomy and hierarchical position as well as attitudinal orientation have been identified as indicators of mediational factors in inter organisational relations. The variation between the prestige and position accorded to the CLDC boundary spanning roles relating to the local authorities and the voluntary sector gives a useful additional measure of their relative weight. While providing insights into certain features of inter organisational relations, this systems approach tends to view these aspects in a political void. It is important to add to the assumptions of relative hierarchies and priorities the underlying determinate, that of power.

ORGANISATIONAL ENVIRONMENTS AND NETWORKS

How does CLDC, in the light of the theories in Chapter 5 relate to its environment? According to a systems perspective it might ideally be categorised as a linking pin organisation, a node through which different networks may be coupled within an environment. The networks identified as linked with the CLDC however, tended to be treated as separate entities: local government being accorded more organisational resources expertise and prestige than the voluntary sector. The lack of an effective link serves to confirm the discontinuity identified by Laumann and Pappi and described in an earlier section of this chapter. It appears that this distinct cleavage, isolating discrete contrasting networks, may be bridged by incorporating media institutions into the scheme. It is evident from the discussions in Chapter 8 that such links for economic reasons, are more likely to be skewed towards the putative focal organisation, CLDC. Despite this bias, the media organisations have a common interest in some links with the voluntary sector, if only from a news gathering aspect. In turn, the voluntary sector, and other networks, see value in a relationship with the press, television and radio in terms of public relations as a means of intelligence and feedback and indeed, as has been noted, as sometimes the only channel for dialogue through its correpondence columns. It is thus possible to conceive the networks in central Lancashire being linked tenuously through a common communications channel, and in the case of central Lancashire this connection would be predominantly, though not exclusively, the Lancashire Evening Post. (See Diagram D for a representation of the network link.)

It is thus possible to postulate that, at certain times when issues are of public or newsgathering interest, networks some of which more

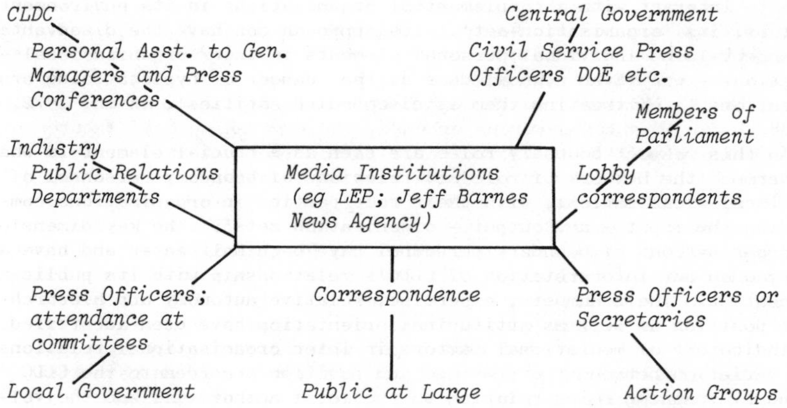

Diagram D

Local Mass Media Institutions as the Network Bridge in Central Lancashire

accurately may be described as action sets (which may be quite ephemeral in nature) may be linked with more permanent networks (industry, central and local government) through the activities of the local media, which then become the real nodal point.

According to the insights of the power perspective, CLDC may be described as a middle ranking, powerful organisation, able to influence its own immediate planning and socio-political environment, that in central Lancashire. In turn, it is influenced by its wider national environmental context. This occurrence is exemplified by changes in government policy, which may be financial or adjustments in political policies, such as a change in the ratio of houses to be built for rent or for sale in new towns. This highly disparate environment is more adequately represented as either a hierarchy of environments or preferably organisations in contact with differential power and classified within networks. Within each network it is possible to conceive of the organisation being dominated, for example by national political or industrial pressures, or dominating as in the central Lancashire local authority network.

The environmental or power distribution in networks may be finely balanced. Local power may be attenuated by governmental or societal expectations such as those required after Skeffington on consultation or participation in planning matters. Where there is network domination or perceived environmental certainty, according to Lawrence and Lorsch's findings, then an organisation will survive with a rigid, formal impersonal structure. Where there is network influence or an uncertain environment then decentralised, more formal, 'personally orientated' organisation is likely to be more successful (Lawrence and Lorsch, 1967).

Such possible organisational/environment incongruities formed one basis for criticisms contained in the Morgan report (Morgan, 1973) (see page 200). Above all, organisations will seek stability in their network relationships and seek to be protected from uncertainty. The most interesting example of an attempt by CLDC to protect itself from instability was the ability to advance its programme in strategic sites within the designated area through Section6(i) applications and gain approval for advanced sewerage schemes, thereby making key features of the outline plan less liable to cancellation (See Waterhouse, 1975).

A useful distinction may be drawn between organisations which hold strategic or subservient positions in different networks or alternatively are seen as dominating one environment or dominated within a separate environment - and those which may be classified as organisations with power to influence their environments, and those only able to respond to their environments. In industrial firms this differentiation was described as between centre firms and periphery firms (Averitt, 1968). It is important that centre-periphery features are extrapolated into other institutions and sectors in society. It is an essential element in the public sector, such as between central and local government (See Local Government Act 1980 and Jones 1980) and in society generally, a mode of analysis which forms the basis of the next section of this chapter.

LOCAL POLITICIANS, MPs AND CENTRAL GOVERNMENT

According to successive legislation since 1946, new towns are centrally selected, and then financed and controlled through the channels of a chosen bureaucratic agency, a development corporation. The CLDC like other development corporations may be regarded as a device by which the civil service is able to be directly involved in physical planning. In effect, this linkage means primarily the department of the environment, through its new towns division, but it also involved to a greater or lesser degree such departments as the Treasury, Department of Industry, Department of Education and Science and the departments responsible for other services, such as housing, hospitals and social services. Much of this tradition of central control in the new town programme emanates from the strong influence of Dame Evelyn Sharp, permanent secretary in the ministry of housing who, according to the Crossman diaries, had little confidence in local government's capacity to plan and execute the programme of new town building. This scepticism is confirmed in Lady Sharp's own words when she states that such a programme was 'beyond their financial competence' and that 'only determined government action and underwriting by government money could secure '(the new towns)' (Sharp, 1972, p.14).

The new towns programme and its inevitable impinging upon local autonomy provides an example of a centre/periphery tension; between that of central government direction and local discretion. The evidence submitted to the Select Committee on New Towns (HMSO, 1975) provides many instances of this strain between some local authorities in which new towns are located and central government. This tension is particularly marked in the evidence of a body which is now incorporated into the association of district councils, ANTLA(The Association of New Town Local Authorities). The districts called witnesses which claimed that local authorities could be more cost effective than development corporations in house building and providing amenities (Expenditure Committee,

1974, p.181). The counties were less hostile, but nevertheless, the counties of Buckinghamshire, Cambridgeshire, Cheshire and Lancashire, Northamptonshire and Salop submitted an analysis outlining the financial difficulties involved in providing amenities in advance of the expected population increase.

The DOE for its part has not acknowledged the separate rights of new town local authorities in the development of new towns. As Aldridge points out:

> .... The parties concerned seemed rather to have been defined as the government, the development corporations, employers and residents, even if the last have been treated as an abstraction. (Aldridge, 1979, p.186)

It is small wonder that there appears to be some disparity between the high minded macro 'a-political' view of the central government and the seemingly parochial and self interested complaints of certain local authorities, who quite naturally felt 'squeezed out' from any influencing process.

How did the local politicians contribute towards the CLNT tensions? Reference has been made in Chapter 10 to the presence of councillors and their statements in the public meetings held by CLDC. Interventions in council or in committee were occasionally reported, but it is conceded that it is difficult to reverse, (or ask for a report back) committee decisions in council since council business is usually a formal endorsement of a committee decision (See Friend and Jessop, 1969, pp.48-49). Most involvement in amenity society activity by district councillors took place in Preston, which was quite naturally a reflection of the impact of the most controversial aspect of the outline plan, the proposed routes of the eastern and western primary roads.

The contrasting roles of three members of the Preston Labour group illustrate the variation of activity possible in relation to CLNT. Councillor Dick Evans, chairman of Preston North Action Group, was one of a number of ward councillors to involve themselves initially in the work of the large committee formed. Despite party pressures he remained an active member and the consequence was his failure to be renominated for a relatively safe seat. The only other councillor to remain a member of the committee was Ron Atkins, MP. Councillor Evans's representation of local interests, as he saw them, in preference to conformity to the party whip, contrasts with the more detached stance of Councillor Ken Bodfish. A young councillor, he bacame chairman of the New Town Committee and represented the Association of District Councils as a witness before the Expenditure Committee on 25 June 1975. An inconsistency in his attitude to nominated bodies is evident, however, when a month after he had attacked the Area Health Authority as 'not representative, not democratically appointed' (LEP, 23 October 1975) he accepted the Secretary of State's invitation on 26 November 1975 to join the Board of a similarly constituted organisation, CLDC. This point was also noted in a letter by Ray Johnson to the Lancashire Evening Post (LEP, 28 November 1975).

It is important to recognise the restraints placed upon councillors, both by their local party organisations, and the council decision making procedure to which reference has already been made. The unusual double role of Councillor Ron Atkins, MP permitted him to surmount the usual restraints of local party discipline, to play a key part in the back bench revolt on Preston Borough's reaction to the new town road proposals, but above all to become a central figure and major irritant in new town affairs.

Though similar rifts in new town development corporations have been reported (6), Ron Atkins was responsible for bringing to the public notice a critical report of the CLDC organisation through tabling questions in the House of Commons to the Secretary of State for the Environment, and informing the press of his correspondence about the report to ministers. From a media content perspective, it is significant that the LEP item, though newsworthy, should only warrant a small single column item on its front page. (Hostile report 'hidden' - MP) which referred to the 'full story on page nine'. This report was a seven column spread with the heading "New town men accused on 'hidden' report" (LEP, 5 November 1975). The research for the report, to which reference was made, was known to the writer through an early interview with the general manager and was based on an arrangement with the Department of Behaviour in Organisations at Lancaster University. A lecturer in the department, Mr Gareth Morgan, conducted this research by interviewing staff, observing meetings and obtaining completed confidential questionnaires from nearly 70 members of the CLDC staff.

This so called 'Morgan report' was a private document, and therefore its contents have only been described through secondary sources. The research was conducted during the early years of the organisations formation and the report itself was submitted to the development corporation in May 1973. A number of people had heard of the existence of the report during the following two years and this information was confirmed by the press report on 6 November 1975, from the Lancashire Evening Post's parliamentary correspondent, John Egan:

> .... At Westminster today Mr Atkins said he had been suspicious for some time that an adverse report had not been allowed out.
>
> The copy which he had obtained now confirmed the complaints he had received from individuals within the corporation that a small group of senior officials were stifling those lower in rank. (my emphasis)

The report, Mr Atkins alleges:

> .... never saw the light of day because it damned the present organisation . . . Its findings confirm the complaints from individuals and professional officers which I have heard during the last few years. (LEP, 5 November 1975)

It appears that a three page summary of the report had been prepared by Mr Atkins and sent to the ministers most directly concerned with new towns; the Secretary of State, Mr Crosland, the Minister responsible for Local Government and Planning, Mr John Silkin and a junior Minister, Mr Gordon Oakes. The report, which is of particular relevance to the study of organisational structure, became public knowledge through a breach of internal confidentiality or, as Mr Atkins described it: "I obtained a copy. I used the word 'unearthed' in my letter to ministers" (LEP, 6 November 1975).

The contents of the report were also summarised some 18 months later, but still within the post-public inquiry influencing period, by Bernard Davies in an article in the weekly professional newspaper 'Planning':

> .... Morgan saw this situation arising primarily out of

the way power is exercised within the corporation. For his analysis showed its structure is highly centralised and hierarchical, with all decisions being closely controlled by the general manager and a small group of senior aides. Inter related tasks are fragmented and distributed between different parts of the organisation. Planning and executive functions are split, thereby eliminating essential feedback between 'the thinkers' and 'the doers'. In this way CLDC's 'learning ability' has been seriously impaired since 'effective thinking may be a product of doing'.

As one member of staff concluded:

.... The effect . . . is to lock people away in little bubbles on the organisation chart.

The central control was most clearly illustrated by the way the outline plan was formulated. Basically, it was the work of three people. Other individuals contributed, but they worked largely in isolation from each other so that the plan even to many of these, ramained 'a mystery'.

Morgan's overall conclusion was that, given the primary tasks facing the corporation, the high authoritarian style in which it was organised and managed was most inappropriate. His report argued that a much more flexible approach was needed if the creative potential of the staff was to be tapped and if the corporation was going to be able to deal with the complex problems posed by its environment. Even in 1973, certain danger signs were already discernible. Some professional staff were beginning to adapt to their situation - to view their jobs in a more routine and sterile manner. It was suggested that 'this trend, if continued, is likely to be increasingly detrimental to the effectiveness of the corporation'.

Significantly, the group holding these negative views were also those who seemed most committed to the work of the corporation. They had been appointed mainly for their specialist expertise and therefore were expecting (and theoretically were expected) to make a significant creative contribution. That they were being prevented from doing this was, to them, far more important than were dissatisfactions over such things as salaries.

Morgan's prime focus was the planning process in a new town and in particular how the outline plan was developed. But, more generally he examined the structure of the organisation and whether CLDC could respond flexibly to the changing situation facing it. He concluded that it was experiencing some very serious problems. One group of staff (19 per cent) who were in general doing very routine jobs or were the very top people in the organisation, thought the corporation efficient. But a second group (33 per cent) - almost entirely middle management - were dissatisfied on a

> number of counts. They were critical for example about the amount of information they had about the Corporation's work overall, about internal communications, the restrictions placed on them and their work, and how tasks were coordinated. In general they felt that their superiors did not understand what they were doing and that the climate within the Corporation did not encourage new ideas. (Davies, 1977, p.6)

It is doubtful whether the report would have been publicised if it had not been adopted as a cause by a Member of Parliament. This action was, with the initiative of the Local Groups' Working Party, the most important observable event to take place during the period between the public inquiry and the Secretary of State's decision. Both incidents illustrate features of organisational behaviour, relationships between the centre and the periphery and some aspects of influencing decisions in society.

The Local Groups' Working Party has been shown as an example of an 'action set', collaborating in a collective effort to attempt to influence a government decision. The Morgan Report also suggests how its findings could account for the style of CLDC's inter organisational relations, particularly with residents' or action groups and the public in contact. As Peter Grimshaw put it:

> .... The malaise of insufficient participation of relevant staff in decision making would inevitably be reflected in the Corporation's external dealings: it is unlikely the 'outside world' would be allowed greater involvement than its own staff. This postulation fits the evidence precisely, for Davies (who, like Morgan, was in the privileged position of having access to the internal workings) concluded, like many others, that the Corporation's commitment to public participation is no more than a verbal and paper one. (Grimshaw, 1978, p.158)

The publicity surrounding the Morgan Report most markedly serves as a central focus on new town decisions, their means of implementation through development corporation and ministerial accountability for such activity. In response to Mr Atkin's questions about the report, which had already been received by the Minister, it was clear that ministers would not publicly intervene in disputes and that Members of Parliament should address complaints directly to Development Corporations. Mr Oakes's written reply stated:

> .... Every new town Development Corporation has full responsibilities for its own management and operation and for staffing matters up to and including the upper salary range level.
>
> The Central Lancashire Development Corporation is no exception. Inquiries of this nature should therefore be made to them direct. (LEP, 14 November 1975)

Taking up this answer in the local press, Ray Johnson commented that the statement:

> .... gives to the Central Lancashire Development

Corporation a degree of autonomy they were never intended to possess. Complacency on the part of local authorities and the general public has allowed development corporations to exceed their powers continually and consistently, unfettered by real challenge from the democratically elected councils on to which they are imposed. (LEP, 28 November 1975)

The question of accountability on new town decisions, highlighted by the statements on the Morgan Report also caused Alan Howard to declare:

.... Confronted with this Leviathan, we have (or thought we had) one remedy - appeal to the Department of the Environment. This remedy has now been taken away from us. Gordon Oakes the junior minister concerned with new towns has declined to give proper answers to Mr Atkins' questions. Such inquiries he says, should be made to the development corporation direct.

.... If a Member of Parliament cannot get satisfaction from a minister, what chance have the general public? From now on, it seems, the central Lancashire development corporation will be its own judge, jury, court of appeal and executioner. (LEP, 24 November 1975).

The New Towns Act provides for a great deal of discretion to the administrative level and in Crossman's phrase 'a kind of autocracy' to the development corporations (Crossman, 1975). In addition:

.... corporations are remarkably exempt from checks provided by such bodies as the Local Government Commissioner and the Comptroller and Auditor General; neither are their deliberations exposed by the Public Bodies Admissions to Meetings Act. (Grimshaw, 1978, p.158)

Mr Atkins's intervention in Parliament, and his unusual double political role, points to his Parliamentary pre-eminence in new town affairs. One should not overlook, however, the leading part played by the MP for Preston South, Mr Stan Thorne, in seeking a postponement of the public inquiry through the initiation of an adjournment debate in July 1974, nor the regular comment in the Leyland or Chorley Guardians by George Rodgers, MP for Chorley at this time. Respective attitudes may be measured by the contributions to the debate on the New Towns (Amendment) Bill on 23 March 1976 relating primarily to the eventual transfer of housing and related assets to local authorities. George Rodgers's speech was slightly critical, yet conciliatory:

.... But I should much prefer this attractive, well planned programme, rather than the sprawl and squalor which have disfigured so many industrial areas of the north west of England.

Naturally there are complaints and queries and, because I favour the broad concept, that is not to say that I have not frequently engaged in battle with the development corporation. Individual projects within a major project must be closely scrutinised at all stages and challenged whenever necessary.

There are other features which create problems. Many of the older residents find it difficult to adapt to the new situation. They resent change, and there are difficulties in superimposing a new population on the old. There will be special problems if the housing stock provided by the development corporation is only partially occupied while local people are homeless. These issues and many others must be and I think will be overcome if the formula of common sense is applied by all authorities at all levels.

The Bill contains the essential ingredient of democracy. In itself, it is not sufficient to meet all the problems which will arise, certainly in my area of Lancashire, and I urge my right hon. and hon. friends to be more generous with this ingredient of democracy. It is only by early and total community involvement that all the questions can be resolved. (Hansard, vol.908, p.75)

Mr Ron Atkins took the opportunity of emphasising his earlier comments about CLDC and accountability. In welcoming the Bill, he expressed concern about the Bill failing to change the structure of the development corporation. Echoing Richard Crossman's views, he stated:

.... I believe that when the structures were first considered years ago there might have been more need for independent bodies of this kind. But they wield enormous impact on the lives of half a million people, and it holds large resources and patronage as well.

The corporation is not accountable to the public and everything we have seen so far shows that it is also unresponsive. It is frequently stated, for instance, that local authorities are not as responsive as they should be to the electors, but the machinery is there for them to influence the administration through their elected representatives from day to day. But there is no such accountability as regards the corporation. If hon. members have criticism to make of the corporations, they will be told by the minister that he has no power to interfere in the day to day running of the corporations.

Those bodies have enormous power, not only directly in their own sphere, in the realm of their own jurisdiction, but as regards local authorities also. Everyone who is on a local authority will know that officers from various local authorities - they form a big part of the central Lancashire new town, covering Preston, Chorley, Leyland and many others - discuss planning regularly with their equivalents in the central Lancashire new town. They reach decisions after weekly or monthly discussions. Therefore, the influence of the corporation is greater. It spreads to the local authorities....

The plans for roads and other communications cancelled out earlier plans proposed by someone who left in

> desperation. Instead, roads were proposed across the town of Preston and other towns, destroying cheap accommodation and destroying in particular terraced houses by their hundreds.
>
> Fortunately, my right hon. friend reversed that decision and the position is now much better than it would have been. However I am still worried because the corporation is as unresponsive as ever. It is an inward looking organisation that still does not respond to the wishes aspirations and needs of the local inhabitants. They are the experts because they know the area.
>
> Unless the situation has changed recently, not one of the leading figures of central Lancashire new town lives in the area which they are supposed to plan. Their decision to live outside is one of the best decisions I have known them to make. What they have to plan for is in many cases not the sort of thing I would like.

The debate also permitted a reiteration of the views of the GMC when the MP for Westhoughton Mr Roger Stott, expressed his scepticism 'about certain aspects of some new towns'.

> ....My constituency is split between Bolton on the north and Wigan on the south. To many people, Wigan may be a music hall joke, but the area has serious problems. It is surrounded by new towns, with Runcorn to the south, Skelmersdale to the west and the central Lancashire new town to the north west. Fantastic resources have been poured into the new towns surrounding the Wigan basin. Wigan has been left to decline and rot. We have a declining population and urban deprivation.
>
> This has been caused by the provision of new towns on all sides of the metropolitan borough of Wigan. In Wigan and Bolton local authorities object to the monolithic growth of Skelmersdale and to the proposals for the central Lancashire new town. People are faced with a growing sense of despair when they compare the roads and the infrastructure of Skelmersdale, Runcorn and the central Lancashire new town with the decaying life style in Wigan. There is a conflict of opinions about what should be done.
>
> I am not against the provision or the development of new towns, but I ask the government whenever they are planning to develop new towns to consider areas like Wigan before taking green fields and building new houses and new factories to the detriment of the older areas.

The remaining member representing party of the designated area was Edward Gardner, MP for South Fylde. Hitherto more subdued and equivocal in his remarks, he was reported to regard the CLDC as having 'breathtaking arrogance' (LEP , 23 November 1976) and in the Commons on 5 April 1977 outlined the reasons for his change of view and those of his constituents:

> .... When I came to the constituency and fought the 1970 general election, I found many people who if not enthusiastic

> were not openly hostile to the concept of the new town. Now . . . I find hardly a friend of the CLNT . . . (CLDC) . . . therefore has a particular duty to be sensitive to the aspirations and ambitions of those who live within its boundaries. Instead my constituents complain, with a frequency which is becoming extraordinary, about what they call the ham fisted approach of officials.

The foregoing pages reflect some of the reported and observable activities of the local politicians and parliamentary representatives. Many councillors preferred to be discreet about their contacts with action group leaders, but were able to use their relationships with CLDC, however tenuous, to suggest meetings for the benefit of their constituetns and to give advice. The local MPs in reflecting the concerns of some of their constituents, particularly about lack of local democratic or parliamentary accountability, may be viewed as agents of the periphery. In this role they are seeking balance and redress for their provincial electorate against the central administration. The lack of accountability for ministers for new town administration provides an acute case of an agent of central government, a development corporation, confronting local, peripheral interest. Yet, as Roger Stott's contribution to the debate on the New Towns (Amendment) Bill illustrates, there is one aspect of this tension which the centre may exploit to its advantage, that of intra regional rivalry.

INFLUENCING DECISION MAKING : AN OVERVIEW

The central Lancashire new town provides an effective example of central government's involvement in physical planning, and it has given an insight into centre-periphery relations and tensions. While Levin has produced a comprehensive description and analysis of decision making relating to the designation of CLNT, (Levin, 1976) the post public inquiry influencing process draws attention to the extent to which pressure groups, or their spokesmen, as agents of the periphery, can carry weight with the central decision makers.

In this context, how is the process of decision making studied? Social scientists have observed and hypothesised the methods and procedures from both individual and organisational perspectives. Basic stages have been identified, for example by Scott, (Scott, 1967) and such models of decision trees and systems suggested. An ideal, rational approach assumes that the problems about which decisions need to be made are perceived; there is a tendency to stress the importance to positive decisions and to overlook the significance of avoiding making a decision or taking a negative decision (Barnard, 1938); and the decision maker

> .... is supplied with a complete range of information and has the computational capacity to exploit this information in order to discover the best possible course of action (Castles et al, 1971, p.16)

In this context it may be pointed out that the lack of validity of the theories underpinning the designation and development of CLNT and the assumptions about population growth in the north west needed to be perceived and accepted. Allowance should also be made for the inertia in central government in changing a project underway and the tendency to avoid reassessment of committed schemes.

Taking a more individual approach, Downs has shown how members of organisations display certain behavioural characteristics of information scanning, levels of perceived satisfactory performance, and the effects of a 'performance gap' on 'research activity'. (Downs,1967). Within an organisation certain tensions occur to affect this search operation and personal bias emerges. Employing Festinger's theory of cognitive dissonance, Downs suggests that a decision maker will screen out data adverse to his interests and magnify those favouring. There will also be a need to allow for departmental bargaining which could favour existing papers in allocating resources, 'trimming' alternatives to achieve courses and those alternatives that remain will be likely to involve as little certainty as possible.

While it is vital to allow for such intra organisational factors, it is also essential, as we have noted, to account for environmental influences and inter organisational bargaining in decision making. In this chapter we have related how peripheral organisations attempted to influence the decision making at the centre. These parties in the influence process have similarly been termed 'partisans' and 'authorities' (Gamson, 1968). according to this model, influence is deemed to have been in operation when the decision making behaviour of the authorities

> .... has been altered from what it would have been in the absence of the influencer and the amount of influence is 'the degree of change'.

Congruent with the political economy or power model of inter organisational relations, the basis of this influence is regarded to be the resources available to the group or their spokesman, and how effective such means may be deployed both in a positive, inducement sense or in a negative, constraint form. The degree of influence, in purely power terms, will be related to the continuum shown earlier in this chapter and where power diminishes, influence is based primarily on persuasive gifts and logical argument and the degree of acceptability of the organisation.

The relevance of the Joint Groups' Working Party's request for reappraisal to the influence process may be interpreted in the light of these observations. CPRE's advocacy was significant, since this organisation has regular contact with the appropriate departments, ministers and MPs on other environmental issues. Such a group thus did not need to acquire a separate acceptability. Individual organisations, such as Grimsargh and Haighton action committee, indeed alleged that there had not been a reply to much correspondence with the Department of the Environment.

Apart from the formal or informal machinery of consultation which links a civil service department into its network, awareness of a problem may be alerted by a political signal, such as MP's questions, letters and publicity given to contentious matters, such as the Morgan Report. Awareness will be modified by selective perception and rationalisation, often based on previous commitment and a belief in 'accepted theories' such as the efficacy of growth centres. In practical terms, however, departmental pressures, the roles of 'experts' or 'advisers' and of previous experience ('organisational memory') muddy the pool of decision making. As Brown suggests, it is

> .... difficult to isolate 'a decision' from the incessant stream of consultants, committee decisions, authorisations

and initialling of papers which make up the day of senior members of organisations (Brown, 1970)

The difficulties experienced by new peripheral organisations influencing decision making may often be related to ignorance of the system of government and the working of civil service departments. In his study of the Ministry of Health, Eckstein pointed out how short term priorities significantly reduced the rationality of decision making. There was a tight timetable for replies to parliamentary questions, and letters from MPs required answers in a given number of days. These activities, together with the treasury estimates, meant that longer term planning issues were driven out by daily routine (Eckstein, 1960).

The involvement of civil servants in the decision making process is a feature of the British system of cabinet government. New town policies and decisions provide an extreme example of legitimate civil service autonomy. Under Section 6(i) of the New Towns Act it is permissible for development corporations to be granted ad hoc orders for compulsory purchase or area schemes. As Grimshaw points out:

> .... In CLNT's case the department allowed the corporation to press ahead with a number of major commitments, thus preempting to a marked degree the Secretary of State's decision; it also failed to curtail growth proposals clearly at variance with the region's greatly diminished needs with, for example, competitive development under way in favourable locations nearby at Westhoughton, and problem torn Skelmersdale a mere ten kilometres from CLNT's boundary. (Grimshaw, 1978, p.158)

Reference has been made to interest group theory in Chapter 4. Their degree of influence on decision making will naturally depend on a number of factors such as expertise and acceptability, but such features will be misdirected unless they are addressed to the real centres of decision making rather than the apparent. It is the centralised nature of British government which makes it essential that, to the effective, interested parties should also develop a centralised power base. It is difficult for local groups to organise such an operation without previous experience, particularly if they are representing areas in the regions. In central Lancashire it was the late realisation of the workings of national pressure groups, largely through the contribution of Robin Grove-White to a day conference, which mobilised an action set in the form of the Local Groups' Joint Working Party. It was advantageous that the CPRE, for whom Grove-White is now director, functions as an 'expressive' group and is seen, as such, to have more weight and acceptability.

Successful groups need to know who directs and determines public policy, and then seek, by informal means, to recruit members or officers. In CLNT much effort was initially directed at evidence for the public inquiry rather than indirect influences. Unlike the Wing campaign against the third London airport, no informal network of 'establishment' contacts were cultivated. Lack of political consensus based on earlier commitment to the new town, and exacerbated by intra regional rivalry, meant that there was no significant political lobby through which to operate. There was thus no prospect of a wholehearted backbench revolt threatened, as in the 'In Place of Strife' White Paper, or with the Roskill recommendation of Cublington as the third London airport. The longstanding advocacy of new towns by the TCPA was not matched to any extent, until the Joint Groups' Working Party made its request for reappraisal under the aegis of the CPRE.

Some political scientists have pointed out that it is the 'successful' groups which become consulted by the administration, and that the less powerful or acceptable groups need to persuade individual legislators to take up their cause, because the administrative avenue is closed to them. Those with influence, they argue, will tend to concentrate on the administration but this route will often be augmented by parliamentary lobbying and public propaganda with the ultimate aim of persuading ministers and the relevant civil servants to make a decision in their favour. The actions of the local MPs in initiating either adjournment debates or parliamentary questions or in the contributions to the New Towns (Amendment) Bill tend to confirm some redressing or the balance of influence between Whitehall and Parliament.

The Members of Parliament in constituencies covering CLNT's designated area were not obvious allies to groups objecting to aspects of the development. Irrespective of party affiliation, all were initially in favour of the concept. Mr Ron Atkins, in particular, had made many press statements in support, yet it was the persuasive power of his constituents, albeit in a very marginal seat, which increased his scepticism of some of the methods of implementation and the transportation element particularly. Although a member of the party of government at the time, it could hardly be said that, as a 'Tribunite' back bench member, Ron Atkins was in a strong position of influence. Yet, it can be argued, that his handling of the publicity linked to the Morgan Report, and the repercussions of the questions on accountability, caused some embarrassment to the administration and were instrumental in the eventual trimming down of the scheme. This action, together with the advocacy of reappraisal by the CPRE, may be seen as two major instances of pressures which may be described as the 'drip effect' in influencing decision making. Such instances may be 'feathers' on a heavily biased scale but they might just have the effect of 'tipping'.

The common theme to emerge is the inherent disadvantage of interest groups on the periphery. Pressure group methods require a central base; public inquiries on the site only serve to divert attention away from the informal methods of influence. MPs can also act as agents for the periphery and, in particular, through parliamentary questions, are able to probe into ministerial decision making, and alert civil servants to matters of disquiet. In the case of CLNT an important factor would seem to be criticisms of the lack of sensitivity and accountability of the development corporation arising from the Morgan Report. These criticisms no doubt stimulated R.W. Phelps's published justification of the organisational design. The 'opening up' of public knowledge of CLNT, linked with a greater sensitivity to new town policies through the activities of the expenditure committee when coupled with the growing concern about the inner cities, are elements which, when combined, suggest enough thrust to trim the project. Yet much of this influence would have been stunted but for the crucial role of the media. The network bridge function served not only to correct the local activists but to link the periphery with the centre through the pivotal activity of the parliamentary correspondent.

SUMMARY

This chapter has outlined the activities of the various local groups following the period of intense activity during and prior to the outline plan public inquiry. It has related their action to the categorisation of pressure or interest groups, and into the analysis of networks. By employing the perspectives offered by organisational analysis, particularly inter organisational relations, the structure and relationships of the development corporation have been examined and assessed. The importance of organisational environments and organisational networks has been stressed, but above all the role of the local parliamentarians in publicising a critical organisational study and its possible part in influencing decision making has been highlighted.

NOTES

1. See Lancashire Hotchpotch, Guardian, 10 June 1975.
2. If further persuasion were needed, a few days later much criticism was aired during the debate on the second reading of the New Towns (Amendment) Bill on Tuesday, 23 March 1976 in the non democratic nature of the CLDC (Hansard, vol.908, vol.75, cols. 306-10).
3. This is a refinement of Potter's two fold classifications, (Potter, 1961) (into sectional or promotional groups) or Childs (Childs, 1930) (into organisations of and organisations for,) into four categories of operational, representative, expressive and propagational groups.
4. Described by Rivers as 'sheer, naked political pressure', (Rivers, 1974, pp.94-95)
5. Organisations that 'exceed others in their political capabilities, that is, in interest in forming or mediating coalitions, in resources available for coercion or exchange, in orientations towards contest and bargaining, in negotiable interests and standards, in multiple contact points, in use made of them by other organisations, and in adaptability to uncertainty'.
6. (e.g. Peterlee, see Planning No. 120, 20 June 1975).

14 Summary and conclusions

INTRODUCTION

The focus of this study, the central Lancashire new town, holds a unique place in British town and country planning. Envisaged on a sub regional scale, CLNT became the last new town whose proposals would be permitted, as modified by the Secretary of State, under the New Towns Acts. At its zenith the proposals contained within its outline plan suggested investment (at 1973 prices) of £900 million - a quarter of which would be public money - to provide for an additional population of 184,000 by 2001. This chapter brings together various themes linked with this major project contained in the previous chapters. It emphasises the key theoretical and empirical strands of the study, draws some conclusions and suggests possible areas for further research.

THE CENTRAL LANCASHIRE NEW TOWN AS A RESEARCH FOCUS

The 1970s became the decade when the 'new town idea' was supplanted by a concern for the inner cities. The turning point between the two rival investment strategies was signalled by the Peter Shore Manchester speech on 17 September 1976, referred to earlier in Chapter 2, and consolidated by the inner city partnership schemes and finally the Inner Urban Areas Act of 1978. This policy change occurred despite the survival tactics employed by the development corporations, the commitment to the new town policies by some politicians and decision makers and the strength of the new town lobby expressed through the Town and Country Planning Association. It is argued that the intra regional rivalries fuelled by the Strategic Plan for the North West and articulated in the outline plan public inquiry, point to the fact that nowhere else in Britain were the stresses evoked by the threatened policy shift more starkly focussed than in central Lancashire. Not only did CLNT provide a final chance to study new town decision making procedures, it also afforded an opportunity to observe large scale participation practices 'post Skeffington'.

In addition within the evolution of regional and sub regional planning theory itself CLNT has an outstanding position. Indeed sub regional planning in the 1960s may be seen as an attempt by central government to influence the highly fragmented local government system in collaborative ventures generally, and more specifically later, in response to anticipated population pressures. In land use and social and economic planning, governments have a unique opportunity to assume direct control. Using the New Towns Act 1965, government was able to designate CLNT to serve as an instrument of sub regional policy. This (unlike many former new towns specifically designed to relieve population pressures) was an expression of overt central power, defined in Chapter 6 as the first 'imperative quasi sub regional plan'.

Likewise in the classification of planning theory, the new town development corporations serve as examples of attempts to implement a type of normative planning (See Gillingwater, 1975, p.87). Normative planning is acknowledged to be an approach to public planning which is not 'objective' but openly involves the formation of attitudes and values inplanning and with mobilising political and technical commitment to such ends. Mobilising such commitments has been a consistent feature of the CLDC's activities and this study has highlighted such practices. Most obvious of these were the applications for compulsory purchase orders and area plans submitted under Section 6(i) of the New Towns Act, which have been fully described in this study.

CLNT - A CONSIDERATION OF THE ARGUMENTS

A major theme throught the study has been the allegations that CLDC has highlighted the lack of local and national accountability of new town development corporations and, in its inter organisational relations and its dealings with local action groups, shown a marked lack of sensitivity. The chapters describing the processes of public participation (Chapters 4, 9 and 10) and the proceedings of the outline plan public inquiry (Chapter 12) have rehearsed the various objections to the new town and its methods and style of operation. Not only have the various action groups expressed their disquiet at their lack of involvement in the early formulation of plans, so have the various constituent 'supporting' district councils. The Section 6(i) procedures were resented by even the most sympathetic local authorities and the overt policy of the CLDC in promoting simultaneous and dispersed development throughout the designated area was even commented upon adversely by Lancashire County Council during the public inquiry.

The policy of dispersed growth was argued for by the development corporation as a vital feature in promoting the attractiveness of the area. This strategy was seen to complement the natural advantages of the area with the existing provision of social facilities, in particular the cultural and artistic investment evidenced by the new Preston Guild Hall complex (incorporating a large concert hall and a well equipped theatre). Opened in 1972, it would be fair to imply that such bold planning and development decisions were made in anticipation of the population growth stimulated by CLNT.

The policy of dispersed growth, entailing development in several parts of the new town simultaneously, so the argument goes, was also justified as a vital feature of the success of the project in encouraging industry, commerce and - of its own volition - population. Without overspill agreements, the natural attractiveness of the area, it was argued, must be maximised and it would not be possible to create a new growth point without the importation of population (Wheatley, 1969). The project therefore demanded and justified the clear need for peripheral greenfield development to encourage this new industry and population: a policy which objectors regarded as being against the interests of the existing population. The new town's justification, now that population growth considerations no longer applied, rested firmly on demonstrating that the project would effect regional regeneration, through the application of growth centre theory, and that there would be an overall net benefit for the whole north west region. It therefore required a convincing demonstration that the undoubted injection of central government funds in central Lancashire would not hasten decline or affect any natural economic buoyancy elsewhere in the region. Only on that basis could the 'sacrifice' of dispersed, simultaneous, peripheral development on greenfield sites be remotely justified.

New towns are reputed to require and achieve better design results than most local authorities. The existing and future inhabitants, it is argued, should thus benefit from the output of the talented personnel which are attracted to a new town by the prospect of cooperating in innovatory schemes and by working to the higher environmental and planning standards which are made possible by the wider planning powers vested in a development corporation, although it is not strictly speaking in the planning authority. In central Lancashire this remit included the task of transforming the somewhat haphazard 'pepper pot' growth into coordinated and accelerated housing and industrial development programmes. The proposed area plans, broadly equivalent to local plans in structure planning terms, were seen to provide for comprehensive rather than piecemeal development and insisted upon better standards of layout and coordination with the public utilities for the provision of social and other facilities. The concentration of such development within the designated area was designed to remove pressure for expansion in the surrounding rural areas, so preserving the concept of a clear transition from urban to non urban zones.

The reason why the advocates of the new town anticipated its success, despite the lack of preferential financial incentives when compared with many other new towns at that time, was in the belief in the attraction of the 'natural advantages' of the area. This optimism drew upon certain theories of the location of industry and in the efficacy of growth centre theory as a cure for sub regional and regional deficiencies (see Chapter 6). By building upon the relatively firm and successful employment base of the sub region, and given effective promotion, it was argued that a considerable number of new employment opportunities could be created. These investments, it was stressed, would not necessarily be located elsewhere in the north west, nor indeed, in some cases in the United Kingdom. The inducement to underpin the promotional campaign and natural advantages, the argument continued, included the possibility of offering a wider range of housing types and locations (for sale or for rent) to attract potential labour, and the ability to offer a number of fully serviced advanced factories or sites in the new, well positioned employment areas.

In summary, the protagonists of the scheme believed that a new town development corporation was the best vehicle for the coordination of all efforts to develop the area.

CLDC -AN EXAMPLE OF ORGANISATIONAL SURVIVAL?

From the date of its formation in 1971, CLDC has been placed within a turbulent, uncertain and often hostile environment. Indeed the point was made in Chapter 1 that in terms of organisational survival alone the corporation is worthy of study. Despite changes in administration from Labour to Conservative and to Labour again during the period of

The facts Granada didn't give you.

If you watched Granada's programme 'A Week on Friday' on 19 June, you can be forgiven for coming away with a rather poor image of Central Lancashire New Town, and the Development Corporation that manages it.

This, however, is not what primarily concerns us.

We have long recognised that it is impossible to undertake large scale development without upsetting someone, somewhere. And we are not afraid of constructive criticism; indeed, we welcome it.

But what does disturb us is that many of the very real achievements of the New Town went unacknowledged. Or at best were covered only sketchily in the programme.

1. Jobs. Since the New Town was set up, we have built 2½ million sq ft of industrial space, and filled over 100 factories in our employment areas. Directly or indirectly, we have been responsible for providing over 5,000 jobs.

2. Villages. The oldest and most mature village the Development Corporation have created is Astley Park, Chorley. It has attracted residents from all over the country, and has shops, a supermarket, a pub, a post office, a well-used village hall, a school, a squash club, a sauna, a solarium, a restaurant, and sheltered accommodation for old people.

3. Housing. Already, we have housed over 3,500 families in rented homes. Over 2,500 families have bought houses of their own, built by private developers

If you saw Granada's programme 'A Week on Friday,' transmitted on 19 June, then you may find some of the facts in this advertisement of interest.

on Corporation land. And we are providing purpose-built accommodation for hundreds of single people.

4. Quality of Life. Recently, we have opened the 700 acres of Cuerden Park to the public. There's an attractive lake at its centre–which the Corporation have stocked with fish–and the park is currently drawing thousands of visitors every week. We have also planted over one million trees and shrubs, well over 400 every working day. Most of them are native, a fact of considerable importance to wildlife.

5. Recreation. The Corporation have sponsored the development of a championship golf course and leisure complex at Ingol, to the north of Preston, with both private and rented houses overlooking the greens. The first of our purpose-built sports halls has recently been opened by the Duke of Gloucester. And playing fields, playing areas, as well as open spaces abound on our developments.

6. Restoration. Far from pulling down buildings left, right and centre, the New Town–together with local councils–have started the restoration of thousands of homes and considerably enhanced the environment in the older urban areas.

Central Lancashire New Town has meant an investment of over £140m in the North West, by Central Government.

It has resulted in new houses, new jobs, new industry, new roads, new shops, new schools, new parks, urban renewal, and even unglamorous things like new sewers.

You may wish the money had been spent differently. But do you honestly wish the money had never been spent at all? Or had been spent not in the North West, but elsewhere?

If you'd like to know more about Central Lancashire–the environment, the factories and the houses for sale–contact Bill McNab, our Commercial Director, who'll be pleased to help you.

Central Lancashire
BRITAIN'S BIGGEST NEW TOWN

CENTRAL LANCASHIRE DEVELOPMENT CORPORATION, CUERDEN HALL, BAMBER BRIDGE, PRESTON. PR5 6AX

The Guardian - 29 June 1981 A response to the continued antagonism expressed by new town opponents ......

Reproduced by kind permission of the Guardian

the fieldwork the successive Secretaries of State permitted its continued existence. Changes in national and regional policies, adverse economic trends and declining population forecasts all pointed to the vulnerability of the project.

CLDC's survival in such a hostile environment was mainly through the skilful use of the 6(i) procedures so that commitments made would tend to pre-empt attempts to curtail the project. Local opposition, it has been pointed out, was largely unaware that new town decisions were made primarily at the centre and naively awaited a public inquiry, which was viewed as the major forum for protest and representation. Through the relentless implementation of piecemeal projects using new town powers the possibilities of delay through 'participation' and involvement was minimised, and opposition in some areas, such as Leyland, Moss Side, became dispirited.

Much of the explanation of such organisational survival is grounded upon the insights of organisational analysis and an understanding of theories of participation. It is to a review of such theoretical and analytical tools used in the research that we now turn.

THE THEORETICAL FOUNDATIONS OF THE STUDY

The earlier chapters in Part II of this study set out the basis for the main disciplinary thrust of the research. They described the separate areas of organisational analysis and participatory theory, both with their various theoretical strands and practices. The study of organisations dispels the naive expectation that dominant institutions will be able to meet the needs of all the governed and indeed the analysis of organisational goals reveals a complex and dynamic area of analysis. A Weberian 'structural' model with its inclusion of rival loyalties and foci of influence may be seen as an appropriate approach to organisations, their structure, and their members' attitudes to organisational power. From the descriptions and justifications of the design of CLDC in Chapters 7 and 13 it is evident that a valid approach could then be that, instead of analysing organisational structure as a measure of an organisation's effectiveness, it will look 'at structure as being the outcome of a political context for control within the organisation'. (Pfeffer, 1981, p.266). By focussing upon organisational environments and the political economy approach inter organisational networks and power relations have been set within the wider context of influence and power structures of society.

The empirical study of inter organisational behaviour is difficult and can only be partial. As the fieldwork observation of events in central Lancashire described in Part IV of this study has shown, apart from extensive non-participant observation of selective amenity societies, it is mainly 'set piece' public events which provide the observable evidence of the quality and balances of inter organisational relations. Such events included public meetings whose procedures were noted and analysed.

The study of organisational networks is a complex one. The overt and covert elements of the networks both require recognition. As stated in Chapter 5, the public inquiry is a public performance of the 'theatre of inter organisational power'. This case study involved observing this predominantly 'correct' ritual when many relationships are, at least partially, formalised so that an audience may observe and researchers note proceedings and collect supporting documentation, proofs of evidence and so on.

The public inquiry has been shown to have different functions and varying perceptions for divergent contributors. The diagram in Chapter 12 indicated how the institution of the public inquiry had a link with the urban regulations system. As the discussion in Chapter 12 of the study has shown,evidence points to a distinct cleavage between the networks of the CLDC and the action groups. In CLDC's case, there have been joint projects with the district councils, such as urban renewal in Chorley and Preston. In the case of the action groups, the drafting of a joint report, the request for reappraisal of the new town and the link up with CPRE for national lobbying are examples of inter organisational decision making.

The interlocking of these disparate sub systems within a local urban relations system has been the function of the local press. Its role as an information or network bridge, as indicated in Chapter 8, has been a crucial one, and there is strong evidence to support the Lancashire Evening Post's centrality on new town issues within the local planning and political communications systems.

An organisational perspective has highlighted the importance of such aspects of inter organisational relations as inter group negotiations and bargaining. This approach, in turn, has brought insights into pressure group activity both at local and national levels. Local government authorities and business organisations operate at both local and national levels. The former have their interests represented nationally through such bodies as the Association of District Councils and County Councils, while the latter employ their relevant trade association, the CBI or Association of Chambers of Commerce. The failure of many action groups to affiliate and harness such equivalent umbrella organisations, and in this research to do so only belatedly, is a significant feature of the study in pointing up power imbalances. There are, of course, costs of such negotiations at national level. As Lowe and Goyder point out, in such cases as the Friends of the Earth or the National Trust, these costs include a certain loss of freedom 'through implicit understandings that agreements will be honoured and that a group will show restraint in its public behaviour' and loss of purity through being involved in compromise. (Lowe and Goyder, 1983, p.178)

Inter organisational relations have also provided an emphasis upon participation. Indeed such relations with the voluntary sector in particular may be viewed as an important new approach to the issue. An organisation's permeability, giving evidence of interchange with its environment, is a useful measure of participation, and aspects of this approach were discussed in Chapters 5 and 6. In this study it is argued that the evidence has shown CLDC's belief in the efficacy of participation was only superficial. In essence, the 'Skeffington ideal' involving a two way process of exchange was 'spurned', as Chapter 9 indicated.

In linking the two elements which the organisational perspective has emphasised, it is possible to show that understanding of participation inplanning requires both an appreciation of inter organisational relationships and a consideration of the processes of decision making at both local and governmental level and the associated centre-periphery tensions. The local MPs in their roles as advocates of the periphery proved most important in their representation of felt injustices and particularly Mr Ron Atkins in giving publicity to a critical report of CLDC's organisational structure.

In essence, the chosen arena for the overt inter organisational relations on the new town is at local, or at least sub regional, level. The actual decision making relating to a major national investment is at the centre. (1)

The complexities and imbalances of decision making in Britain have been thrown into sharp relief through the idiosyncratic nature of British new towns. Much of their uniqueness is grounded in the early direction and ideology of the new towns programme and its method of implementation. The ability of ministers using the new towns legislation to make significant land use decisions by direct powers contained in the Act has caused, within the locations of these developments, a great deal of mistrust with their existing inhabitants. This 'efficient' practice was spelled out by Richard Crossman when he wrote in his diary

> .... New towns of course are Dame Evelyn's greatest creation. She is enormously proud of them and convinced that they wouldn't have been built without the completely autocratic constitution of the corporations, which we finance and whose members we appoint. The fact that they can get on with their job without consulting public opinion is the great thing in their favour, according to the Dame. Maybe this kind of autocracy was necessary in the first generation of new towns. (Crossman, 1975, p.127)

The maintenance of this attitude of Dame Evelyn Sharp within the DOE could do much to account for the continuance of new town policies in Britain generally and the survival, despite adverse trends, of CLNT in particular.

On the other hand, one should not discount the increasing concern felt in the last few years with urban problems focussed particularly upon inner cities. Social unrest and racial tensions, fuelled by the experience in the United States, were more the concern initially of the Home Office which later became linked with the Department of the Environment in initiating a number of projects. Regional planning reports, notably the Strategic Plan for the North West, suggested the concentration of investment on the older urban areas and the establishment of the inner city 'partnership' schemes provided for a degree of local government dialogue with an understanding that local residents should be involved. The establishment of the Urban Development Corporations, however, indicates a residual 'toehold' for the advocates of the more direct, autocratic approach to the arrest of urban decline.

CONCLUSIONS

Central Lancashire new town, the final development in an important phase of British regional and town and country planning policy has been examined, and the development corporation's relationship observed, as a case study which has provided widerinsights into aspects of British institutions and society. Its role as a direct arm of government in regional policy is an example of policy survival against adverse evidence. It is argued that this inertia is grounded in planning ideologies. Planning professionals and founding fathers, visionaries such as Ebenezer Howard, have given the decentralisation and anti urbanism implicit in the new towns programme a dominant place in the ideological equipment of the civil service. This ideology was given official weight by the Barlow report of the Royal Commission on the distribution of the industrial population and, it is argued, thus became an orthodoxy difficult to challenge.

Thus the bureaucratic control from the centre in the DOE was underpinned by ideological support from the planning profession and the primary interest group in this field, the TCPA. New towns, as an example of normative planning, were given credence by the adoption of untested economic 'growth point' theories when their original remit, that of providing for population overspill, had been supplanted.

CLDC provides an outstanding example of organisational survival and the tactics adopted have been described. Organisational analysis has provided important insights into such defence mechanisms. Goal displacement is a common phenomenon in the study of organisations; related and more relevant here is the occurrence of goal succession (Sills, 1957). Organisations seek out new goals when original ones cannot be achieved, given an approach to organisational goals which is specific to each organisation. Even more relevant here, and congruent with the views of organisations developed in Chapter 5, is the 'dynamic goals approach' which emphasises the setting of goals, not as a static element, but one which stresses the importance of interdependence of complex organisations within a wider society (Thompson and McEwan, 1973).

CLDC's management of its organisational environment was also dependent upon the public's perception of the role of the outline plan public inquiry. A naive view of the function and decision making power of a public inquiry can explain how local activists and groups may be diverted away from the actual centre of decision making to the local arena. Above all, a major contribution of the research is the employment of organisation theory in providing a wider understanding of participation in planning and of decision making. The political economy approach to organisations specifically takes as its central tenet the analysis of power differences and the importance of the conflicts which exist between interests, between organisations and between the centre and the periphery. Such an approach relates closely with participation as 'containment and bargaining' (Thornley, 1977, p.47).

This 'containment' to local levels did not hold beyond 1975 in this research, however, and Chapter 13 has described the efforts of some local groups attempting to influence decision making at the centre, having become wary of accepting at face value the process of rational decision making following the public inquiry (See Chapter 12). This realisation that the interplay of group pressures at the centre was important, became a significant feature of the political maturation of the local groups. There was a need for them to progress up the group power hierarchy.

The findings of this study suggest further areas of research. The boundary roles of social development in development corporations and personnel management in industry and parallels between 'industrial relations' and 'urban relations' may be fruitful areas of development. While the greenfield new towns of the post 1945 era decline, new similar institutions of central government, the the urban development corporations have been constituted. These organisations, in turn, based at present in the London docklands and Merseyside will require study: their effectiveness monitored, their relationships with local authorities and local groups scrutinised.

SUMMARY

This concluding chapter has emphasised the importance of the central Lancashire new town as a focus of study, both in terms of its position in the development of British planning and in the opportunities it presented to study inter organisational behaviour and interaction. Following a consideration of the theoretical foundations of the research, the chapter discussed CLNT as an example of policy survival and emphasised how organisational analysis can provide a fresh insight into the theories and practices of participation in planning.

NOTES

1. 'One way in which government has sought to manage and contain pressures from environmental groups is to deflect them away from the centre of government where the major decisions are made about the direction of the economy, the legislative programme and the allocation of resources. Participation has been encouraged instead in a number of peripheral environmental agencies and in the administration of planning powers by local government. It should be stressed that these are not the places where the major decisions affecting the environment are made. These decisions are made in the Treasury, the Department of Transport, the Ministry of Agriculture, the Department of Industry, the Department of Energy and the Department of the Environment, as well as in Brussels.' (Lowe and Goyder, 1983, p.180)

Bibliography

Ahamed, S.M. and Howard, A., Minority Report on Draft Outline Plan for Central Lancashire. 19th December 1973.

Aiken, Michael, Organizational Environment, Permeability and Organizational Structure: A Study of Forty-Four Local Governments in Belgium. Paper prepared for Eighth World Congress of Sociology: Toronto, Canada, August 1974.

Aiken, Michael and Hage, J, 'Organizational Interdependence and Intra-organizational Structure', American Sociological Review, vol.33: pp.912-30.

Albrow, Martin, Bureaucracy, Macmillan, London 1970.

Aldrich, Howard E., 'Organizational Boundaries and Interorganizational Conflict', Human Relations, vol.24, 1971, pp.279-93.

Aldrich, Howard E., Organizations and Environments, Prentice-Hall, Englewood Cliffs, New Jersey, 1979.

Aldrich Howard E. and Mindlin, S., 'Uncertainty and Dependence: Two Perspectives on Environment' in Lucien Karpik (ed.) Organization and Environment, Sage, London 1978.

Aldridge, Meryl, The British New Towns, Routledge and Kegan Paul, London 1979.

Almond, G. and Verba, S, The Civic Culture, Little, Brown, Boston 1965.

Annan, Report of the Committee on the Future of Broadcasting, Cmnd 6753: HMSO, London 1977.

Apgar, Mahlon IV (ed.), New Perspectives on Community Development, McGraw-Hill, London 1976.

Argyle, Michael, The Psychology of Interpersonal Behaviour, Penguin Books.

Arnstein, Sherry, 'A Ladder of Citizen Participation', Journal of the American Institute of Planners, vol.35, 1969, pp.216-24.

Ash, Maurice, 'Planning, growth and change: the new towns - versus - inner cities fallacy', Town and Country Planning, vol.44, 1976, pp.55-61.

Averitt, Robert T., The Dual Economy: the dynamics of American industry structure, W.W. Norton.

Bachrach, Peter and Baratz, M.S., 'The Two Faces of Power', American Political Science Review, vol.56, 1962, pp.947-52.

Bachrach, Peter and Baratz, M.S., Power and Poverty: Theory and Practice, Oxford University Press, London 1970.

Bachrach, Peter and Baratz, M.S., 'Two Faces of Power' in Castles, F.G., Murray, D.J. and Potter, D.C. (eds.) Decisions, Organizations and Society, Penguin/Open University Press, Harmondsworth 1971.

Bachrach, Samuel B., and Lawler, E.J., Power and Politics in Organizations: The Social Psychology of Conflict, Coalitions and Bargaining, Jossey-Bass, London 1980.

Baer, Michael A., 'Political Participation in New Towns', British Journal of Political Science, vol.8, pp.237-45. 1978.

'Bains Report', The New Local Authorities, Management and Structure, HMSO, London 1972.

Banfield, E.C., Political Influence, Free Press of Glencoe, New York 1961.

Barker, Anthony, Public Participation in Britain: a Classified Bibliography, Bedford Square Press, London, 1979.

'Barlcw Report' Report of the Royal Commission on the Distribution of the Industrial Population, Cmnd 6153, HMSO, London 1940.

Batty, Michael, 'The Impact of a New Town', Journal of the Town Planning Institute, vol.55, pp.428-35, 1969.

Barnard, Chester, The Functions of the Executive, Harvard University Press 1938.

Beith, Alan, 'The Press and English Local Authorities', Oxford University, B.Litt. thesis, 1968.

Benewick, Robert, 'Politics without ideology: the perimeters of pluralism' in Robert Benewick, R.N. Berki and B. Parekh (eds.) Knowledge and Belief in Politics, Allen and Unwin, London 1973.

Benson, J. Kenneth, 'The Interorganizational Network as a Political Economy', paper presented to Eighth World Congress of Sociology, Toronto, August 1974.
see also
in Karpik (ed.) Organization and Environment, Sage, London, pp.69-101.

Benson, J. Kenneth, 'Organizations: A Dialectical View' in Zey-Ferrell, Mary and Aiken, Michael (eds.) Complex Organizations: Critical Perspectives, Scott, Foresman, Glenview, Illinois 1981.

Bergin, Francis J., Practical Communication, Pitman, London 1976.

Blau, Peter M., Bureaucracy in Modern Society, Random House, New York 1956.
The Dynamics of Bureaucracy, University of Chicago Press, Chicago 1963.

Blau, Peter M. and Scott, M.R., Formal Organisations, Routledge and Kegan Paul, London 1963.

Blau, Peter M. and Shoenherr A., 'New Forms of Power' in Salaman, Graeme and Thompson, Kenneth, (eds.) People and Organisations, Longman, London 1973.

Blondel, Jean, Voters, Parties and Leaders: The Social Fabric of British Politics, Penguin, Harmondsworth 1969.

Blumler, Jay G., 'The Political Effects of Mass Communication', Unit 8 Mass Communication and Society, Open University, Milton Keynes 1977.

Boaden, Noel, Goldsmith, Michael, Hampton, William and Stringer Peter, Planning and Participation in Practice: A Study of Public Participation in Structure Planning, Progress in Planning, vol.13, pp.1-102, Pergamon Press Ltd., Oxford 1980.

Boaden, Noel, Goldsmith, Michael, Hampton, William and Stringer, Peter, Public Participation in Local Services, Longman, London 1982.

Bollens, John C. and Schmandt, Henry J., The Metropolis: Its People, Politics and Economic Life, (Second Edition), Harper & Row, New York.

Booth, Simon, 'A Crisis in Maturity', Town and Country Planning, vol.43, pp.540-52, 1975.

Boydell, P., 'The Roles of the Lawyer in the Planning System', Journal of Planning Law, vol.31, pp.590-3. 1978.

Breed, Warren, 'Social Control in the Newsroom', in Schramm, Wilbur (ed.) Mass Communications, University of Illinois Press, Urbana 1960.

Broadbent, T.Andrew, Planning and Profit in the Urban Economy, Methuen,

London 1977.
Broadcasting, White Paper on the Future of Broadcasting, HMSO, London 1966.
Broady, Maurice, Planning for People, NCSS., London 1968.
Brooke-Taylor, G. 'The Social Development Dimension', Town and Country Planning, February, vol.45, pp.73-76. 1977.
Brown, G. Sutton, A Preliminary Plan for Lancashire, Lancashire County Council, 1951.
Brown, R.G.S., The Administrative Process in Britain, Methuen, London 1970.
Bruce-Gardyne, Jock and Lawson, Nigel, The Power Game: An Examination of Decision-making in Government, Macmillan, London 1976.
Bryant, Richard, 'Community Action' in Kimber, Richard and Richardson, J.J., (eds.) Pressure Groups in Britain, Dent, London 1974.
Burgess, Tyrell and Travers, Tony, Ten Billion Pounds: Whitehall's Takeover of the Town Halls, Grant McIntyre, London 1980.
Burke, Edmund M., 'Citizen Participation Strategies', Journal of the American Institute of Planners, vol.34, pp.287-94.
Burns, Tom and Stalker, G.M., The Management of Innovation, Tavistock, London 1961.
Butler, David and Stokes, D., Political Change in Britain, Macmillan, London 1969.
Buxton, Richard, Local Government (Second Edition), Penguin, Harmondsworth 1973.
Castles, F.G., Murray, D.J., and Potter, D.C., (eds.), Decisions, Organizations and Society, Penguin/Open University Press, Harmondsworth 1971.
Catanese, Anthony J., Planners and Local Politics: Impossible Dreams, Sage, London 1974.
Childs, Harwood L., Labor and Capital in National Politics, The Ohio State University Press, Columbus 1930.
Civic Trust, The Local Amenity Movement, Civic Trust, London 1976.
CLDC (Central Lancashire Development Corporation), Draft Outline Plan, Preston 1973.
CLDC, Outline Plan, Preston 1974.
CLDC, Central Lancashire Development Corporation, Research and Intelligence Unit, Master Sample Social Survey, Preston 1974a.
CLDC, General Manager's Proof of Evidence, Public Inquiry into Outline Plan, November 1974b.
CLDC, A Social Atlas of Central Lancashire, CLDC, Preston 1976.
CLDC, Implementation Strategy, CLDC, Preston, October 1978.
Cockburn, Cynthia, The Local State: Management of Cities and People, Pluto Press, London 1977.
Colignon, Richard and Cray, David, 'New Organizational Perspectives: Critiques and Critical Organizations' in Zey-Ferrell, Mary, and Aiken, Michael, (eds.), Complex Organizations: Critical Perspectives, Scott, Foresman, Glenview, Illinois 1981.
Collins, Randall, Conflict Sociology, Academic Press/Harcourt Brace Jovanovich, New York 1975.
Cowan, Robert, 'The Public Inquiries Fraud', Town and Country Planning, vol.49, pp.109-10, April 1980.
Cowley, John et al, Community or Class Struggle?, Stage 1, London 1977.
Cowling, T.M. and Steeley, G.C., Sub-Regional Planning Studies: An Evaluation, Pergamon, Oxford 1973.

Cox, Harvey and Morgan, David, City Politics and the Press, Cambridge University Press, Cambridge 1973.
CPRE, Briefing document, 21st December 1976.
Cresswell, Peter, The New Town Goal of Self-Containment, Open University Press, Milton Keynes 1974.
Cresswell, Peter and Thomas, Ray, 'Employment and Population Balance' in Evans, Hazel, (ed.), New Towns: the British Experience, Knight, Charles, London.
Crossman, Richard H.S., The Diaries of a Cabinet Minister Vol.I., Minister of Housing, 1964-66, Hamilton, Hamish and Cape, Jonathan, London.
Crozier, Michel, The Bureaucratic Phenomenon, University of Chicago Press, Chicago 1964.
Crozier, Michel, 'The Relationship Between Micro and Macro Sociology', Human Relations, vol.25, pp.239-51.
Crozier, Michel and Friedberg, Erhard, 'Organisations as a Means and Constraints of Collective Action' in Warner, Malcolm, (ed.), Organizations Choice and Constraint: Approaches to the Sociology of Enterprise Behaviour, Saxon House, Farnborough 1977.
Curran, James, 'Capitalism and Control of the Press, 1800-1975' in Curran, James, Gurevitch, Michael, and Woolacott, Janet, (eds.), Mass Communication and Society, Arnold, Edward, London 1977.
Curran,James and Seaton, Jean, Power Without Responsibility: The Press and Broadcasting in Britain, Fontana, London 1981.
Dahl, Robert A., Who Governs? Yale University Press, New Haven 1961.
Dahl, Robert A., 'Pluralism revisited' in Ehrlich, Stanislaw, and Wootton,Graham, (eds.), Three Faces of Pluralism: Political, Ethnic and Religious, Gower, Farnborough 1980.
Dahrendorf, Ralf, Class and Class Conflict in an Industrial Society, Routledge and Kegan, Paul, London 1959.
Dalton, Melville, Men Who Manage, Wiley, New York 1959.
Davies, Bernard, 'Battle with Bureaucracy: the Central Lancashire Story', Planning, vol.207, pp.6-7, 11th March 1977.
DEA, The North West: A Regional Study, HMSO, London 1965.
Dearlove, J., The Politics of Policy in Local Government, Cambridge University Press, Cambridge 1973.
Dennis, Norman, Public Participation and Planners' Blight, Faber and Faber, London 1972.
Dennis, Norman, 'In Dispraise of Political Trust' in Sewell, Derrick W.R., and Coppock, J.T., (eds.), A Perspective on Public Participation in Planning, Wiley, New York 1977.
Dill, W.R., 'Environment as an Influence on Managerial Autonomy', Administrative Science Quarterly, vol.2, pp.409-43.
DOE, Circular 52/72, Town and Country Planning Act: Part II. Development Plan Proposals: Publicity and Public Participation, HMSO, London 1972.
DOE, New Town Circular No. 276, dated 15th September 1972a.
DOE, North West 2000: Regional Policies for the Present and Future, A Summary Report by the North West Joint Planning Team, HMSO, London 1974.
DOE, Strategic Plan for the North West (SPNW), HMSO, London 1975.
Donaldson, Peter, Economics of the Real World, BBC/Penguin, Harmondsworth 1973.
Donnison, David, 'The Economics and Politics of the Regions', The Political Quarterly, vol.45, pp.179-89, April-June 1974.

Donnison, David, with Soto, Paul, The Good City: A Study of Urban Dev--elopment and Policy in Britain, Heinemann, London 1980.

Downs, Anthony, Inside Bureaucracy, Little, Brown, Boston 1967.

Dunleavy, Patrick, 'Social and Political Theory and the Issues in Central-Local Relations', in Jones, George, W., (ed.) New Approaches to the Study of Central-Local Government Relationships, SSRC/Gower, Farnborough 1980.

Eckstein, H., Pressure Group Politics: The Case of the British Medical Association, Allen and Unwin, London 1960.

Edelstein, Alex A., and Blaine, Schultz, J., 'The Leadership Role of the Weekly Newspaper as seen by Community Leaders: a Sociological Perspective' in Dexter, Lewis A., and White, David M., (eds.) People, Society and Mass Communications, Collier-Macmillan/Free Press, New York 1964.

Emery, F.E. and Trist, F.L., 'The Causal Texture of Organizational Environments', Human Relations, vol.18, pp.21-32,1965.

Etzioni, Amitai, A Comparative Analysis of Complex Organizations, Free Press, New York 1961.

Etzioni, Amitai, Modern Organizations, Prentice-Hall, Englewood Cliffs, New Jersey 1964.

Evan, William M., 'An Organizational-Set Model of Interorganizational Relations' in Tuite, Matthew F., Chisholm, Roger, and Radnor, Michael, (eds.), Interorganizational Decision making, Aldine Publishing Co., Chicago 1972.

Expenditure Committee, Thirteenth Report, New Towns, vols. I, IV and V, HC 616, I, IV and V., HMSO, London 1974.

Fagence, M.T., Citizen Participation in Planning, Pergamon, Oxford 1977.

Ferris, J., Participation in Urban Planning: The Barnsbury Case; a Study of Environmental Improvement in London (Occasional Papers in Social Administration No. 48)., Bell, London 1972.

Festinger, Leon, 'Cognitive Dissonance: Scientific American, (W.H. Freeman)., vol. 207, pp.93-102., October 1962.

Finer, S.E., Private Industry and Political Power, Pall Mall, London 1958.

Finer, S.E., 'Groups and Political Participation' in Kimber, Richard and Richardson, J.J., (eds.), Pressure Groups in Britain, Dent, J.M., London 1974, also in Parry, Geraint, (ed.), Participation in Politics, Manchester University Press, Manchester 1972.

Foley, Donald, 'British Town Planning: One Ideology or Three?', British Journal of Sociology, vol.2, pp.211-31, 1960.

'Franks Report', Report on the Committee on Administrative Tribunals and Inquiries, Cmnd. 218, HMSO, London 1957.

Freeman, Linton C. et al, Metropolitan Decision-Making: Further Analyses from the Syracuse Study of Local Community Leadership, University College of Syracuse, New York 1962.

Friend, J.K., and Jessop, W.N., Local Government and Strategic Choice, Tavistock, London 1969.

Galbraith, John Kenneth, The New Industrial State, Penguin, Harmondsworth 1969.

Gamson, William A., Power and Discontent, The Dorsey Press, Homewood, Ill. 1968.

Gans, Herbert J., 'Planning and Political Participation', Journal of the American Institute of Planners, vol.10, pp.3-9, 1953.

Garin, R.A., 'A Matrix Formulation of the Lowry Model for Intra-Metropolitan Activity Location', Journal of American Institute of

Planners, vol.32, pp.361-64, 1966.

Garnham, Nicholas, 'Contribution to a political economy of mass-communication', Media, Culture and Society, vol.1., pp.123-46, 1979.

Gerth, H.H., and Wright Mills, C., From Max Weber: Essays in Sociology, Routledge, London 1948.

Gibson, Tony, People power: Community and Work Groups in Action, Penguin, Harmondsworth 1979.

Gillingwater, David, Regional Planning and Social Change, Saxon House/ Lexington Books, Farnborough 1975.

Glasson, John, An Introduction to Regional Planning, Hutchinson, London 1974.

Glidewell, Iain, Final Submission on behalf of the Development Corporation (transcript), CLDC, Preston 1975.

Godschalk, David R., Participation, Planning and Exchange in Old and New Communities: a collaborative Paradigm, Centre for Urban and Regional Studies, University of North Carolina, Chapel Hill 1972.

Golding, Peter, The Mass Media, Longman, London 1974.

Goldsmith, Michael, Politics, Planning and the City, Hutchinson, London 1980.

Goldthorpe, John H., Lockwood, David, Bechhofer, Frank and Platt, Jennifer, The Affluent Worker: Industrial Attitudes and Behaviour, Cambridge University Press, Cambridge 1968.

Goodey, Brian, Social Planning in New Communities, Oxford Working Paper No. 3 in Planning and Research, Oxford 1970.

Goodin, Robert E., Manipulatory Politics, Yale University Press, New Haven 1980.

Gouldner, Alvin W., Patterns of Industrial Bureaucracy, Free Press, New York, Collier-Macmillan, London 1954.

Greater London Plan, (Abercrombie, Patrick), HMSO, London 1944.

Grimshaw, Peter N., 'The decline and fall of CLNT: a case study in planning gone wrong', The Planner, vol.64, pp.156-8, September 1978.

Groombridge, Brian, Durant, John, Hampton, William, Woodcock, Geoffrey and Wright, Anthony, Adult Education and Participation, Universities' Council for Adult and Continuing Education, Sheffield 1982.

Gross, N., Mason, W.S. and McEachern, A.W., Explorations in Role Analysis, John Wiley, New York 1958.

Gulic, L., and Urwick, L., (eds.), Papers on the Science of Administration, Columbia University, New York 1937.

Gurevitch, Michael, and Blumler, Jay G., 'Linkages between the Mass Media and Politics: a model for the analysis of political communications systems', in Curran, James, Gurevitch, Michael, and Woolacott, Janet, (eds.) Mass Communication and Society, Edward Arnold, London 1977.

Gwilliam, K.M., 'The Indirect Effects of Highway Investment', Regional Studies, vol.4, pp.167-76, 1970.

Hall, Peter, Gracey, H., Drewett, R., and Thomas R., The Containment of Urban England: Vol. I, Urban and Metropolitan Growth Processes or Megalopolis Denied, P.E.P./Allan and Unwin, London 1973.

Hall, Richard H., et al, Interorganizational Relationships, (Mimeo), University of Minnesota, Minneapolis 1973.

Hall, Stuart, "Culture, the Media and the 'Ideological Effect'", in Curran, James, Gurevitch, Michael and Woolacott, Janet, (eds.), Mass Communication and Society, Edward Arnold, London 1977.

Hampton, William and Beale, Wendy, 'Public Participation in Planning: the Contribution of Adult Education', Adult Education, vol.48, pp.401-4, 1976.

Handy, Charles B., Understanding Organizations, Penguin, Harmondsworth 1976.
Hanson, Royce, 'Issues in democratic development of new towns', Ekistics, vol.201, pp.82-5, 1972.
Harloe, Michael and Horrocks, Meryl, 'Responsibility without power: the case of Social Development', in Jones, D, and Mayo M, (eds.) Community Work I., Routledge and Kegan Paul, London 1974.
Hayward, Jack E.S., 'Institutional Inertia and Political Impetus in France and Britain', European Journal of Political Research, vol.4, pp.350-52, 1976.
Heap, Desmond, The New Town Planning Procedures, Sweet and Maxwell, London, 1968.
Heap, Desmond, An Outline of Planning Law (6th edn.), Sweet and Maxwell, London 1973.
Heclo, Hugh and Wildavsky, Aaron, The Private Government of Public Money, Macmillan, London 1974.
Heider, F., 'Attitudes and Cognitive Organization', Journal of Psychology, vol.21, pp.107-12, 1946.
Heraud, Brian J., 'Social Class and the New Towns', Urban Studies, vol.5, pp.33-58, 1966.
Heraud, Brian J., 'New Towns: A Philosophy of Community' in Leonard, Peter, (ed.), The Sociology of Community Action, Sociological Review, Monograph 21, 1975.
Hill, Dilys, Participating in Local Affairs, Penguin, Harmondsworth 1970.
Hill, Dilys M., Democratic Theory and Local Government, Allen and Unwin, London 1974.
Hill, Michael J., The State, Administration and the Individual, Fontana, London 1976.
Hindess, Barry, The Decline of Working Class Politics, MacGibbon and Kee, St. Albans 1971.
HMSO, See 'Bains Report', 1967.
HMSO, See 'Skeffington', 1969.
HMSO, Select Committee on New Towns, HMSO, London 1975.
Holland, Stuart, Capital Versus the Regions, Macmillan, London 1976.
Horrocks, Meryl, 'Social Planning in New Communities' in Built Environment, vol.1, pp.551-54, November 1972.
Horrocks, Meryl, 'Social Development Work in New Communities', Occasional Paper, No. 27. University of Birmingham, Centre for Urban and Regional Studies, Birmingham 1974.
Hovland, C.I., and Weiss, W., 'The influence of source credibility on communication effectiveness', Public Opinion Quarterly, vol.15, pp.635-50, 1951.
Howard, Alan, Letter to all Liaison Committee members, 1st February 1974.
Howard, Alan, 'The Great Participation Fallacy', The Planner,pp.163-4, September 1976.
Howard, Ebenezer, Garden Cities of Tomorrow, Swan Sonnenschein, 1902, also
Faber, London 1965.
Hunt, John, Managing People at Work, Pan Books, London 1981
'Hunt Report', Report of the Committee on Intermediate Areas, Cmnd 3998, HMSO, London 1969.
Hunter, Floyd, Community Power Structure, University of North Carolina Press, Chapel Hill 1953.
Jackson, Ian, The Provincial Press and the Community, Manchester

University Press, Manchester 1971.
Janowitz, Morris, 'The Study of Mass Communication', International Encyclopedia of the Social Sciences, Vol. 3, 1968.
Jenkins, Simon, 'The Press as Politician in Local Planning', Political Quarterly, vol.44, pp.47-57, 1973.
Jennings, M. Kent, Community Influentials: The Elites of Atlanta, Free Press, New York 1964.
Jewell, M., 'Is there an Alternative to the Public Inquiry?', Journal of Planning and Environment Law, vol.32, pp.216-22, 1979.
Johnson, James, 'A Plain Man's Guide to Participation', BEE (Bulletin of Environmental Education), vol.103, pp.11-16, November 1979.
Jones, George W., Borough Politics, Macmillan, London 1969.
Jones, George W., 'Varieties of Local Politics', Local Government Studies (New Series), vol.1, pp.17-32, 1975.
Jones, George W., (ed.), New Approaches to the Study of Central Local Government Relationships, SSRC/Gower, Farnborough 1980.
Journal of Planning and Environmental Law, 'Inquiries without Lawyers', vol.32, pp.518-23, August 1979.
Jowell, Roger, A Review of Public Involvement in Planning, Social and Community Planning Research, 1975.
Karpic, Lucien, 'Multinational enterprise and large technological Corporations', Revue Economique, vol.23, pp.1-46, 1972.
Karpic, Lucien (ed.), Organization and Environment: Theory, Issues and Reality, Sage, London 1978.
Katz, D., and Kahn, R., Social Psychology of Organizations, Wiley, New York 1966.
Katz, Elihu, and Lazarsfeld, Paul F., Personal Influence, Free Press, Glencoe, Ill. 1955.
Kay, Adah, 'Planning, participation and planners' in Mayo, Marjory, (ed.), Community Work I., Routledge and Kegan Paul, London 1974.
Klapper, J.T., The Effects of Mass Communication, Free Press, Glencoe 1960.
Kolarska, Lena, 'Review of Interorganizational Studies', Mimeo 1980.
Kornhauser, William, The Politics of Mass Society, Routledge and Kegan Paul, London 1960.
Kraus, S., and Davis, D., The Effects of Mass Communication on Political Behaviour, Pennsylvania State University Press, University Park 1976.
Lancashire County Council, Review of the County Development Plan, Preston 1962.
Lancashire County Council, Future Development of Central Mid-Lancashire (Preliminary Technical Report by the County Planning Officer), Preston 1964.
Lane, Tony, and Roberts, Kenneth, Strike at Pilkingtons, Fontana Books, London 1971.
Laski, H.J., 'The Pluralistic State' in Nicholls, D.A. (ed.), The Pluralist State, Macmillan, London 1975.
Laumann, Edward O., and Pappi, Franz U., Networks of Collective Action, Academic Press, New York 1976.
Lawrence, P.R., and Lorsch, J.W., Organization and Environment: Managing Differentiation and Integration, Harvard University Press, Cambridge, Mass. 1967.
'Layfield', Committee of Inquiry into Local Government Finance, Cmnd. 6453, HMSO, London 1976.
'Layfield' Appendix 6, Local Government Finance Appendix 6: The Relationship between Central and Local Government: Evidence and Commiss-

-ioned Work, HMSO, London 1976.
Levin, Peter H., 'The Planning Inquiry Farce', New Society, vol.14, pp.17-18, 1969.
Levin, Peter H., 'Commitment and Specificity in Urban Planning: A Study of Administrative, Technical and Political Process', Town Planning Review, vol.43, pp.93-115, 1972.
Levin, Peter H., 'Opening up the Planning Process' in Hatch S., (ed.), Towards Participation in Local Services, Fabian Tract 419, Fabian Society, London 1973.
Levin Peter, Government and the Planning Process, George Allen and Unwin, London 1976.
Levin, Peter, and Donnison, David, 'People and Planning' in Cullingworth, J.B., (ed.), Problems of an Urban Society, Vol. 3: Planning for Change, George Allen and Unwin, London 1973.
Litwak, Eugene and Hylton, Lydia H., 'Interorganizational Analysis: A Hypothesis on Co-ordinating Agencies', Administrative Science Quarterly, vol.6, pp.395-426, 1962.
Losch, A., The Economics of Location translated by Woglom, W.H., from Die raumlich Orgnung der Wirtschaft (1940), Yale University Press, New Haven, Conn., 1954.
Lowe, Philip and Goyder, Jane, Environmental Groups in Politics, Allen and Unwin, London 1983.
Lowry, Ritchie P., Who's Running This Town?, Harper and Row 1962.
Lukes, Steven, Power: The Radical View, Macmillan, London 1974.
March, J.G., and Simon, H.A., Organizations, Wiley, New York 1958.
Marshall, John D., (ed.), The History of Lancashire County Council, Martin Robertson, Oxford 1977.
Marx, Karl, and Engels, F., The German Ideology, Lawrence and Wishart, London 1938.
Mayer, Thomas F., A continuous model for influence processes in small groups, Ph.D. thesis, Stanford University, Stanford 1966.
Mayo, Elton, The Social Problems of an Industrial Civilization, Routledge and Kegan Paul, London 1949.
MacMurray, Revor, 'New Towns Participation', Town and Country Planning, vol.42, pp.27-30, January 1974.
McKenzie, Robert T., 'Parties, Pressure Groups and the British Political Process' in Kimber, Richard, and Richardson, J.J., (eds.), Pressure Groups in Britain, Dent, London 1974.
McKie, David, A Sadly Mismanaged Affair: A Political History of the Third London Airport, Croom Helm, London 1973.
McLeod, Jack M., Becker, Lee B., and Byrnes, James E., 'Another Look at the Agenda-Setting Function of the Press', Communication Research, Vol. 1, no. 2, April 1974, Sage, London.
McNeil, Kenneth, 'Critiques of Dominant Perspectives' in Zey-Ferrell, Mary, and Aiken, Michael, (eds.), Complex Organizations: Critical Perspectives, Scott, Foresman, Glenview, Ill. 1981.
Mercer, Alan, Personal Interview, Lancaster, 27th November 1973.
Merton, Robert K., Social Theory and Social Structure, Free Press, Glencoe, Ill. 1957.
Merton, Robert K., and Lazarsfeld, P.F., 'Mass Communication, popular taste and organised social action' in Bryson, L., (ed.), The Communication of Ideas, Harper and Row, New York 1948.
Meyer, Marshall W., and Associates, Environments and Organizations, Jossey-Bass, San Francisco 1978.
MHLG, Circular on Social Development XT/290/5/2, London 1963.

MHLG, Study for a City, London 1967.
Michels, Robert, Political Parties, Dover, Mineola 1959.
Milbrath, L., Political Participation, Rand McNally, Chicago 1965.
Miliband, Ralph, The State in Capitalist Society, Weidenfeld and Nicholson, London 1969.
Miliband, Ralph, 'The Power of Labour and the Capitalist Enterprise' in Urry, John, and Wakeford, John, (eds.), Power in Britain, Heinemann, London 1973.
Miller, Delbert C., International Community Power Structures, Indiana University Press, Bloomington 1970.
Moodie, G.C., and Studdert-Kennedy, G., Opinions, Publics and Pressure Groups, Allen and Unwin, London 1970.
Morgan, Gareth, The Organisation and Management of the Central Lancashire Development Corporation: A Research Report, Department of Behaviour in Organisations, University of Lancaster, Lancaster 1973.
Mosca, G., The Ruling Class, McGraw-Hill, New York 1939.
Mouzelis, Nicos P., Organisation and Bureaucracy, Routledge and Kegan Paul, London 1967.
Murdoch, Graham, and Golding, Peter, 'For a Political Economy of Mass Communications' in Miliband, Ralph, and Saville, John, (eds.), The Socialist Register 1973, Merlin Press, London 1974.
Murphy, David, The Silent Watchdog: the Press in Local Politics, Constable, London 1976.
Murray, David J., 'Informal Political Systems', Unit 25, Understanding Society: A Social Science Foundation Course, Open University, Milton Keynes 1971.
New Society, 'Against the City' leader 25th May 1975, vol.32, p.522.
New Society, 'Into the New Towns' leader 16th October 1975, vol.34, p.130.
New Society, 'Share pushers', 15th June 1978, vol.44, p.584.
New Society, 'Power in Parliament' leader 14th August 1980, vol.53, p.299.
Newton, Kenneth, Second City Politics, Clarendon Press, Oxford 1976.
New Towns Committee, 'Reith Report', HMSO, London 1945.
Nicholls, D.A., (ed.), The Pluralist State, Macmillan, London 1975.
North West Planning Council, An Economic Planning Strategy for the N.W. Region (Strategy I), HMSO, London 1966.
North West Planning Council, Strategy II: The North West of the 1970s, HMSO, London 1968.
OEO (Office of Economic Opportunities), Community Action Programme Guide, Washington, October 1965.
Olien, Clarice N., Donohue, George A., and Tichenor, Philip J., 'The Community Editor's Power and the Reporting of Conflict', Journalism Quarterly, vol.45, pp.243-52, 1968.
Olson, Mancur, The Logic of Collective Action, Harvard University Press, Cambridge, Mass. 1965.
Pahl, Ray E., Whose City?, 2nd Edition, Penguin Books, 1975.
Parsons, Talcott, Structure and Process in Modern Societies, Free Press, Glencoe, Ill., 1960.
Pearson, Frank, Foreward to 'The Central Lancashire New Town', North West Industrial Review, vol.4, p.11, Manchester 1973.
Perman, David, Cublington: A Blueprint for Resitance, Bodley Head, London 1973.
Perrow, Charles, Organizational Analysis: A Sociological View, Tavistock, London 1971.
Perrow, Charles, Complex Organizations: A Critical Essay, Scott,

Foresman & Co., Glenview, Ill., 1972.

Perrow, Charles, 'Zoo Story' or 'Life in the organizational sandpit', Perspectives on Organizations, Unit 15, People and Organisations, Open University, Milton Keynes 1974.

Pettigrew, Andrew, 'Information control as a power resource', Sociology, May 1972.

Pfeffer, Jeffrey, Power in Organizations, Pitman, London 1981.

Phelps, Richard W., 'New City is Born' in 'Financial Times', 12th April 1972.

Phelps, Richard W., 'The Central Lancashire New Town', North West Industrial Review, vol.4, pp.11-13, Manchester 1973.

Phelps, Richard W., 'Genesis of a New City' in Apgar, Mahlon, (ed.), New Perspectives on Community Development, McGraw-Hill 1976.

Phelps, Richard W., The Management of New Towns, New Towns Association, London 1977.

Phillips, D.L., Knowledge from What?, Rand McNally, Chicago 1971.

Phillips, D.L., Abandoning Method, Jossey-Bass, San Francisco.

Pickvance, C.G., 'On the Study of Urban Social Movements', The Sociological Review, vol.23, pp.29-49, February 1975.

Planwatch, Memorandum on the Central Lancashire New Town, January 1974, Preston.

Playford, J., 'The Myth of Pluralism' in Castles, F.G., Murray, D.J., and Potter, D.C., (eds.), Decisions, Organizations and Society, Penguin/Open University Press, Harmondsworth 1971.

Polsby, Nelson, W., Community Power and Political Theory, Yale University Press, New Haven, Conn., 1963.

Polsby, Nelson, W., Community Power and Political Theory - Second, enlarged edition, Yale University Press, New Haven, Conn., 1980.

Potter, Allen M., Organized Groups in Britain National Politics, Faber and Faber, London 1961.

'Reith Report', New Towns Committee Final Report, Cmnd. 6876, HMSO, London 1946.

Rhodes, R.A.W., Control and Power in Central-Local Government Relations, Gower, Farnborough 1981.

Ricci, David, Community Power and Democratic Theory: The Logic of Political Analysis, Random House, New York 1971.

Richardson, A., 'Tenant participation in council house management' in Dale, R., and Walker, R., Local Government and the Public, Leonard Hill 1977.

Richardson, Harry W., Regional and Urban Economics, Penguin, Harmondsworth 1978.

Richardson, J.J., and Jordan, A.C., Governing under Pressure, Martin Robertson, Oxford 1979.

Rivers, Patrick, Politics by Pressure, Harrap, London 1974.

Rollison, Stanley H.A., New Towns Act 1965, Section 5D; CLNT Outline Plan Inquiry into Objections and Representation, Department of the Environment, London 1975.

Rollison, Stanley H.A., Personal Interview, 11th May 1977.

Rose, Paul L., and Barnes, Michael, (eds.), Blundell and Dobry's Planning Appeals and Inquiries (2nd Edition), Sweet and Maxwell London 1970.

Rose, Richard, Politics in England Today, Faber, London 1974.

Ross, Simon, 'Personal Column' in Town and Country Planning, vol.41, pp.332-3, 1973.

Ryan, M., The Acceptable Pressure Group: Inequality in the Penal Lobby: A Case Study of the Howard League and RAP, Saxon House, Farnborough

1978.
Salaman, Graeme, 'Towards a Sociology of Organisational Structure', The Sociological Review, vol.26, pp.519-54, 1978.
Salancik, Gerald R., in Staw, Barry M., and Salancik, Gerald R., (eds.) New Directions in Organisational Behaviour, St. Clair Editions, Neuilly-sur-Seine 1977.
Sarason, Seymour B., et al., Human Services and Resource Networks: Rationale, Possibilities and Public Policy, Jossey-Bass, San Francisco 1977.
Saunders, Peter, Urban Politics: A Sociological Interpretation, Hutchinson, London 1979.
Saunders, Peter, Social Theory and the Urban Question, Hutchinson, London 1981.
Schaffer, Frank, The New Town Story, Paladin/Granada, London 1972.
Schattschneider, E.E., The Semi-Soverign People, Holt-Reinhart, 1960.
Scott, W.G., Organisation Theory, Irwin, Homewood 1967.
Self, Peter, 'New Towns and the Urban Crisis', Town and Country Planning, vol.48, pp.16-18, 1979.
Selznick, Philip, TVA and the Grass Roots, University of California Press, Berkeley and Los Angeles, 1949.
Senior, Derek, 'Planning and the Public' in Cowan, Peter, (ed.) The Future of Planning, Heinemann, London 1973.
Senior, Derek, 'Letting megalopolis happen', Town and Country Planning, vol.44, pp.148-50, 1975.
Sewell, W.R.Derrick, and Coppock, J.T., (eds.), Public Participation in Planning, Wiley, London 1977.
Seymour-Ure, Colin, The Political Impact of the Mass Media, Constable, London 1974.
Sharp, Evelyn, 'The Government's Role' in Evans, Hazel, (ed.), New Towns: The British Experience, Charles Knight, London 1972.
Sills, D., The Volunteers: Means and Ends in a National Organization, Free Press, Glencoe, Ill. 1975.
Silverman, David, The Theory of Organisations, Heinemann, London 1970.
Simmie, James M., Citizens in Conflict: The Sociology of Town Planning, Hutchinson, London 1974.
Simmie, James M., Power, Property and Corporatism: The Political Economy of Planning, Macmillan, London 1981.
Skeffington, People and Planning (The Skeffington Report) Report of the Committee on Public Participation in Planning (for MHLG), HMSO, London 1969.
Smith, Brian C., Policy Making in British Government, Martin Robertson, Oxford 1976.
Smith, Brian C., and Stanyer, Jeffrey, Administering Britain, Fontana/Collins, London 1976.
Spiegal, Hans B.C., and Mittenthal, Stephen D., 'Neighbourhood Power and Control: Implications for Urban Planning', Columbia University/Clearinghouse, New York 1968.
SPNW, See DOE 1974.
Stacey, Margaret, Tradition and Change, Oxford University Press, London 1960.
Stacey, Margaret, et al., Power, Persistence and Change: a Second Study of Banbury, Routledge and Kegan Paul, London 1975.
Stanyer, Jeffrey, Understanding Local Government, Fontana/Collins, London 1976.
Stranz, Walter, 'Regionalism and dispersal: time for a counter attack', Town and Country Planning, vol.44, pp.204-7, 1975.

Strauss, A., et al., 'The hospital and its negotiated order' in Friedson, E., (ed.), The Hospital in Modern Society, Macmillan, New York 1963.

Taylor, Frederick W., Scientific Management, Harper, New York 1911.

TCPS, 'Public Participation in Planning, Statement by Town and Country Planning Association, 26th November 1981.

Telling, A.E., Planning Law and Procedure, (4th Edition), Butterworth, London 1973.

Terreberry, Shirley, 'The Evolution of Organizational Environments', Administrative Science Quarterly, vol.12, pp.590-613, 1968.

Thomas, Ray, London's New Towns, Political and Economic Planning, London 1969.

Thomas, Ray, and Cresswell, Peter, 'The New Town Idea', Urban Development Unit 26, Open University, Milton Keynes 1973.

Thompson, James D., Organizations in Action, McGraw-Hill, New York 1967.

Thompson, James D., and MacEwan, W.J., 'Organizational Goals and Environment: Goal-setting as an interaction process' in Salaman, Graeme and Thompson (eds.), People and Organisations, Longman, London 1973.

Thornley, A., Theoretical Perspectives on Planning Participation, (Progress in Planning Series), Pergamon, Oxford 1977.

Tuite, Matthew F., 'Toward a Theory of Joint Decision Making' in Tuite, Matthew, Chisholm, Roger, and Radnor, Michael, (eds.), Interorganizational Decisionmaking, Aldine Publishing Co., Chicago.

Tuite, Matthew F., Chisholm, Roger and Radnor, Michael, (eds.), Interorganizational Decisionmaking, Aldine Publishing Co., Chicago, 1972.

Tunstall, Jeremy, The Westminster Lobby Correspondents, Routledge and Kegan Paul, London 1970.

Tunstall, Jeremy, Journalists at Work, Constable, London 1971.

Tunstall, Jeremy, 'New Organization Goals and Specialist Newsgathering Journalists' in McQuail, Denis, (ed.), Sociology of Mass Communications, Penguin, Harmondsworth 1972.

Tunstall, Jeremy, The Media are American: anglo-American media in the World, Constable, London 1977.

Turk, Herman, Organizations in Modern Life: Cities and Other Large Networks, Jossey-Bass, San Francisco 1977.

Turner, C.S., Evidence on behalf of Planwatch: Outline Plan Public Inquiry, Preston 1974.

Turner, C.S., Supplementary Proof of Evidence on Transportation for Planwatch, Preston 1975.

Turner, Graham, 'It matters who you have at the top', New Society, vol.33, pp.244-46, 1975.

UCAE, Report of the Working Party on Participation and Adult Education, Leicester 1981.

Warner, Malcolm, 'Decision-making in American T.V. Political News', The Sociological Review Monograph, No.13. Sociology of Mass Media Communications, University of Keele, pp.169-79, Keele 1969.

Waterhouse, Robert, 'Lancashire Hotchpotch' in The Guardian, 10 June 1975.

Watson, W., 'Social Mobility and Social Class in Industrial Communities', in Gluckman, M., (ed.), Closed Systems and Open Minds Oliver and Boyd, Edinburgh 1964.

Weber, Alfred, Theory of the Location of Industries translated by Friedrich, C.J., from Uber der Standort der Industrien (1909)

Chicago University, Chicago 1929.
Weber, Max, The Theory of Social and Economic Organization (1922), Free Press, New York 1964.
Weiss, Joseph W., 'The Historical and Political Perspective on Organizations of Lucien Karpik' in Zey-Farrell, Mary, and Aiken, Michael, (eds.), Complex Organizations: Critical Perspectives, Scott, Forsman, Glenview, Ill. 1981.
Westergaard,John H., and Resler, Henrietta, Class in a Capitalist Society, Penguin, Harmondsworth 1976.
Whale, John, The Politics of the Media, Fontana, London 1977.
Wheatley, Sir Andrew, (for the Minister of Housing and Local Government) The Draft Central Lancashire New Town (Designation) Order: Report of an Inquiry para. 22 (reported answer by the Minister's Official, Mr. I.V. Pugh to a question put to him).
White, D.M., 'The Gatekeeper: a case study in the selection of news', Journalism Quarterly, vol.27, pp.383-40, 1950.
Wiles, R.M., Freshest Advices: Early Provincial Newspapers in England, Ohio State University Press, Columbus 1965.
Willings, Willing's Press Guide, T. Skinner, East Grinstead 1982.
Wirtz, H.M., Social Aspects of Planning in New Towns, Saxon House, Farnborough 1975.
Woodcock, Geoffrey L., A Study of the Influences on Shop Floor Opinions in a Period of Industrial Relations Change. Unpublished M.A. Thesis, University of Liverpool, Liverpool 1972.
Woodcock, Geoffrey L., 'Realistic Pluralism', The Industrial Tutor, vol.2, pp.17-26, 1976a.
Woodcock, Geoffrey L., 'Condundrum in Lancs', New Society, vol.38, pp.360-61, 1976c.
Woodcock, Geoffrey L., Participation - A Select Bibliography, paper presented to Conference of Universities Council for Adult Education, Edinburgh, Institute of Extension Studies, Liverpool 1980.
Woodcock, Geoffrey L., and Emerson, David,'Planning and Adult Education' Adult Education, vol.49, pp.384-87, 1977.
Wootton, Graham, Pressure Politics in Contemporary Britain, Lexington Books, Farnborough 1978.
Wraith, Ronald E., 'Planning Inquiries and the Public Interest', New Society, vol.18, pp.145-47, 1971.
Wraith, Ronald E., and Lamb, Geoffrey B., Public Inquiries as an Instrument of Government, Allen and Unwin, London 1971.
Wright, Anthony, Local Radio and Local Democracy, Independent Broadcasting Authority, London 1981.
Zald, Meyer N., 'Organizations as Polities: An Analysis of Community Organization Agencies', Social Work, vol.11, pp.56-65, October 1966.
Zald, Meyer N., (ed.), Power in Organizations, Vanderbilt University Press, Nashville, Tenn., 1970.
Zey-Farrell, Mary, and Aiken, Michael, Complex Organizations: Critical Perspectives, Scott, Foresman, Glenview, Ill., 1981.